The Complete Guide to Buying, Maintaining and Servicing a Horse Trailer

The Complete Guide to Buying, Maintaining and Servicing a Horse Trailer

NEVA KITTRELL SCHEVE
WITH THOMAS G. SCHEVE

Howell Book House
New York

Copyright © 1998 by Neva Kittrell Scheve
Howell Book House
Published by Wiley Publishing, Inc., New York, NY
No part of this publication may be reproduced, stored in a retrieval system or transmitted in any form or by any means, electronic, mechanical, photocopying, recording, scanning or otherwise, except as permitted under Sections 107 or 108 of the 1976 United States Copyright Act, without either the prior written permission of the Publisher, or authorization through payment of the appropriate per-copy fee to the Copyright Clearance Center, 222 Rosewood Drive, Danvers, MA 01923, (978) 750-8400, fax (978) 646-8700. Requests to the Publisher for permission should be addressed to the Legal Department, Wiley Publishing, Inc., 10475 Crosspoint Blvd., Indianapolis, IN 46256, (317) 572-3447, fax (317) 572-4447, E-Mail: permcoordinator@wiley.com.

Trademarks: Wiley, the Wiley Publishing logo, and Howell Book House are trademarks or registered trademarks of Wiley Publishing, Inc., in the United States and other countries, and may not be used without written permission. All other trademarks are the property of their respective owners. Wiley Publishing, Inc., is not associated with any product or vendor mentioned in this book.

Limit of Liability/Disclaimer of Warranty: While the publisher and author have used their best efforts in preparing this book, they make no representations or warranties with respect to the accuracy or completeness of the contents of this book and specifically disclaim any implied warranties of merchantability or fitness for a particular purpose. No warranty may be created or extended by sales representatives or written sales materials. The advice and strategies contained herein may not be suitable for your situation. You should consult with a professional where appropriate. Neither the publisher nor author shall be liable for any loss of profit or any other commercial damages, including but not limited to special, incidental, consequential, or other damages.

For general information on our other products and services or to obtain technical support please contact our Customer Care Department within the U.S. at 800-762-2974, outside the U.S. at 317-572-3993 or fax 317-572-4002.

Wiley also publishes its books in a variety of electronic formats. Some content that appears in print may not be available in electronic books.

Library of Congress Cataloging-in-Publication Data

Scheve, Neva Kittrell.
    The complete guide to buying, maintaining and servicing a horse trailer / Neva Kittrell Scheve with Thomas G. Scheve.
        p.   cm.
    ISBN 0-87605-686-9
    1. Horse trailers.   I. Scheve, Neva Kittrell   II. Title.
SF285.385.S34   1998
636.1'083—dc21   97-38167
                                                                 CIP

Manufactured in the United States of America

10 9 8 7 6

Book Design by A&D Howell Design

CONTENTS

Preface vii

Acknowledgments xi

Introduction xiii

Chapter 1 Trailering from the Horse's Point of View 1

Chapter 2 Purchasing a Horse Trailer 11

Chapter 3 Trailer Styles, Types, and Variations 21

Chapter 4 Loading and Unloading Features and Options 53

Chapter 5 Interior Features and Options 73

Chapter 6 Controlling the Interior Environment 99

Chapter 7 Exterior Features and Options 111

Chapter 8 Mechanical Parts 123

Chapter 9 Capacity 149

Chapter 10 Construction Materials 159

Chapter 11 Living Quarters 181

Chapter 12 Used Trailers: Buying, Selling, and Trading Up 189

Chapter 13 Buying a New Trailer 207

Chapter 14 Tow Vehicles and Hitches 221

Chapter 15 Driving Tips and Horse Safety 237

Chapter 16 Operation and Service 257

Appendix 295

Index 299

PREFACE

When Tom and I started our trailer sales dealership in 1983, it was to be a part-time venture to help finance my passion for horses. Tom's background in advertising and marketing, my interest and experience with horses, and our combined previous involvement in other retail businesses made for a unique combination for a horse trailer dealership. The horse trailer industry has changed dramatically since then, and we would like to think that our influence has been responsible for some of the improvements.

We named our dealership the Sport Horse Trailer Company, and we were originally Trail-et dealers. Trail-et's sales manager was a good teacher, one of the few real horsemen who also knew trailers, and he was a big help to us. He was the first to suggest to me that the design of the trailer is important for the good of the horse. I was the first to teach him about warmblood horses, which were rather new in this country in the 1980s. Since I was involved in dressage and combined training, it became our market area of expertise, and we became a Top Ten dealer our first year in business. We were always asking Trail-et for custom-built larger trailers because an "extra tall" trailer was 7 feet tall back then, not nearly large enough for the horses in our market. Soon Trail-et made 7 feet 4 inches the standard height for its walk-through (Thoroughbred) trailers and 6 feet the standard width.

Our sales increased yearly, and we were approached by Tom Holdeman of Merhow Trailers. He had just taken over Merhow Trailer Manufacturing, a respected company that had been founded by his father and uncle. He was looking for dealers to sell his new, modernized version of the Merhow trailer, which had been a quality trailer for 25 years but was beginning to look dated in comparison with the flashy new trailers coming on the market. Although the trailer he presented to us was promising, there were many features that I felt would keep it from being accepted by discerning buyers. He agreed to make any changes that I suggested, and a great working relationship was born. The "Sport Horse" edition was the first trailer that was built specifically for us and for the warmblood market. Tom Holdeman also enlisted our help in advertising and marketing, which resulted in a campaign to educate the buyer about the importance of the design and construction for the well-being of the horse. The Sport Horse trailer was a huge success, and we broke all previous sales records. Many of our customers kept in touch and gave us feedback. If problems occurred, changes were made so that the trailer kept improving.

The Merhow Verylight trailer, a lightweight trailer designed for average to smaller horses, also came out of our association with this company.

Word of mouth from our satisfied customers allowed us to expand our sales nationwide and to Canada and Mexico. Our part-time business became full-time, and we moved onto a sales lot in a small town near Cincinnati, Ohio. Over the years customers came to us with stories and experiences of their own. We share some of them in this book. Some stories were funny or cute, and some were downright bizarre, but most involved problems that people had in the past and wanted to avoid with a new trailer. We heard more horror stories than we ever wanted to hear, but they taught us that a horse is capable of anything in a trailer, even the impossible! The most important discovery we made was that certain common design features prevalent on existing horse trailers could actually increase the chance of injury or accident. We also discovered that we could reduce many problems by incorporating common sense into the design of the trailer by looking at the trailer from the horse's point of view.

During our years in Cincinnati, we took on more trailer brands and, at one time or another, we represented just about every major trailer on the market. We were able to find out firsthand which trailers held up better and which ones had problems, how manufacturers handled warranties, which manufacturers had the most customer satisfaction, and which trailers returned to haunt us. In the end, we chose the best manufacturers and had prototypes made of our own designs, using the knowledge we had acquired over the years. It was important that the trailer be easy for me to use, since I am fairly representative of our typical customer, and that my own horses would travel comfortably and safely. The result of this effort was the Equisport, a deluxe trailer designed especially for warmbloods and other large horses, and the Thorosport, a safe economical trailer for all other horses.

When we moved to North Carolina in 1992, our own education was further enriched when Richard Mansmann, V.M.D., Ph.D., then affiliated with the University of North Carolina, contacted us about his special interest—improving the internal air quality of the trailer and reducing the shipping stress of horses. He supplied us with a wealth of information about the negative effects of shipping horses and had his own suggestions for improving the health and well-being of horses during travel. He had seen our Equisport trailer and thought it was the first trailer he had seen that addressed this issue through its design.

Since our customers were clamoring for more information about trailering, we published *The Hawkins Guide: Horse Trailering on the Road*, which is an indepth study of the legal aspects of horse trailering, combined with emergency travel information, and *The Hawkins Guide: Equine Emergencies on the Road,* which I coauthored with James Hamilton, D.V.M.

Neither Tom nor I planned to become so involved in the horse trailer business. We have continued to work to improve the quality and safety of our trailer, and the new EquiSpirit is the result of improvements to our past trailers and a new relationship with the Hawk Trailer Company.

Tom and I both enjoy sharing our knowledge. We travel to major conventions and local clubs to speak about what we have learned about horse trailering and to gather more knowledge from those we meet. This book is a culmination of all that has come before.

NEVA K. SCHEVE

ACKNOWLEDGMENTS

We wish to thank the following people who have been extremely helpful in supplying information for this book: James Hamilton, D.V.M.; Richard Mansmann, V.M.D., Ph.D.; Bob Fisher, engineer, Merhow, Indiana; Bryant Jones, Sundowner Trailers; Robert B. Peliti Jr., Four Star Trailers; Brian Timm, Hawk Trailers; Dave Weimer, North Shore Conversions; Tami L. White, Cherokee Trailers.

The following companies have generously supplied information about their products: Dexter Axle, Elkhart, Indiana, a special thank-you for supplying the service information contained in chapter 16; and to DrawTite Hitch for their support not only of this book, but also for our other projects; and Cor Tec, Washington Courthouse, Ohio. For locations of demonstration photographs, we thank Windy Hill Farm, Pinehurst, North Carolina, owned by Marilyn and Peter Soby, and Southern Pines Tack and Saddler, Southern Pines, North Carolina.

For models, we thank LouAnn Earp, Cassie Mason, and Phyllis Lynch.

For horse models, we thank Tristan 095 and Rio, owned by LouAnn Earp; Gem, owned by Marilyn Soby; Parr's Sparkle, owned by Barbara Scheve; Vespi, owned by Kay Redding; Tina, owned by Allison Territo; Aspasia II, owned by Mary Jo Mattheis; and Rebel and Sunday, owned by Neva Scheve.

Jeep Grand Cherokee supplied by McBreyer Chrysler, Plymouth, Dodge, Jeep, Inc., Southern Pines, North Carolina.

We found that the following publications provided useful medical information:

Racklyeft, D. J. and D. N. Love. "Influence of Head Posture on the Respiratory Tract of Healthy Horses." *Australian Veterinary Journal*, 67, no. 11 (November 1990).

Schott, Harold C., II, DVM and Richard Mansmann, VMD, PhD. "Thoracic Drainage in Horses." *The Compendium,* 12, no. 2 (February 1990).

Smith, B. L. et al. "Managing Transport Stress in Horses." *AESM Proceedings* (University of California, Davis, 1991).

INTRODUCTION

The perfect horse trailer just doesn't exist. Not because it isn't possible, it's that if a manufacturer were to build such a trailer, hardly anyone would be able to afford it. However, even though the perfect trailer doesn't exist, with some smart shopping it is possible to find some that come fairly close.

The objective of this book is to help the buyer make an informed decision when buying a horse trailer, not to recommend one brand over another. In fact, no brand names are mentioned at all. Since there are no advertisers to please, we are free to talk about every aspect of trailering from a candid and impartial point of view. Every major manufacturer has been contacted and given the opportunity to supply information. The information contained herein is as accurate a portrayal as can be possible in a changing and largely unregulated industry.

CHAPTER 1

Trailering from the Horse's Point of View

For the conscientious horse owner, the first consideration in buying a horse trailer should be the needs of the horse or horses that will be riding in it. The next consideration should be the needs of the buyer. Finally, after the trailer is chosen to fulfill those needs, the tow vehicle should then be selected.

Because transporting horses has become more of an everyday occurrence, it is easy to forget that trailering can be a source of anxiety for the horse. Problems, such as unwillingness to load, scrambling, and breaking halters and other equipment, are so commonplace that most horse owners have come to accept them as the norm. Some of these problems, however, can be avoided by using design features in the trailer that respect the character of the horse. Also, a well-designed trailer will reduce the amount of stress to the horse, therefore, possibly avoiding major health problems or crippling injuries. In order to understand how the trailer design can help eliminate trailering problems, we must look at the natural behavior of the horse and how his instincts make trailering a stressful situation.

Born to run wild and free just like their ancestors, these mares are racing for the pure joy of it!

Stress

Horses, like all living creatures, are subject to stress throughout their lives. Stress can be defined as an external stimulus that is beyond the control of the animal. Reactions to this external stimulus can be classified as behavioral response, autonomic nervous response, and neuroendocrine response.

"Behavioral response" is the way the animal reacts to its environment. The behavioral response to stress is for the animal to reduce the quantity of stress by avoiding the object of the stress.

"Autonomic nervous response" is the physiological preparation of the body to act on its behavioral response. Elevated heart rate, vascular resistance to blood flow, gastrointestinal smooth muscle contractions, and secretion of epinephrine or adrenaline are some of the body's reactions. This response is usually brief and in most cases is beneficial to the horse since it helps him avoid the stress by "fight or flight." When these physiological reactions continue over a long period, because the horse cannot escape the object of the stress, his health may be affected.

"Neuroendocrine response" affects the neuroendocrine system, which regulates reproduction, metabolism, growth, immunity, and behavior by releasing hormones. Stress can affect all these functions and may have a negative impact on the horse, especially long-term or chronic stress. Chronic stress may cause changes in immune function that predispose the animal to disease.

The very nature of the horse makes it stressful for him to enter a small enclosed box that will start, stop, turn, bump, and speed on the highway at 65 miles per hour. The horse is a creature made for open spaces and solid ground, where his instinctive flight response can be lifesaving when he must get away. Therefore, the horse can become claustrophobic when he feels restricted in a small space, meaning that he can't escape the threat of "danger."

The horse has evolved to survive as a member of a herd, and though the horse has been domesticated for several thousand years, herd behavior is still instinctive. Since the horse is a prey animal, his flight or fight response has been refined to perfection. It is this instinct that causes the horse to behave and learn differently from an animal that is instinctively a hunter, such as a dog or a cat.

Wild horses live in herds because there is safety in numbers. Separation from the herd can cause anxiety in the horse because he feels vulnerable by himself. We see this anxious behavior in our domesticated horse when we take him away from his pasturemates.

In a perfect wild horse world, if a cougar—or other predator—is sighted by even one member of the herd, all the horses run. Each horse in the herd does not have to individually see the cougar to believe the response of the one who does. The behavior response enables all the members of the herd to alleviate the object of the stress, the cougar, by avoiding it—in this case by running away. The autonomic nervous response facilitates that response by physiologically elevating the horse's adrenaline level and other functions to make it possible for him to run away, or to stand and fight if necessary. When the object of that stress, the cougar, has been beaten or outrun, the horse survives another day, the physical systems return to normal, and all is well. It is the innate flight or fight response of the horse that we must deal with, not only in all our training of the domestic horse, but also in maintaining his health and well-being.

The dogs may not be as dangerous as a cougar, but these horses aren't going to stick around to find out! "Flight" is much more instinctive to a prey animal than "fight."

If the object of stress to the horse cannot be eliminated and the neuroendocrine system continues to react to the stress, the body begins to suffer ill effects. Stress can be caused by many external influences, both physical and emotional, not only by a cougar on the prairie. Exposure to disease, noxious gasses, dust or mold, extreme temperature changes, suppression of instinctual behavior, abuse, hunger, thirst, fear, and separation anxiety are examples of stressful factors that can become detrimental to the health of the animal. Any of these situations, by themselves or in combination, are possible during trailering. The stress of trailering can affect the horse in obvious ways such as an unwillingness to load onto the trailer to the more dangerous behavior of thrashing around in the trailer and suffering external injuries. More insidious effects can be dehydration and heat exhaustion, colic, shipping fever, and other illness. Fluctuating hormones can adversely affect mares who are in foal. Also, trailer accidents can be responsible for the acute and life-threatening stress of traumatic injuries.

Of course, horses travel all the time without incident, and trailering can be a safe and enjoyable pursuit for all involved. A horse that has had a safe and relaxed trip will have that much more to give in his performance, and there will be no emergency vet bills to pay. In the past, and with few exceptions, the design of the trailer itself has been more concerned with the convenience of the human rather than the comfort of the equine. This has not necessarily been on purpose, since there has not been much information available about the effects of trailering stress on the horse. Recently, however, interest within the veterinary community about the effect of stress on the horse during trailering has lead to research on the subject. Even though veterinarians know about the physiology of the horse, they don't know a whole lot about the differences among trailers, and so far the research done on horses in the trailer, in our opinion, is inconclusive. Very little research has been done by the trailer industry itself, but trailers are beginning to be designed to meet the market demands of an increasingly educated buying public; consequently, many improvements have been made in the last few years. Recently, however, there has been a disturbing trend to follow fads in design and construction materials, usually with the best intentions, that does not always benefit the well-being of the horse or the safety of the handler.

Negative Effects of Stress

A good relationship between horse and human must be a compromise. The modern horse must learn to control his natural tendency to flee, and as responsible caretakers, we must take precautions to lower the horse's stress levels so he does not harm himself or others. For those who transport horses, that responsibility includes understanding the most common ways the horse can be affected by trailering.

Because the stressed system of the healthy horse returns to normal when the stress is removed, short-term trips are not usually characterized by illness since the environmental or emotional stress is of short duration. Injury is the most common problem here, since injuries can happen simply from loading and unloading. Traffic accidents or equipment failure can happen at any time, even on a very short trip, so precautions should always include planning for such eventualities.

Long-term trips are another matter. As a rule, a trip of 10 to 12 hours or more is considered long for a horse. Depending on individual temperament, experience, and health status, some horses will suffer from stress in a shorter time, and some horses will travel well for a longer period.

Recent veterinary studies have concluded that the natural way for the horse to remove foreign material from his respiratory tract is to lower his head and cough. For a healthy horse, this is a fairly routine matter in everyday living. A healthy nonstressed horse that is exposed to dust and mold or noxious gasses may return to normal and suffer no long-term ill effects. When the horse is not able to lower his head over time and cannot remove these contaminants, the respiratory tract begins to suffer. Horses that were used in these studies had measurable contaminates and fluid in their lungs after 12 hours of being crossed-tied so they could not lower their heads. The studies were continued over 72 hours, checking the horses at 48 and at 72 hours. The ill effects worsened over the longer times.

When the respiratory tract is stressed in this way, the weakened system is more susceptible to bacteria and disease. With the addition of travel stress and exposure to other horses, then life-threatening "shipping fever" and/or other serious ailments can occur. The horse that is suffering pretrip from an illness, injury, or chronic pulmonary disease will have even more trouble coping physically.

It is not realistic for the environment inside the trailer to be completely free of contaminants, but the cleaner the air, the better for the horse. Even the cleanest hay will have some dust or mold that will contaminate the air in such close quarters. Feeding out of a hay net over the horse's head will increase the exposure unnecessarily. Each time the horse takes a bite, he shakes out the dust all over himself. He cannot help but breathe the flying debris. *Manger trailers* (trailers with a built-in hay manger) are no better since the horse must share his small headspace with the object of the contamination—the hay. More important, the horse cannot lower his head to remove the debris from his lungs in a manger trailer.

There are other contaminates inside a horse trailer besides hay. Ventilation is crucial to remove the harmful noxious gasses that are created by urine and manure, which are harmful to the horse's respiratory tract.

In our years of experience, it has been the green or the nonrespectful horses that have taught us the most about trailer problems because they quickly let us know there is something to worry about in this business of trailering. Problems in trailer design will be made self-evident when injuries occur because the horse is having trouble adjusting to the pressure of this ominous trailer. Those horses that are well trained and calm usually travel in even the worst of trailers without complaint, although they can still suffer unnecessary injuries or illness that are not normally recognized as stress from trailering. Once the physical environment has been made user-friendly for the horse and the horse has been properly trained to trust the trailer and the handler, loading and traveling will be a much safer activity. Articles in magazines and books provide information about nonstressful trailer training, so ignorance is no longer a reason for the horse to be trained by force to load into a trailer.

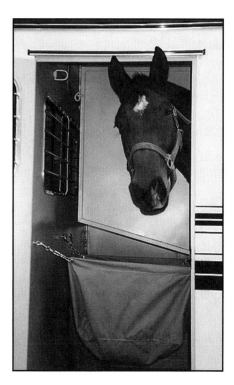

Relaxed and happy, this horse has a better chance to have a safe, nonstressful trip.

Criteria for Selecting a Trailer According to the Nature of the Horse

Many of the causes of stress to the horse, and to the people involved, can be eliminated by the design of the trailer and the proper choice of the hitch and tow vehicle. Many of the design features we discuss are self-evident when one accounts for the nature of the horse as discussed.

No matter the construction material, the number of horses being hauled, or the price of the trailer, three major criteria for trailer selection should apply.

SIZE

Because the horse can easily become claustrophobic, the trailer should have enough room and light inside for him to feel comfortable, therefore, reducing his stress level. A dark interior may cause him to balk when loading because the horse's eyes do not adjust quickly to light changes, and walking from daylight into a dark trailer can be frightening. Windows, doors, and light-colored interior paint make the trailer seem open and inviting to the horse. Height, width, and length should be proportionate to the size of the horse. He should be able to use all four of his legs to keep his balance. This means he must be able to spread his legs apart when he needs to and to slide them forward and backward with freedom of choice as this little box propels him down the highway, twisting and turning. He must have enough headroom so he doesn't feel cramped and can use his head and neck for balance. It is also very important that he be able to lower his head and cough to expel hay dust and other contaminants from his respiratory tract.

VENTILATION

This mention of the respiratory system leads to the next important criteria—ventilation. As previously mentioned, the environment inside the trailer is easily contaminated by dust and mold spores from hay and shavings and noxious gasses from urine and manure. Extreme temperatures, hot or cold, may also cause stress to the horse. The environment can be controlled by smart management techniques and a properly ventilated trailer. Adequate windows or slats and roof vents are necessary to provide a friendly climate for the horse. (These subjects will be discussed in detail in chapter 6, "Controlling the Interior Environment," and in chapter 15, "Driving Tips and Horse Safety.")

SAFETY IN DESIGN

A trailer must be safe for the horse and the handler. There should be no sharp objects or edges that could cut or injure a horse. All latches, tie rings, butt bars, breast bars, and so forth, should be strong enough to withstand wear and tear from the largest, strongest horse that will be hauled in that trailer. The entrance to the trailer should be nonthreatening to the horse, and the handler should be able to exit the trailer quickly if need be without the horse following. Dividers, posts, butt bars, and breast bars should operate freely and be easily removable in an emergency. Ramps should be solid, low, non-slip, and long enough to provide a measure of safety from a kick to the head of a person leaning down to lift the ramp. Step-up trailers (no ramp) should be wide enough to allow the horse to turn around to unload headfirst instead of backing out. A front unload ramp is even better. The floor and underbraces must be in perfect condition—there is no compromising on this point. All lights, brakes, and breakaway brake should be in working condition—the same for tires and suspension. The construction material should be strong enough to handle the size, weight, and strength of the horse(s) and equipment being hauled in it, and to hold up as well as possible in a traffic accident. It goes without saying that the tow vehicle and the hitch should be adequate to haul the trailer and its full load.

These three criteria are the minimum to expect from a horse trailer. Additional features are available that can greatly improve the well-being of the horse and handler. One of the most important features available in the last few years is rubber torsion suspension. This type of suspension is far superior to the drop-leaf suspension and not only reduces shock and stress, but also has other safety features. (More about this in chapter 8, "Mechanical Parts.") It is our opinion that rubber torsion suspension, more than any other factor, is responsible for lowering stress levels in horses.

Insulation, removable hay bags, mats, screens, bar guards on windows, removable or no rear center post, and water tanks are features that can affect the safety and stress reduction of the horse and may not always be expensive. A list of more expensive features includes interior fans, air-ride suspension, closed-circuit TV cameras, and even air-conditioning. Nice, but not always affordable for the average person.

Purchasing a Horse Trailer

At one time a horse was considered "old" at 10. Horsemen de-wormed their horses with tobacco. Tack was made only of leather. As little as ten years ago, colic surgery was rather experimental. Chiropractic, acupuncture, massage, and other alternative therapies for horses, even though they are still controversial, were unavailable. Up until now, tradition has been the rule of thumb in the horse business, but finally we are changing some of those traditions with knowledge and technology. National equine magazines cover almost every breed, discipline, and health condition. Bookstores and tack shops are filled with medical volumes, training books, and even mystery novels about horses.

Anyone can buy or rent a video on just about any subject in the equine world. Cyberspace is buzzing with horse talk. Good people want to know how to be good horse people.

Unfortunately, the availability of horse trailer information has not quite kept up with the rest of the horse world, and old habits die hard. Too many horse people have opinions about trailering that are not based on facts, mainly because real facts are hard to find. Many, but not all, horse trailer manufacturers are engineers who like to build things but have no personal experience with horses. Consequently they try to please the buyer, who may not be buying for the right reasons. Because the industry is small, a lost sale can be devastating to a dealer (one who sells trailers) or manufacturer (one who builds them), so they may sell the customer what he asks for, even though they know it may not be the best trailer for the buyer's needs.

Except for business licenses, horse trailer dealers and manufacturers need no equine-related qualifications to sell or build horse trailers, and though most are well qualified, there is no guarantee that a dealer or manufacturer has the proper knowledge to be advising other people about what to buy.

Horse trailer dealers are almost always in the business because they like it, certainly not to get rich. Most have, or used to have, horses themselves. Just like trainers, grooms, riders, and caretakers, some are really good horsepeople and some are not. Also, some work better than others with people. For these reasons prospective buyers should be well informed before shopping for a trailer, to insure that they buy the right trailer.

If a manufacturer built a horse trailer with walls of cardboard and the horses traveled upside down, he would be allowed to sell it. As long as this trailer was equipped with features that complied with the United States Department of Transportation specifications for road safety (lights, brakes, etc.), no law enforcement official would pull it off the road. However, no design regulations exist that are concerned with the safety and welfare of the horse. Furthermore, in all our research we were not able to find any statistics kept about horse trailer accidents or injuries by any government agency, insurance company, or trailer manufacturer.

The horse trailer industry is self-regulated by customer demand and tough competition. Many new improvements to horse trailers have come about because of better-informed customers and their ability to pay for the features they want. Consequently, the industry is quickly improving, and more good, safe, trailers have become available in all price ranges.

These horses have the same basic needs but require different trailers to satisfy our criteria of room, ventilation, and safety. The gray Arabian mare, Vespi, is 14.1h and weighs 875 pounds. The Hanoverian, Tristan, is 18+h and weighs over 1,600 pounds. Although Vespi will fit into almost any trailer on the market, a trailer for Tristan must meet the special needs of his large size.

Needs of the Horse

We have already established that the horse should be our first consideration in choosing the right trailer. All horsemen understand the importance of saddle fit, bridle fit, and blanket fit, but how about trailer fit? How big is the horse that will be hauled in the trailer? If more than one horse will be riding in it, consider the largest one. Does the trailer give that horse enough headroom? Is it tall enough so he can stand comfortably and not bump his head when loading? Not usually considered, but just as important as height, are the length and width. The horse should have enough room to use his head and neck for balance and to lower his head to cough out dust and debris he may inhale in the trailer. He should be able to spread his legs both forward and backward to stand easily without having to lean or scramble to find his balance. Many horses have learned to scramble and climb the walls from being hauled in a trailer that is too narrow. Once this behavior is learned, it is hard to overcome, but usually giving the horse more room will allow him to unlearn this behavior. Remember the horse has four legs and is quite capable of free standing in a trailer if the driver is considerate enough to drive carefully. (Tied, of course—but more about that later.)

How much does this horse weigh? A 16.2-hand Thoroughbred may need a tall trailer, but the 16.2-hand warmblood or draft horse will also need a wide trailer. These types will also be much heavier than a Thoroughbred. Don't underestimate the power that comes with the extra weight and larger muscles, and the ability to do a lot of damage just from being a horse. The construction material should be strong enough to handle the largest and strongest horse that will be hauled in the trailer. Tie rings, butt bars, ramps, and so forth should be able to stand up to the wear and tear of the behavior of a disagreeable horse. Putting a large horse into a lightweight trailer can be like carrying bricks in a plastic bag.

It is impossible to make decisions based on breed alone, since size within a breed can vary greatly. These two horses are both Quarter Horses. Sparkle (left) is an average-size mare at 15.2h and 1,150 pounds; Rebel (right) is 16.3h and weighs 1,415 pounds.

How old is this horse? Is it a young, untrained horse, or an old, experienced traveler? More seasoned travelers can put up with a less-than-perfect trailer, but the younger one will need the confidence builder of a trailer that is open and horse-friendly. If more than one horse will be hauled in the trailer, consider the one who has the most needs.

You will find that it is much easier to train a green horse to load when the trailer is light, roomy, and nonthreatening. Solid, non-slip flooring and ramps are essential, since no horse wants to step on something that does not feel firm to his step. (Instinct again!)

What kind of temperament does this horse have? Quiet, easygoing horses can be seen riding in the scariest trailers without a care in the world, trusting those people who have so carelessly put them in danger. These good-natured animals seem to endure a lot before they really protest. Personality types range from the even-tempered to the really nervous horses that work themselves up so quickly that they can become colicky on a short trip. A jittery horse or one with some strange idiosyncrasy can really benefit from appropriate trailer design.

Those people who have average to small horses, 16 hands and under, have a wealth of choices for horse trailers and the tow vehicles needed to haul them. The

This trailer, 7'4" tall and 6' wide, is classified as an extra-tall and wide trailer. Tristan is obviously cramped, and the butt bar is too low for him. Vespi has plenty of room, but the stall is too long for her. The butt bar could easily be moved forward for her with the addition of extra brackets. If you own horses of such different sizes, buy a trailer for the bigger one and make adjustments for the smaller one. (Tristan should be wearing a head bumper.)

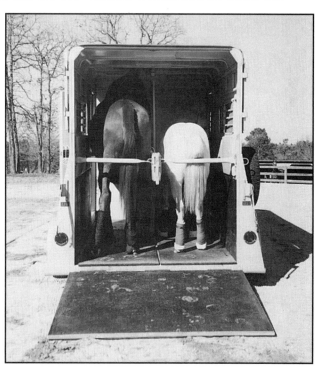

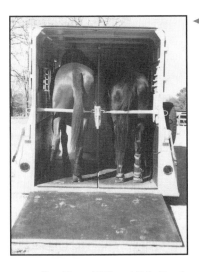

◄ There is adequate room in this same trailer for Rebel at 16.3h. With these two horses on the trailer, we have over 3,000 pounds of horse! The construction of a trailer that must hold such large horses must be strong enough to hold up to the extra stress of the greater weight.

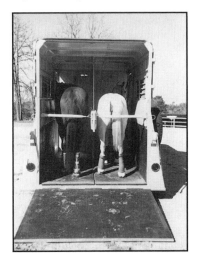

Sparkle at 15.2h and little Vespi are quite comfortable in this trailer. Both horses have 3' of width and plenty of room to spread their legs for balance without interfering with each other. These two could also fit in a smaller trailer, but it is better to have more room than less. ➤

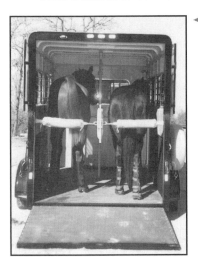

◄ This trailer is larger than the first trailer. It is 7'6" tall and 6'8" wide. Tristan (18+h) and Rebel (16.3h) fit as well in this trailer as Sparkle and Vespi fit into the other one. The butt bar is still too low for Tristan, and the center divider could be a bit higher. This can be accomplished with adjustable brackets. If the butt bar and dividers were permanently raised, they would be too high for smaller horses that would be able to get under them.

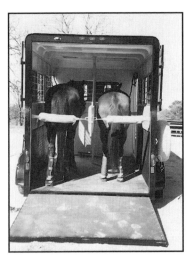

Both Quarter Horses can ride comfortably in this double extra-wide and extra-tall trailer. Even though Sparkle (right) is an average 15.2h, she can benefit from the extra space. ➤

selection gets smaller when the horse gets larger, and the buyer needs to devote extra energy to finding the right trailer.

Up and Down the Road

Ann asked her friend, Judy, to go with her to pick up her newly purchased Thoroughbred mare. Ann has a stock trailer with a window in the front, so she could see the horse through her rearview mirror. They loaded the new mare with no problems and started off. It wasn't long before Ann looked into the mirror to check on the mare, but she could not see her! She stopped the truck, jumped out, only to see the mare get up off the floor and stand up. She checked out the mare, found nothing wrong, and got back in the truck. The moment the truck started moving, the mare went down again. Ann got out. The mare got up. Ann started the truck again. The mare went down. Ann stopped. The mare got up.

She didn't live very far away, so Ann decided to continue on home, even though the mare was lying down in the trailer. When she got home, the mare got up and stood quietly until Ann could open the doors to unload her. She put the mare in her new stall and immediately called the former owner. "When I brought the mare home," Ann said, "she kept lying down whenever the rig was moving! Do you know why that would happen?" "Oh," the former owner replied, "I forgot to tell you. She always hauls that way!"

Needs of the Buyer

Whoever said "I wouldn't know what to do with a million dollars" obviously never had a horse. Budget is usually the first consideration when buying a horse trailer. Smart shopping can get you the features you need without buying more trailer than you have to, but buying the wrong trailer is never a bargain.

How many horses do you have? Don't buy a trailer with space for more horses than you really need. One-horse trailers are not very common, but if you are absolutely certain you will never have more than one horse and you want to haul it with a lighter tow vehicle, why not? Also, you have a good excuse not to haul someone else's horse to a horse show!

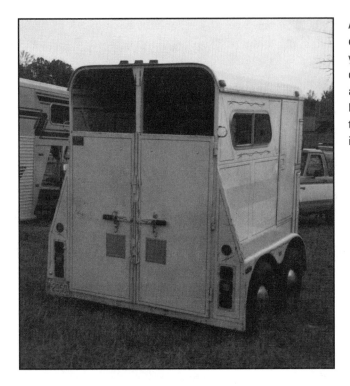

A nice used trailer like this one may suit your needs if you don't do a lot of long-distance traveling. The light and ventilation could be better, but the structure is sound and the mechanical parts are all in good condition.

How many horses will you be hauling in the future? You can always trade up when you can afford it, so think about resale value if that's a possibility.

Two-horse trailers are the most common type of trailer and fit the needs of most people. Even if you will only be hauling one horse, you have extra room for storage, and the resale value will be much higher than for a one-horse trailer. Horse trailers carrying four or more horses may require extra consideration for licensing, and the choice of tow vehicles becomes more specialized. Unless you actually need to haul four or more horses at one time or you need the extra room for a carriage or some other equipment, don't spend the extra money unless you want to.

Note: If you live in an area where natural disasters may require evacuation, such as a hurricane or forest fire, it would be wise to have a trailer space for each horse (and multiple trailers, if necessary) so that all can be moved out in one emergency trip.

How often will you be using this trailer? If you travel frequently, your trailer is an important tool, and durability and ease of use are important considerations. If you

Professionals need to have horses that are fresh and ready to go when they get to a competition. For an active competitor, a trailer must be able to hold up to the abuse of many miles on the road, and it must be a stress-free ride for the horse.

will use the trailer only occasionally to take your horse to the vet or to a lesson, a good used trailer that you can pull with your everyday vehicle will do the job. (As long as the tow vehicle is rated to safely pull the load.)

If you compete, camp, trail ride, haul horses for hire, or use your trailer for other reasons that put a lot of miles on your trailer, storage becomes more important. Dressing rooms, tack/feed compartments, and even living quarters may be necessary features.

The tow vehicle and hitch that you will be using must be rated to pull the weight of the loaded trailer. Accidents can, and have, occurred in the driveway before the combination is even off the farm, so "I'm only going a few miles," isn't an excuse for cutting corners on safety. (Tow vehicles will be discussed in chapter 14, "Tow Vehicles and Hitches.")

Growing, Growing, Gone!

The Evans family, Mom, Dad, Emily, and Joan, ages 17 and 18, had purchased two Trakehner fillies at a sale. They owned a two-horse steel trailer that had been used for the daughters' Pony Club horses, and they loaded their new fillies and took them home.

Time went by and the fillies grew to be mares, both well over 16.3 hands tall. When it was time to take them out for their first show, they were loaded into the same little trailer that had brought them home from the sale. Not much thought was given to the fact that these mares fit rather tightly in this trailer, and the whole family piled into the Suburban and went to the show.

Everything went fine until they were almost home. Mr. Evans had slowed down to turn into their own driveway when a commotion was heard from behind, and the trailer started jumping. He stopped the truck and the whole family jumped out to find both mares standing on the road. The mares had kicked out the back doors of the trailer! Both doors were off and the center post was bent, causing the whole frame of the trailer to twist. Miraculously, both mares were unhurt, but Mr. Evans suffered a broken wrist in the excitement. However, if he hadn't been driving so slowly to turn into the driveway, the outcome would have been much more disastrous. Even though the trailer was in good condition and had been strong enough for their previous horses, the Evanses had not realized that their "fillies" had outgrown the trailer and that they were now big enough and strong enough to tear it apart.

3

Trailer Styles, Types, and Variations

Watch out for bad advice. A person has a small dark trailer, barely roadworthy. He is lucky enough to have an easygoing, mild-mannered horse, and he uses the trailer for years. The "accident waiting to happen" hasn't—yet! A new horseperson asks him for advice, and he tells the novice that a trailer just like his will do fine.

Another person has a few nicks and bruises on his horses, but he believes that this is part of trailering. He doesn't particularly care if a horse is a problem loader; he forces the horse to load anyway or just gets another horse. When the novice asks him for advice, he replies, "Save money and get the cheapest trailer. Any horse that doesn't load into it belongs in the can!"

A longtime horse person who had a ramp-load trailer ten years ago is convinced that all ramps are bad because hers was steep and slippery, so she tells everyone who asks that a step-up trailer is the only way to go.

A conscientious horseperson spends a great deal of money for a new slantload trailer. He feels his horses are traveling better than ever before, and he is convinced that a slantload trailer is the very best thing that ever came along. He spreads the word, "Slant! Slant!" He has not considered that the suspension on his new trailer is much better than on his old trailer with the drop-leaf type and that this may be a greater factor in the horse's comfort than standing on a slant.

Choice of horse trailer usually depends on the discipline. For example, western riders prefer one type; hunter-jumper people prefer another. Dressage and event people have certain ideas, and all breeds have their own fashions.

But these differences should not be so wide, because a horse is a horse no matter what breed or discipline, and his requirements need to be met to maintain his well-being, so he can perform at his best.

Even some of the most experienced horse people get used to trailering their own way and don't give much thought to improving things until a major problem occurs. It is unreasonable to expect people to keep up with the development of the horse trailer industry and to be familiar with problems other than the ones they have experienced themselves. When individuals are trying to find information, it becomes the luck of the draw if they get good advice or not. Unfortunately, it's hard to tell who knows and who doesn't!

Another source of confusion is the inconsistency in the industry. The quality of trailers built by the same company can vary from year to year. Because of changes in design, materials, personnel, management, and ownership, a trailer built by one company in 1989, for example, may be of a completely different caliber in 1993.

Because we have recommended choosing a horse trailer from the horse's point of view, we evaluate trailers from that perspective first. There are three major types of trailers: manger models, walk-through models, and slantload models. All three have advantages and disadvantages.

Styles of Trailers

MANGER

Manger models have a fixed, built-in hay manger in the head area of the trailer. Underneath the manger, there is usually a tack compartment. There is a solid wall in front of the horse's legs. These trailers have traditionally been popular with western riders with small- to average-size horses, therefore, some of these older trailers are only 6 feet tall and 5 feet wide. Newer models usually come standard $6^1/_2$ feet tall and $5^1/_2$ feet wide. Optional height and width is available on almost all new trailers.

It would be very difficult to get out of this escape door in a hurry! Most manger trailers have small doors similar to this one.

The advantages of this type of trailer favor people rather than the horse. Since there is enclosed, lockable tack storage under the horse's heads, the trailer is more compact, and more gear can be hauled without purchasing a longer and, therefore more expensive, trailer with a separate tack area or dressing room.

The disadvantages of this type of trailer affect the horse and outweigh the advantages. Since the horse's head is confined in a small area with the hay, he must breath hay dust and debris. He cannot lower his head to cough and clear his respiratory tract. This may not be a problem on short trips, but the more time the horse travels in the trailer, the more hazardous the situation. Vents and windows become very important in manger-type trailers.

The next problem concerns the wall in front of the horse's legs. When the trailer stops, the horse bumps into the wall and cannot slide his legs forward to maintain balance, especially when the stop is sudden. Sometimes, the horse will jump into the manger because he has lost his equilibrium. Even if he does not resort to this behavior, he may be more stressed trying to keep his balance throughout the trip.

You think that a horse jumping into the manger would be a rare occurrence, but we have found this to be a fairly common problem in hauling horses in a manger trailer. The horse usually has to get himself out of the situation, since it is impossible for a person to get in there with him without risking life and limb. Injuries are common, both to the horse and handler, and the trailer can get damaged as well. When we consider the flight-or-fight response, the most logical reason for this behavior would be that the frightened horse sees the window in front of him and believes it is the way out.

The manger trailer usually has a small escape door for the handler to walk out if he leads the horse into the trailer. This door leads out over the fender, and it is very awkward for the person to get out easily. If the horse is behaving badly, this can be dangerous. It doesn't seem possible, but many fractious horses have squeezed out these little doors, usually with injuries. For more information regarding manger trailers, see chapter 5, "Interior Features and Options."

Saved in the Nick of Time

Linda was leaving the horse show with her horse trailer in tow. She was still on the show grounds when she looked in her rearview mirror to take a last look at the trailer before heading down the highway. Her manger door had popped open, so she got out of the truck to close it. When she got closer to the trailer she could not believe her eyes.

The lead rope had come untied and slipped out the open feed door. When she had started driving, the lead rope had wrapped around the wheel and was starting to pull her horse up into the manger! He was starting to be pulled out the feed door. This is an extreme example, but a good reason to always drive a little way, like down the driveway, and stop to check your trailer before pulling out onto the road.

WALK-THROUGH

The walk-through–type trailer has a breast, or chest, bar to stop the horse from going out the large walk-out door intended for people. The head area is open from ceiling to floor, creating one open area from head to tail. Sometimes this trailer is called a "Thoroughbred" type because it is popular with the English market, which has been dominated by the Thoroughbred horse. Even older trailers of this type are commonly an "extra tall" height of 7 feet, but new ones are usually taller, making 7 feet no longer "extra tall." There are some popular brands of older walk-through trailers still out there, but even though they are tall, some of these trailers are only $5^{1}/_{2}$ feet wide, and a few are only 5 feet wide. Nowadays, the newer models are usually 6 feet standard interior width and with even more spacious dimensions optional.

The one disadvantage to the walk-through trailer is that you do not have a place to put saddles and other tack where they cannot be absolutely safe from the horse or separately locked away. For this luxury it is necessary to have a separate dressing room or lockable tack area, which costs more money but makes for a really workable trailer.

From the horse's point of view, the walk-through trailer has many advantages. Because it is more open, it is less threatening to the horse and his claustrophobic nature. He can brace himself with his front legs by putting them forward without the interference of a solid wall, so he is less likely to panic and go up and over the bar. Sometimes a horse will go over the breast bar, but this happens much less often than going up into a manger. A good quick-release latch on the bar will make

A walk-through trailer with a dressing room. Canvas hay bags are removable and encourage the horse to reach down for his hay.

it easier to get the horse down, resulting in fewer injuries and less damage to the trailer.

Because the horse can stretch his head and neck over the breast bar, he is better able to clear his respiratory tract. Hay nets that are tied above the horse's head can be a problem, but if the hay is stored in solid feed bags positioned lower than his head, he will not be as subjected to hay dust falling on his head and flying around in his air space. For more information about hay bags, see chapter 5, "Interior Features and Options."

The large walk-out door is safer for the handler to exit when he leads a horse into the trailer. A door on each side of the trailer is preferable to a door on one side only, not just for handler safety but so that each horse can always be safely reached (for food, water, surveillance, a pat on the head, or an emergency) without removing the other horse(s).

A few manufacturers build two-horse walk-through models that have a front unload ramp. For the special horse that has had a history of bad trailer experiences, a young horse, or a mare and foal, this type of trailer can make it very easy to safely unload a horse, but usually the extra expense for such a two-horse trailer is unnecessary.

SLANTLOAD

Slantload trailers have become the trend in the last decade. Let's examine why. Slantload trailers were originally built to put more horses in a shorter trailer. This idea was first readily accepted by western riders and polo players, who generally have average-size to smaller horses. It was reasoned that since most horses stand in a slanted position when given the chance in an open or stock-type trailer (true), they must feel better balanced in that position (maybe). Slantload trailers also became popular about the same time as rubber torsion suspension came on the market, a fact that may have distorted the conclusions. Keep in mind that there has been no controlled testing or research to measure the effect of both the type of trailer and the differences in suspension on the well-being of the horse. If we look at slantloading from the horse's point of view, we may see a different picture.

Legally, trailers cannot be more than $8\frac{1}{2}$ feet wide on interstate highways and some other designated roads, usually truck routes. Other roads have an 8-foot width restriction, so most horse trailers are 8 feet wide, including fenders and other exterior protrusions. The minimum space for the wheels on each side of the trailer is one foot, usually covered by the fenders on the outside of the trailer. If the width of the trailer spreads over the space for the wheels, there must be a "wheel well" inside the trailer to protect the interior from the wheels. If the interior width of the trailer is 6 feet, there will be no wheel well; therefore, the inside walls will be smooth and the entire interior is usable to the horse. If the trailer has a 7-foot interior width, there will be 6 inches of wheel well on each side of the trailer, and the wheel well will take up an entire foot of wall and floor space on each side if the interior width is 8 feet. In other words, if the wheel well is located inside the horse area, the horse has only 6 feet of floor space no matter the trailer width.

It is for this reason that most slantload trailers are built on 102-inch axles. This way, the interior floor space can be expanded to about 6 feet 9 inches without wheel wells. Furthermore, the wheel wells take up less space if the trailer is expanded even more. However, the trailer may not be legally driven on all roads.

This is an 8' wide slantload on a 96" axle. There is 1 foot of wheel well on each side of the interior, leaving only 6' of floor space in most of the stalls. There is a rear tack area and no front unload ramp, which makes it impossible for most of the horses to turn around to come out headfirst.

Different manufacturers have different ways to install the dividers. Sometimes the dividers are put in at a slight angle almost straight across. In this case, more horses can fit in the trailer, but the overall stall length is limited to the width of the trailer. Sometimes the dividers are installed at a much steeper angle to lengthen the stall area, but if this angle is too steep, the stall can have a distorted aspect. In any case, the dividers are placed according to other considerations besides where the horse has a "better" sense of balance. When the horse is put into the stall, the choice of where he wants to stand has been eliminated. If the stall is too short for him, he ends up with his nose stuck into a corner, and if the trailer has been widened to make longer stalls, he will usually have either his back or front legs rubbing into the wheel well.

This trailer is built on 102" axles, which allows for 6'9" of floor space with no wheel wells. This type gives more usable floor space, but horses over 16h will be cramped in this trailer.

Is there really a place where a horse is more comfortable in the trailer? No one knows for sure. It is true that a horse will stand on a slant in an open trailer, but tie him next to the wall in a barn, and he is sure to stand with his hindquarters away from the wall in exactly the same way he will stand in the trailer. Maybe the horse just prefers not to have his entire body next to the wall, and it's not a "center of balance" after all that makes him stand that way.

Many horse people have determined that their horses haul better when the divider is removed and the horse is allowed to stand on a slant; therefore, a slantload is better. More than likely, the reason is that the horse has more room and feels less claustrophobic. Some research has determined that the horse has a better heart and respiratory rate when hauled in a slantload trailer. The problem is that such research does not consider other factors. Slantload trailers are new enough on the market so that they have many other features that improve hauling. They are usually lighter in color, taller, quieter, and most important, have rubber torsion suspension. When a horse that has been hauled in a smaller, darker, noisier, and bouncier trailer is put inside a newer slant, the new features, not exclusively the slant, add a great deal to the horse's comfort.

With each deceleration the horse must brace on the leading foreleg, and with each acceleration he must brace with his trailing hind leg, or he must lean on the divider. Therefore, he will not be absorbing the impact evenly throughout his body. A straight-load trailer will allow the horse to absorb the impact more evenly through the spine from front to back. We have seen horses become lame from long distances in a slantload, and sometimes less evident stiffness and soreness occur that are not commonly attributed to the trailer but are caused by it nonetheless.

Using our criteria of plenty of headroom and legroom, this style of trailer can be satisfactory for smaller breeds since they won't be so cramped. A horse that is 16 hands or over must travel with his nose in the corner, thus restricting his movement so that he does not have enough room to find his own balance. It is not uncommon to see large horses in slantloads traveling with bent necks or with the windows open so they can put their heads outside for more room. This is a good way to invite eye injuries from flying debris. A large horse can be made more comfortable by taking out a divider and giving him the space of two stalls, or the trailer can be custom designed to make the stalls up to 4 feet wide to accommodate his special needs.

What are the advantages of a slantload trailer? Because more horses fit in a shorter length trailer, it is possible to haul more horses in a smaller trailer. Three horses can be hauled in a tag-a-long trailer, making it unnecessary to go to a four-horse gooseneck if it isn't needed. Horses usually are happy to load into the openness of a slant, and the horses can be turned around and led out headfirst. Removable dividers make the trailer more easily converted and customized. Also, the slant design gives more room for tack storage and dressing rooms, both at the front of the horse area and at the rear corner.

Are there more disadvantages than already discussed? A few, but some forethought to design can solve some of them.

Once three or more horses are loaded into the trailer, the middle one becomes unreachable if a problem occurs, unless the back horse(s) is unloaded. This can be solved by adding front unload ramps that make it possible for each horse to be unloaded individually.

Many slantload trailers are step-up models. The larger the trailer, the heavier the suspension system. This often causes the trailer to sit higher off the ground. A

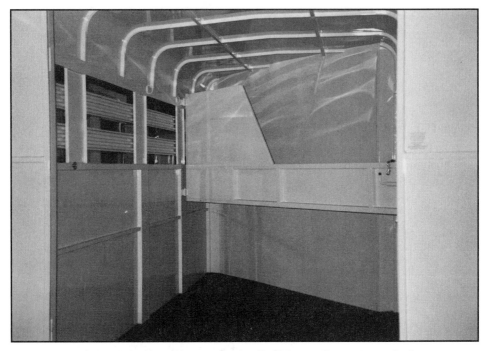

This trailer is only 6' wide inside and has no wheel wells. Three small- to average-size horses can ride in this trailer. There is no front unload ramp, but the horses can turn around to walk out headfirst.

The step-up on this trailer is 21" from the ground. It is a four-horse slantload with no front ramp and a rear tack. At least the back two horses in this trailer will have to back out of the trailer and blindly step down from this very high step. The front horses may have enough room to turn around after the others have been unloaded, but they will have to jump out.

longer trailer may also need to sit higher for ground clearance. In either case, the step-up becomes very dangerous for horses that must back out. Make sure that each horse can come out of the trailer headfirst. A rear ramp on such a trailer will most likely, but not always, be very steep for backing out.

Some manufacturers measure the stall length from corner to corner, but unless you want your horse to travel with its head stuck into the corner, measure the stall length from front center to back center. This is the actual comfortable space your horse will have. Since horses measuring 16 hands and over should have at least 10 feet of stall length, you won't find a slantload with stalls this long from center to center unless the stalls are slanted at a steep angle. In this case, the stall space gets distorted and the stalls should be made much wider. (In a trailer for multiple horses, one or two stalls may be positioned so that they miss the wheel well. If the trailer is 8 1/2 feet wide, these particular stalls may be long enough for a large horse.)

The width of the stalls varies from manufacturer to manufacturer. Unless all the horses being hauled in the trailer are very small, we recommend that the stalls be no less than 3 feet wide and wider if possible, especially for large horses. For more information on measuring the usable space in a slantload trailer, see chapter 9, "Capacity."

There are three trends that we have seen in slantload trailers that we believe should be avoided. Nowadays, some slantloads are being built with mangers instead of

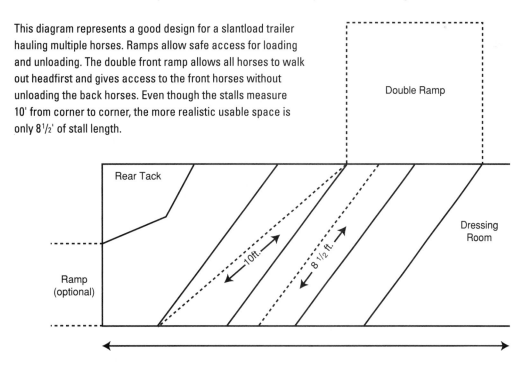

This diagram represents a good design for a slantload trailer hauling multiple horses. Ramps allow safe access for loading and unloading. The double front ramp allows all horses to walk out headfirst and gives access to the front horses without unloading the back horses. Even though the stalls measure 10' from corner to corner, the more realistic usable space is only 8 1/2' of stall length.

feed bags. This really takes up floor space and makes the stalls too short for even an average-size horse. The second trend is for three-horse and larger trailers to be built without a front ramp and with a rear tack space that makes it impossible for the horse to turn around to unload. All the horses must back out one at a time, the rear horse first, and so on. The third trend is for people to haul their horses backward in a slant because they heard somewhere that horses haul better backward. Never haul a horse backward in any trailer that has not been built for it. The balance of the trailer can be severely impaired and cause the trailer to be dangerous on the road.

Variations

FOUR-HORSE AND LARGER

Four-horse and larger trailers are also available in manger, walk-through, and slantload types. All have the same criteria for selection as two-horse trailers. Walk-through and manger types are available in head-to-tail configurations (all horses facing to the front) and walk-through types are also offered in a centerload design (front horses facing backward, back horses facing forward).

CENTERLOAD

Centerload trailers are longer than four-horse head-to-tail trailers but shorter than six-horse head-to-tail trailers. This extra length comes from the space between the front and back horses where the side ramp is located. The extra length is a minor problem for the four-horse because there are so many advantages to the centerload. When the centerload is built with a side unload ramp (best to be able to be used from both sides) and a rear entry with a ramp, it is the most horse-friendly configuration for hauling multiple horses.

Whether horses *like* to haul backward is open to discussion. When horses are hauled loose in an open trailer, they will often face backward. The reasons may or may not be that they feel more balanced that way, and some people believe that horses can brace themselves better on their hindquarters when the trailer stops. This sounds logical, but for every stop there is a start, and the horse must brace on the front legs at least half the time. There could be many other reasons for riding backward that only horses know about, such as avoiding exhaust fumes, but we believe that they like to keep an eye on the noisy traffic behind them. (Could it be that simple? Naaa!) Whatever the reason, facing backward is just as good as facing forward, and some horses may prefer one over the other. The horse absorbs the shock of acceleration and deceleration from back to front, in the direction of its spinal column. To repeat a word of caution: *Never* haul a horse backward in a trailer that is not designed for it. More about that in chapter 15, "Driving Tips and Horse Safety."

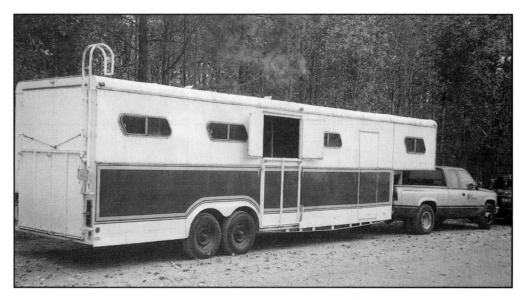

This is an example of a typical centerload trailer. The rear horses can load onto the trailer from the back ramp, and the front horses load onto the side ramp and back into the front stalls. This particular trailer does not permit access unless the ramps are down. The front door leads into the dressing room, not into the horse area.

Six-horse centerloads are three stalls wide, and four-horse centerloads are two stalls wide. The front horses haul backward facing the rear horses, who haul forward. The front horses can be led onto the side ramp and then backed into the front stalls. If there is a rear entry, the back horses can be loaded from the rear, just like any other rear-loading trailer. Since the horses then face each other, they have the benefit of knowing where all the members of their "herd" are at all times during the trip. This factor, along with almost unlimited headroom, is a stress-reducing advantage. Each horse can be individually attended to or unloaded without disturbing the other horses in the trailer. A trailer like this works great for hauling a number of horses to a one-day horse show or event where there is no stabling. The horse that is being used can be taken off the trailer separately while the others stay in the trailer. The horses can be interchanged all day long, one, two, or more, at a time.

Some four- and six-horse centerload trailers do not have rear-entry doors. All horses must be led into the trailer from the side and backed into each stall. This is still an acceptable design, but if there is a problem with a horse that does not want to back into a stall, the rear entry provides a better alternative.

Some centerload trailers have box-stall conversion packages that allow the dividers and center post to be removed, and stall partitions can be arranged across the trailer to make box stalls. This works well for hauling mares and foals or for two horses over long distances. Driving enthusiasts who need to haul one or two horses and a carriage might find this type of trailer ideal.

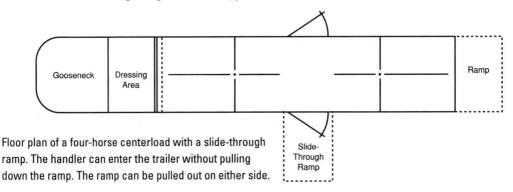

Floor plan of a four-horse centerload with a slide-through ramp. The handler can enter the trailer without pulling down the ramp. The ramp can be pulled out on either side.

Although most trailers come in two-horse and multiples of two, there are trailers for those who have special needs.

ONE-HORSE

One-horse trailers are not very common, but they can be an advantage to the person who will never haul more than one horse. They can also be hauled by a lighter tow vehicle, and you always have an excuse not to give a ride to anybody else's horse. The resale value is very low, however, and they are not much cheaper than a two-horse. Most manufacturers have taken them out of standard production, but some will build a custom order.

TWO-HORSE INLINE

Another less common trailer type is the two-horse inline. This trailer is one-horse wide, but two horse lengths long. One horse loads from the back into the front, a door is closed behind him, and the second horse goes in behind that door. The wheels of a tag-a-long inline are quite often arranged in the four corners instead of two together on each side. The tongue on a tag-a-long trailer is attached in a "wagon wheel" or "cut under" configuration, which turns the front wheels independently and the rear wheels follow, like a wagon. This results in a very light tongue weight, which allows the trailer to be hauled with a lighter tow vehicle. Also, the longer wheelbase on the trailer adds stability to a tow vehicle with a shorter wheelbase. The downside is the difficulty in backing up. Gooseneck inline trailers are traditionally built, with tandem wheels and a normal gooseneck hitch. The trailer is also as long as a four-horse trailer, but only one-horse wide instead of two.

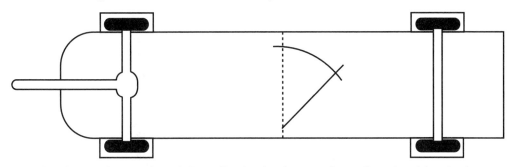

Floor plan of a tag-a-long two-horse inline trailer showing the cut-under configuration of the wheels.

An inline trailer allows two horses that do not necessarily get along to be hauled in the same trailer. They can be completely separated from each other by the solid door between them without sacrificing space in either horse's area. This is a great way to haul a stallion and a mare, or two stallions together. The disadvantage of backing the first horse out the entire length of the trailer can be fixed by a front unload ramp. Inline trailers are rarely built anymore but are available as a custom order from some manufacturers. Resale value is low, so if you want to sell a used one, you probably won't get much for it. On the other hand, if you want to buy a used one, you can probably get a good deal if you can find one.

THREE-HORSE SIDE-BY-SIDE

If you need a trailer for three large horses, a three-horse side-by-side can be a better option over a slantload. This trailer type is available as a bumper pull or gooseneck type, and the stall length can meet the needs of the large horse. The stall width will be slightly narrower than in a two-horse, but the length and headroom are more important. Wheel wells may be a problem, but if they are under the horse's head instead of in the stall area, they won't interfere with the standing floor space. Usually a three-horse side-by-side can be converted to a two-horse with very wide stalls. For people who have living quarters in the trailer, the extra width of the three-horse side-by-side will add extra square feet in the living area without adding more overall length. Three-horse side-by-side gooseneck trailers can be built with front or backward facing stalls.

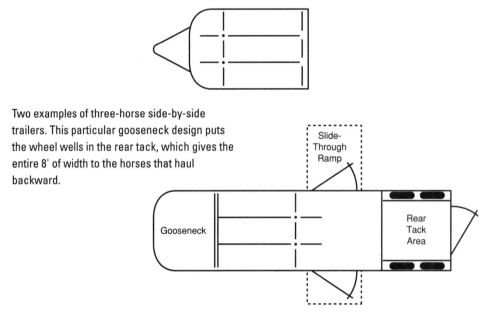

Two examples of three-horse side-by-side trailers. This particular gooseneck design puts the wheel wells in the rear tack, which gives the entire 8' of width to the horses that haul backward.

STOCK AND STOCK-COMBO

Till now we have been talking about trailers built exclusively for horses. When the budget does not allow for a horse trailer that meets the three requirements of room and light, ventilation, and safety, there is an alternative: stock or stock-combo trailers.

The stock type of trailer is built for hauling livestock, has slats instead of windows, and is usually open without dividers inside. Since it does not have a claustrophobic atmosphere, the horse will be more willing to load into the trailer and he can be turned around to unload headfirst. The standard stock trailer may not have dividers, but they can be installed as an optional feature to separate horses.

The stock-combo trailer has a solid front nose with front windows or vents. Simple dividers offer separate stalls for horses, and the sidewalls are slatted. Manger models with tack compartments or dressing rooms are available. Some have rear ramps.

This kind of trailer offers many advantages. The first is the price. Most stock trailers are heavily constructed of steel to withstand the hard work of hauling

This stock trailer has a good structure and gives good light and ventilation. It would be better if it were a light color, especially the roof.

livestock. Steel is the least expensive construction material so the price can be kept down by the simple design and basic features.

The openness of the stock trailer meets the roominess and ventilation requirements for horses. Unlike cattle, horses should be tied and separated by dividers, which are available in several configurations. Sixteen- to 20-foot stock trailers can have two straight stalls in the front with a space in the back for one or two more horses, or two box stalls using a full door in the center. Slant dividers can also be used.

The disadvantages of the stock or stock-combo are the result of the economical price. They are usually built tough enough for hard farm use, but livestock trailer manufacturers do not have as much concern for animal safety features. Be on the lookout for sharp edges, protruding objects, and other horse hazards. Some manufacturers build only with livestock in mind, selling mostly to the agricultural market, and other manufacturers are more inclined to build stock and stock-combo trailers for the equine market.

Overall quality of stock trailers differs greatly among brands. Aluminum stock trailers are also available, but unless you have a dual purpose for the trailer, such

Stock-combo trailers are half horse trailer and half livestock trailer. This is a good example of a nice usable trailer that could be used for hauling short distances (under 5 hours). It would be better if there were roof vents and windows or vents in the nose.

This is a very nice aluminum stock trailer that has rubber torsion suspension and removable Plexiglas slat covers. However, there is only room for three small- to average-size horses or two large horses, and it is almost two times the cost of a comparable steel or hybrid two- or three-horse trailer.

as cattle, the cost of an aluminum stock trailer will be the same as a very good horse trailer.

More horse-friendly features can be added to stock trailers, but then the price starts escalating. Most stock trailers are built with drop-leaf suspension, but some manufacturers offer optional rubber torsion suspension, which greatly adds to the comfort of the horse, driving safety, and the life of the trailer. (More about suspension in chapter 8, "Mechanical Parts.") Ramps and escape doors, spare tires, dividers, and so forth are features that can be added to a stock trailer. Removable Plexiglas or plywood can be used to enclose the trailer in cold weather, but don't jeopardize the ventilation.

When hauling horses in a stock trailer there are a few things to consider. It may seem highly unlikely and overly cautious, but debris can fly into the trailer and cause eye injuries. Putting protective fly masks on the horses is an inexpensive alternative to vet bills or loss of an eye.

The horse should be tied in the trailer and not allowed to walk around while the vehicle is moving. A child likes to stand up in the front seat, but it is not safe, so we don't let him. Even though the horse would like to walk around, his shifting weight can unbalance the load, possibly causing loss of control of the vehicle.

Now it is time to look at the trailer from the human point of view. All the above models are available in tag-a-long or gooseneck styles. Which one is right for you?

Types of Trailers

TAG-A-LONG

The tag-a-long is also called "bumper pull" style, but since the trailer is not supposed to be attached to the bumper of the tow vehicle, but to a hitch installed on the frame, the term is a misnomer. Tag-a-long trailers are the most common type with two-horse capacity, and there are good reasons for this:

- They are less expensive than gooseneck trailers.

- There is a wider choice of tow vehicles that can be used to haul a tag-a-long other than a pickup truck.

- More people have them, so it is easier to find an emergency lift from a friend if your tow vehicle breaks down. It is also easier to get a tow truck that is capable of hauling it.

- The tag-a-long follows the path of the tow vehicle, making it easier to make normal turns without fear of tearing a trailer fender or pulling the trailer wheel over a curb.

- The tag-a-long is less intimidating for first time or infrequent users.

- It takes up less space for storage.

- Licensing is less complicated. It is possible to keep the combination under 10,001 pounds, therefore avoiding the decision to make a declaration of "commercial."

- When the trailer is correctly hitched to a vehicle that is properly rated, the two-horse trailer is as safe as a gooseneck. It is very common to see tag-a-long trailers that are not hitched safely, and accidents happen because of carelessness, not from any fault of the trailer. More about hitches in chapter 14, "Tow Vehicles and Hitches."

The tag-a-long has some of the following disadvantages:

- When hauling more than two horses, stability becomes a problem, and a gooseneck is a better choice. Tongue weight becomes heavier on the

A trailer this long will not have the stability of a gooseneck trailer of the same capacity. To safely tow a tag-a-long trailer that holds more than two horses, it is very important to have a weight-distributing hitch that is properly rated to pull the load.

rear of the tow vehicle, and special precautions must be taken. Some-times a triple axle, although rare, will alleviate some of the tongue weight, but the maneuverability of the trailer suffers. Some three-horse slant or side-by-side units can work satisfactorily as a tag-a-long, but it is most important that the tow vehicle and hitch be properly rated to haul the load.

- There is not as much room for sleeping quarters as in a gooseneck trailer.

GOOSENECK

Owners of gooseneck trailers are so attached to them that they are always quick to say that "It's the only way to go!" Although there are many advantages to a goose-neck trailer, it is not always right for everybody.

There are two types of gooseneck hitches. The most common type is the "ball hitch" and the other, less common type, is the "mini-fifth wheel." The ball hitch coupler drops down onto a ball that is located in the truck bed. The mini-fifth wheel has an elevated wheel-like notched hitch installed in the truck bed. The kingpin on the trailer slides into the notch when the truck is backed into it. This is just like the fifth-wheel hitch you see on the big tractor-trailer rigs, only smaller. The mini-fifth wheel is usually seen on larger trailers, such as six horse and more, but it is available for all goosenecks if desired.

A typical gooseneck trailer and pickup truck.

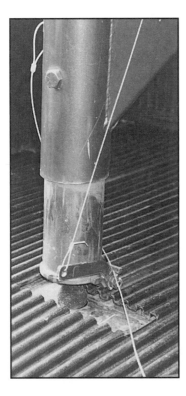

Ball hitch. This drop-down coupler has the benefit of a cable attached to the release lever. When it is time to unhitch the trailer, the owner does not need to get into the bed of the pickup truck. The cable runs out near the jack, where it can be pulled as the trailer is being jacked up.

A mini-fifth-wheel hitch.

The Department of Transportation in many states distinguishes between these two types of hitch by requiring safety chains for ball hitch goosenecks but not for mini-fifth wheels. At the time of this writing, 26 states require safety chains for ball hitch goosenecks, a fact that has not been widely known, even by those who enforce the law.

The gooseneck-type trailer offers the following advantages:

- The tongue weight of the trailer rests directly onto the bed of the truck over the rear axles, which means that the truck is able to carry more weight with better stability, an important factor when hauling more than two horses.

- The trailer starts turning when the truck turns, cutting corners more quickly than the tag-a-long. This feature gives the entire unit a very tight turning radius, although if the trailer is turned too tightly too often, excess wear will occur on the tires, wheels, and axles.

- Ball hitch gooseneck trailers are available with couplers that allow hitching without getting into the bed of the trailer, which makes them easier to hitch up than other trailers. You can see the ball in the truck bed while you are backing up to the trailer coupler.

- The area in the gooseneck can be used for sleeping or extra storage without adding extra length to the floor of the trailer. Living quarters are best built into gooseneck trailers.

A gooseneck may not be for everybody. Some disadvantages are the following:

- Expense. A gooseneck can cost on the average $2,000 more than a tag-a-long of the same capacity, and it must be pulled by a pickup truck. It is unnecessary to spend this extra money for the trailer and a truck to pull it if you are only hauling two horses and you don't need the extra space for sleeping or storage.

- The tight turning radius makes it more difficult to make normal turns without cutting corners too sharply. Many a fender has been left on a signpost.

- It is a real pain to hitch up one of the couplers, which requires getting into the bed of the truck to hitch and unhitch.

- Since fewer people have gooseneck hitches, it is more difficult to find someone to give an emergency tow. Also, it is more difficult to find a tow company that has the equipment to tow a large combination in the case of a breakdown. Mini-fifth wheels are even more difficult in this situation since very few people have them.

- Depending on the state in which you live, licensing can be more complicated. Most gooseneck combinations will be over 10,001 pounds GVRW, and "commercial" declaration may be necessary. See chapter 8, "Mechanical Parts."

- Neophytes may find the large size more intimidating.

- Trailer storage may be a problem.

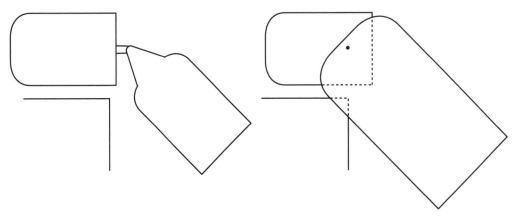

A tag-a-long follows the path of the tow vehicle when making a turn. The gooseneck cuts the corner more quickly, so it is necessary to make wider turns.

Dressing Rooms, Living Quarters, and Tack Areas

All the previously discussed styles and models of trailers are available with dressing rooms. The standard dressing room is 4 feet long, for both tag-a-long and gooseneck models. Almost all manufacturers will custom build the dressing room to almost any length. Gooseneck models are best suited for the extra length needed for living quarters to be installed. However, it is possible, but not common, to put some type of simple living space in a tag-a-long.

Dressing rooms are a very popular option. They are one of those conveniences that people "think they don't need until they have one." Dressing rooms usually double as tack areas with saddle racks and bridle hooks. Saddle racks that are removable offer the option of using them only when you need to.

It is not the most common way to design a dressing room, but it makes the doorway somewhat accessible from both sides of the trailer.

It is easy to sweep out the dirt from this dressing room floor.

This dressing room is difficult to sweep because of the lip around the door frame.

Dressing rooms can be quite plain and functional or fancy enough to have wall paneling and carpeting. It can be made more convenient.

- Indoor-outdoor carpeting should be mold resistant. Linoleum or some other smooth washable surface is easier to sweep than carpeting.

- The dressing room is easier to clean if the door opening is flush at the bottom. If there is no lip, it is much easier to sweep out the dirt. Lay a separate rug over carpeting so that you can pick it up and shake out all the dirt that gets tracked in. This will protect the carpeting underneath and keep it looking good longer.

- A step or running board makes it easier to get in and out.

- Windows and vents in the dressing room roof help avoid the buildup of heat inside and protect tack from mildew.

- A wall mirror is good if you do a lot of showing out of your trailer.

- Options such as hat racks, blanket racks, shelves, brush boxes, and bench seats with storage space underneath can offer many benefits to those who use the trailer for showing, camping, or even everyday tack storage.

An extra opening window in the bulkhead wall allows light and air to pass through the dressing room into the horse area.

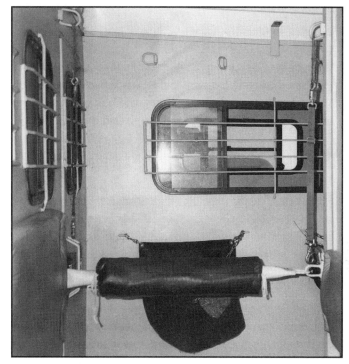

We like trailers to have windows in the front of the horse area for light and ventilation if possible. One of the drawbacks of the dressing room is that it blocks the airflow to the horse because the "bulkhead" wall is solid between the horse area and the dressing room. It is possible to put a window in this wall, allowing the air to flow from the front window to the horse area. If a window is not an option, it should be possible to put a couple of vents in the wall.

For those who use the dressing room area for sleeping or for storing things that do not need to smell like horse tack, you have the option of adding a separate tack area to models that do not already have one under the manger. The tack area can be built between the horse area and the dressing room area in walk-through trailers and slantloads. Doors allow access from the outside, and it is even possible to have a door between the dressing room and the tack area. A rear tack area can be added to slantload trailers by using the triangular space left by the last horse stall; the area can be accessed from the back of the trailer. Sometimes this tack compartment has walls that can be taken out if they are not being used.

This kind of rear tack area is convenient for the people involved but can be bad for the horses. Since it takes up part of the rear loading area, it makes it impossible to turn a horse around and walk him out. All the horses in the trailer must back out

In this trailer a separate tack compartment keeps tack out of the sleeping area.

unless there is a front unload ramp. If the trailer is a high step-up, this can be a hazard. We have already talked about this in chapter 3, but it bears repeating.

Living quarters can be as simple as a mattress in the gooseneck or a luxurious home away from home with duct air-conditioning, deluxe bathrooms and kitchens, and pullout sections to add extra width. The additional length and all the appliances and cabinetry also add extra tow considerations. Traveling in style can be fun. You can have everything you are willing to pay for. Living quarters will be discussed more thoroughly in chapter 11, "Living Quarters."

When a dressing room is added to a two-horse trailer tag-a-long, the extra length of the trailer may provide further stability to the combination. Also, when backing up, a longer trailer is easier to control than a shorter trailer, which tends to jack-knife quickly.

Note: Never sleep in a dressing room with a heater that is not approved for such use, and always leave vents and windows open. The buildup of carbon monoxide can cause death!

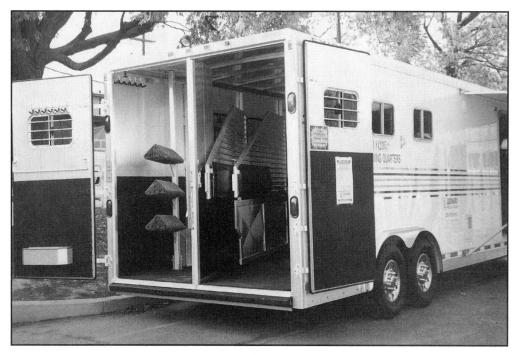

A rear tack in a slantload is very convenient but makes a difficult step down for a horse. This trailer does not have a front ramp for unloading horses.

A smaller "weekend" package can have a lot of conveniences without adding much length. A 7 ½' dressing room in a gooseneck trailer can hold a king-size bed, microwave, refrigerator, fold-down table, sink, shower, and toilet.

This aerodynamic nose takes up more space in the gooseneck area than a flatter nose.

This trailer is designed so the aerodynamic nose adds space instead of taking it away.

AERODYNAMIC VERSUS FLAT NOSE

Both gooseneck and tag-a-long trailers are available with a flat nose or an aerodynamic pointed or rounded nose. Theoretically, the pointed or rounded nose cuts through the air better than the flat nose and offers less wind resistance, therefore, improving gas mileage for the tow vehicle and adding tow stability to the rig. The amount of gas savings can be more significant for someone who travels many miles than for a person who stays close to home and travels infrequently. Depending on the manufacturer's design, pointing or rounding the nose may either add or take away headroom for the horse. A gooseneck area may also lose some space. Usually, the aerodynamic nose will be more expensive than the flat nose. If this is the case, the expense may not justify the gas savings if you don't drive a lot of miles. If you are trying to decide between two trailers and all things are equal except for a more expensive aerodynamic nose, the flat nose will be fine unless you travel enough to save enough gas to pay for the extra expense. If the price is the same, choose the aerodynamic nose.

We have explored all the models and types of horse trailers. Perhaps by now you are beginning to form a picture of the type of trailer you want to buy, but first, we need to look at all the features and options that are available.

Loading and Unloading Features and Options

They say that the most dangerous parts of flying in an airplane are the takeoff and the landing. The same can be said for loading and unloading a horse into a trailer. Most trailer injuries to horse and handler happen during these times. Although there is no guarantee that injuries will not happen no matter what kind of trailer you have, the probability can be greatly reduced by choosing a trailer that is horse-friendly.

Rear Entry

STEP-UP VERSUS RAMP

Step-up trailers do not have a ramp, and the horse "steps up" into the trailer. This kind of rear-entry system is more common on manger, slant, and stock-type trailers. The advantage of a step-up trailer is the belief that a horse will more readily step up into a trailer since horses are often afraid to step onto a ramp. However, the disadvantages to owning a step-up far outweigh this one advantage.

Every time you put a horse onto a trailer, he must also exit it. If he has to back out of a step-up, he has to step down—usually blindly. Each time the trailer is moved to a different place, the height of the step-down is also different. When he sightlessly feels his way out of the trailer, it is easy to miscalculate his footing. A horse that is new to a step-up may actually be afraid to come out, but even an experienced horse may fall out and, in the worst-case scenario, slip a leg under the trailer. This can mean devastating injuries not only to the leg, but also to the spinal column, resulting in expensive vet bills, loss of use, or even the loss of the horse. Although horses are obviously hauled in step-up trailers every day without incident, in our experience this type of accident happens enough to consider an alternative. Horses are also commonly injured by bumping their legs on the trailer when they are stepping in, especially when there is a problem loading. No horse should ever be put into any trailer without leg protection, but it is even more necessary in a step-up model.

The risk of a step-up can be eased by allowing the horse to turn around and unload headfirst or walk out the front by a front unload ramp. This is one situation where the slantload has an advantage, since unloading can be done in either of these two ways (unless there is rear tack area to make it impossible for all the horses to turn around). Open stock trailers also have enough room to turn the horse around.

"My horse won't step onto a ramp!" is one of the most common complaints we hear from potential customers. It is true that horse trailer ramps were pretty rickety in past years, and no one could blame a horse for being unsure about stepping onto such unsteady footing. After all, uncertain footing can mean mortal danger to the wild horse, so we are again asking the horse to overcome his natural fear when the ramp is unsteady, slippery, or steep.

Actually, the problem is not ramps in general, but ramps in particular. Many manufacturers build trailers with good ramps, but not all. By shopping, it is possible to

A stock-combo step-up that is open enough to allow the horses to turn around to walk out headfirst.

find a trailer with a ramp that is solid, not slippery, and low to the ground. This kind of ramp is not as threatening to the horse, and quite often he doesn't even notice it. A horse that is new to trailering or had a bad experience earlier may not trust it at first but will easily walk on once he has had a chance to test it with one footstep.

A good ramp is a safety net for the horse. By making a smooth transition from the ground to the trailer, fewer mishaps can take place when loading or unloading. Yes, a horse can step off to the side of a ramp, but if it is low to the ground, it usually isn't more of a problem than stepping off any other step. If he is wearing leg protection, he most likely will not hurt himself. If he falls off the side of the ramp when unloading, it will not likely cause the devastating type of injury that can happen if he slides a leg under the trailer. Even if he falls down and slides a leg under the ramp, the ramp can be lifted; the trailer cannot.

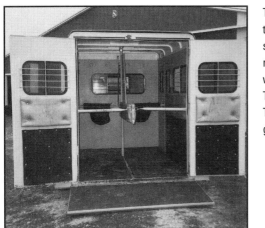

Three examples of good ramps. All are very low to the ground and have non-slip surfaces. All are very steady even though the ground is uneven. The ramp of this trailer is wider than the doorway, which gives a better safety margin on the sides. This trailer is very light and inviting to the horse. The full-height doors on the side keep him from going off to the side.

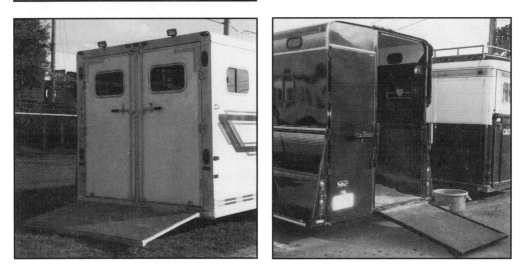

These two trailers show that slantload trailers are available with nice ramps.

A good ramp must meet the following criteria to be horse-friendly:

- It must not be steep. A short ramp will more likely be too steep, although some trailer manufacturers lower the ramp at the hinge so that the angle is acceptable, even though the ramp is short.

- It must not be slippery. Some ramps have struts, which give good footing, but they sometimes break off with use, especially the wooden ones. Different kinds of mats on the ramp offer different kinds of footing, some better than others. Hard, smooth mats will get very slippery, especially when wet with urine or manure, but they are easy to clean. Nubby mats may be harder to clean, but offer better footing in all kinds of conditions. Some foreign-made trailers come with a rush matting that seems to be non-slip, but gets to be slick or slippery if it is covered in manure. It is also very hard to clean.

- It must cover the entire width of the trailer opening or more. Ramps that are not wide enough make it easy for the horse to fall off the side. Some trailers have ramps that are wider at the bottom hinge to give more leeway for the horse as he unloads.

- Springs should be smooth, with no parts sticking out to cut the horse or cause hoof damage.

- Springs should not be installed on the sides of the trailer and ramp unless they are completely out of the way when the ramp is down. When the ramp is down, springs are hazardous on the front corner of the ramp.

- The door latches should not stick out the sides of the ramp when it is down. This can be a source of injury to the horse, and the horse can step on them, bending or breaking them.

This ramp is low and non-slippery, but the springs on the side can catch a horseshoe if the horse puts a leg out when unloading. Because the ramp does not lie on the ground, it is shaky when a horse steps on it to go into the trailer. Many horses are afraid of a ramp like this. The ramp on the trailer in the background folds up over half doors—a nice addition to a stock-combo trailer.

The side springs are out of the way on this ramp, but they do not help lift the ramp. This ramp is so heavy that it is very difficult for one person to lift. The struts help to give traction for the horse, but as you can see, one is broken, a very common problem with wooden struts.

- The latches should be strong enough to withstand the horse forcefully backing into the ramp when the trailer is closed. Butt bars or chains should protect against this, but always be prepared for the possibility that one of them could break.

To make the ramp more user-friendly for the handler, there are a few things to consider. For example, a long ramp will generally be heavier, but the slope will be less steep and the horse will have an easier time loading and unloading. The weight of the mat, and/or the hinge system will determine how easy it is to lift. Some trailer ramps are spring-assisted and can be easily lifted by one person. One trailer manufacturer has so much tension in the springs that once the ramp is started up, the ramp can actually lift itself the rest of the way and slam shut. This is a wonderful feature, but one must be careful not to let it slam behind an unsuspecting horse. It may be too much of a surprise. Conversely, be careful of a ramp that is so heavy it falls open when the latches are undone. Even if you don't get your foot smashed, you are going to have to get three friends to close it again.

This ramp is so slippery and steep that it is difficult even for a person to walk down it. A horse doesn't stand a chance!

A short ramp will be lighter and easier to lift, and it will usually, but not always, be steep. There is also a slight, but added risk of getting your head close enough to the horse's hooves to get kicked when leaning over to pick up the ramp. A ramp that folds over closed rear doors solves this problem.

With all these things to think about, it seems that buying a ramp trailer may not be worth all the trouble, but it really isn't so hard to find a trailer with an acceptable ramp and the increased safety for the horse makes it worth the effort.

One more type of ramp can be a compromise between the two styles. A few trailers have a ramp that slides under the trailer when not in use and is held there by brackets. The horse can be loaded without the ramp if desired, and then the ramp can be pulled out for unloading. This feature is not used enough by manufacturers.

REAR DOORS AND WINDOWS

Whether the trailer is a step-up or a rampload, many different types of rear doors and windows are available.

Half doors are one of the most common types of rear doors. Each horse stall has an individual door that is only one-half to three-fourths the height of the trailer, leaving an open space above. These doors most commonly latch onto the center post of the trailer, and each door works independently. Sometimes there are top tail door covers that close above the half doors, and sometimes there is a canvas door cover that attaches with snaps or by some other means.

These half doors are acceptable enough and have been used since the first horse trailers were built. When the doors are open, they flare out to the side, providing a barrier that discourages the horse from going off to the side. Each door can be closed individually, and after the first horse has been loaded the door can be closed while the next horse is being loaded. Half doors are generally used on step-up trailers, but it is possible to have a ramp that lifts up and closes over the doors after the doors are closed—a good option.

The major issue concerning half doors is discussed in detail in the section on dividers and center posts. The doors are latched to the center post, a feature that, although very common, has its problems. Some trailers have a different and better system to latch the doors that doesn't require the use of a center post.

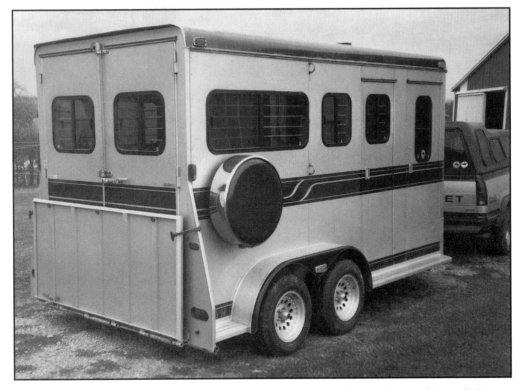

Full-height doors with a short ramp over. The windows in the doors can be opened to provide ventilation. The top door frame where the latch is attached is small enough not to interfere with the actual doorway height. Some trailers have a very large frame that makes the entry way shorter than the interior height.

Many trailers have an open space over the rear doors, allowing a certain amount of ventilation. If ventilation is so important, why would anyone want top doors, called "tail door covers" or "storm doors," which close the trailer up? Because when the trailer is being hauled down the highway, air is pulled in like a vacuum, and dirt, debris, and rain can actually fly into the trailer from behind. That's how those tractor-trailer rigs get so dirty in the back. Also, with their extensive range of vision, horses can see that something is coming up behind them, and seeing the loud trucks and cars coming nearer can frighten some horses, adding unneeded stress.

A variation of the twin doors/ramp over in a less expensive stock-combo trailer, except these are attached to a center post. The slats provide ventilation while making the doors tall enough to fully enclose the horses. The butt bars on this trailer sit too far to the back, so they do not leave a space for the tail to fall between the butt bar and the door. The horses can also push against the back doors, especially in this case because the butt bars are too low for these horses.

Tail door covers protect the horse from the environment and act in the same way that blinders do for driving horses. Horses don't react to something if they don't see it. Tail door covers are not usually airtight, and you don't want them to be, because you want some airflow. Sometimes though, it gets too hot to keep the doors closed, especially in stop-and-go traffic. Generally tail door covers are removable, and the easier it is to do this, the better. Better still is the type of door cover that can be tied back in an open position while traveling. The best system, however, is the tail door covers with windows that can be opened or closed as the situation dictates, making it unnecessary to remove the door covers themselves. Canvas tail door covers (also called tail curtains) can also be removed as needed.

Tail door covers should always be latched back to the side of the trailer when the horse is being loaded. They should never stick out unless they are attached to the half door so they don't swing. A sharp corner can cut a horse if he goes off to the side and runs into it. We have even seen horses run off to the side under the door cover and lift it off the hinges. Human heads are also within bumping distance of door cover height.

Ramp with tail door covers. The door covers attach directly to the ramp since there is no rear center post. These door covers can be latched open when the trailer is in transit. The door hinges on this trailer should not stick out so far on the side.

Trailers that have ramps instead of doors can also have tail door covers. They can be closed and latched directly onto the closed ramp or onto a center post.

Beware of tail door covers that have sharp edges and corners.

Five piece Dutch doors are a combination of all the above. Two small "Dutch" doors in the middle, door covers on top, and a short ramp that only reaches up to the doors create the five pieces. These are rather popular. People like that the small doors can close the horse in quickly before the butt bar is fastened. After the door is closed, it is possible to reach under and fasten the butt bar. Also the ramp is short and quite likely easy to lift. However, this kind of ramp is usually steeper than a longer one.

Dutch doors used to be our favorite type of rear door, but we have changed our minds through the years. A butt bar should be strong enough and easy enough to

Five-piece Dutch doors. These particular Dutch doors do not fold back any more than pictured, and they tend to blow shut in a breeze. This problem can be solved by installing hold-backs.

fasten so that closing the door first should not be necessary. The latches on the door may not be strong enough to keep a strong horse from bursting through if the butt bar is not attached. Also, if the horse is leaning on the door, it is not always possible to put up the butt bar without smashing an arm or finger in the process. Again, this type of door configuration requires a center post.

It may seem like a remote possibility, but leaning over to pick up a short ramp puts one's head very close to the horse's hooves. The short Dutch doors allow a fractious horse to kick out far enough to be dangerous to a person who is lifting the ramp.

Another type of rear door are the full-height twin doors, which work like the half doors, but cover the full height of the rear opening. These doors should have windows that can be opened or closed, according to the circumstance. As with half doors, the latches can attach to the center post, but we recommend an independent latching system that does not involve the center post. When these doors are open, they also flare out, making a full-height barrier for the horse on the side. These doors can be used on a step-up, or they can have a fold-over ramp. With them, handlers have all the advantages of half doors plus the advantage of never having to worry about what to do with the top door covers.

The one disadvantage of full-height doors takes a bit of explanation. When there is no center post on which to latch the doors closed, there must be another system to accomplish this. What is commonly used is a three-point latch—the kind of heavy-duty latch that is used on the large commercial semi trailers. The three "points" of this latch are on the top of the doorway, the bottom of the doorway, and in the middle of the doors. In order to have a place to install the top bracket, there must be a frame at the top of the doorway. This frame will take up some of the true height of the trailer entryway. There is nothing wrong with this system, in fact, it is a very good one, but one must account for the actual clearance height of the entryway because it may be less than that of the overall trailer. For instance, a trailer that has a 7-foot-6-inch interior height may only have 7 feet of true height in the doorway if the frame drops down 6 inches from the top. The frame may also include the sides of the entryway, making the actual doorway narrower than the actual interior width. The degrees of difference will vary, depending on the manufacturer. If you are contemplating a trailer with this kind of door, make sure the all-around framing width is acceptable for your needs. Interior padding on the top of the frame can protect the horse somewhat if he throws up his head and bumps it when unloading.

A bonus with this framing system is the fact that the exterior running lights can be installed on the frame, where they are more visible than on the top of the roof, the more usual place.

Slantload and stock trailers are usually equipped with one large door that opens from one side, through which the horse enters. The door can be installed with the three-point latch that is installed on the same frame system used for the full-height doors with no center post. It is on the side instead of in the middle, however. There are other types of latch systems available for a full-width door.

Full doors work for slant and stock trailers since there is no need for a butt bar or door to keep one horse from coming back out while the others are still loading. A full door does not work very well in a regular side-by-side loading trailer. If this type of door has been installed in an existing side-by-side trailer, separate butt bars should be installed so each horse can be kept in the trailer until it is his turn to unload. A full door should have opening windows or slats for ventilation.

HOLD-BACKS

Door hold-backs, sometimes called tie-backs, are one of those features that you can't do without once you have used them. Trailer doors are always banging shut when the wind picks up, and it is not only annoying but painful as well when that tail door cover hits you on the head. Hold-backs come in many different styles,

This type of hold-back pulls apart
with a slight tug.

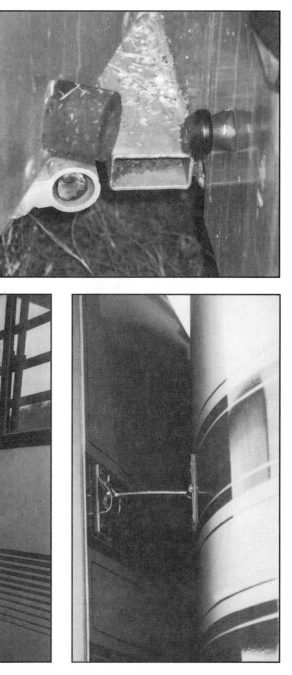

It is possible to travel with the door covers open
with this kind of hold-back.

This is the most common type of hold-back. If
the trailer has a thin skin, the tie-back should be
attached to the frame, or it will easily pull off.

and all have the same purpose, holding the door open. Some are little aluminum arms located on the trailer side that fit into a slot found on the door, or sometimes the arm is in the door and the slot is on the trailer side. Some are arms that stick into a rubber grommet where they hold until the door is slightly tugged. Another kind works like a door latch: the latch fits through a slot in the arm, and a pin holds it there until the pin is removed. This last type works very well for tail door covers. Hold-backs are available on most trailers either as a standard feature or as an option. They can be installed on tail door covers, feed doors, escape doors, and dressing room doors.

There are a few problems with hold-backs. The aluminum arm and slot types work very well, but they can bend easily or even come off if someone inadvertently tries to pull the door away without unlatching it. The rubber grommet type does not always hold the door if the wind gets too strong. If you are purchasing a trailer with hold-backs, test them for ease of use and for proper installation. If the hold-back seems to be strong enough to work the way you think it should, make sure it is bolted to the trailer securely enough so that it will not pull off when it is put to the test.

Front and Side Ramps

A few two-horse trailers and a number of three-horse-and-more trailers offer front unload ramps. A front unload ramp is located in front of the horse, which allows him to walk out forward instead of backing out. They are called "front" unload ramps even if they actually come off the side of the trailer. The best ones open on a slight angle, which enables the horse to come out without excessive bending. An anxious horse may want to jump off the side instead of taking the time to bend to walk down a narrow ramp. A ramp that folds down will take the place of a door on one side of the trailer, so access is limited to that side of the trailer unless the ramp is down. A ramp that slides out from under the trailer makes it possible to also have an access door on that side.

Front unload ramps on two-horse trailers can be a benefit for horses that have had bad experiences backing out of trailers, injured horses, young horses, and mares and foals. Actually, any horse can benefit from walking out headfirst, but it is not a necessary option on a two-horse trailer for most horses.

Four- and six-horse straightload, head-to-tail trailers can benefit from an unload ramp for the front two. If those horses can come out the front, they do not have to move back the whole length of the trailer to get out. This kind of ramp also allows the front horses to be unloaded without disturbing the back horses.

This unload ramp is steep, slippery, and heavy. Since there are no hold-backs on the top door cover, a horse and handler can easily get hit by the door as it blows in the breeze.

Slantload trailers are commonly equipped with a front unload ramp, which allows the front horse to walk out without unloading the back horses, and the rest of the horses can also be led out the front. Double unload ramps, wide enough to cover two stalls, allow two of the front horses to unload individually. Double unload ramps are also wider and have a better safety margin. Since it is important to have access to each horse individually and to be able to unload each horse without removing the others, front unload ramps increase the safety margin and should always be a part of a slantload of three horses or more.

Side ramps are different from front unload ramps in that they are located in the middle of the trailer, and horses can also be loaded onto the trailer by the same ramp. This type of ramp is most often found on centerload trailers and other trailers that haul the horses backward. The horses are loaded into the trailer from the side ramp and then backed into the stalls. Those horses are then able to walk out the same ramp. Horses that have been loaded from the rear of the trailer and are facing the front, may also walk forward out the side ramp.

It would not be possible to build a workable centerload trailer without a side ramp. The ramp can either fold down or slide out from under the trailer. The fold-down ramp will limit handler access to the trailer unless the ramp is down or there is a separate escape door on the same side as the ramp. Usually a ramp is on one side only, and a human door on the other, although it is possible to have a fold-down ramp on each side. The slide-out ramp is located under the trailer and can be pulled out when needed. A handler has access to doors on both sides without having to worry about the ramp. In most cases, the slide-out ramp will be usable from either side. Since a slide-out ramp is stored under the trailer, it is susceptible to road salts and other elements. It is important to keep the ramp clean to insure a long life.

A ramp on one side is workable, but having ramp access to either side is much more convenient. Finding a place to park a large trailer is not always easy, and worrying about parking with the ramp side out makes it somewhat more difficult.

What Are the Chances of This Happening?

A large warmblood horse was being hauled to the horse show in a new slantload trailer that was not quite roomy enough for him. When the owner arrived at the show grounds, she opened the feed door in front of him. He must have seen the open door as a way out, because he tried to jump out through this little door! He got his head, neck, and front legs out the door and then he got stuck. He was hanging behind his front elbows and was hardly able to support himself with his back legs.

Everyone was helpless to do anything for this horse. After a while, someone thought to put a hay bale under his back legs so that he had something to stand on, but even though this helped, he was still not able to get out of his terrible situation. He could not get back out of the window. A nearby body shop was called to cut the trailer apart. A veterinarian was called because the horse began showing signs of stress. He was having trouble breathing, and he was getting lethargic.

The veterinarian stacked several bales of hay under the outside window so that he could stand on them to better assess the condition of the horse. Someone noticed that the horse was trying to reach the hay bales, so they were stacked up even higher to support his front legs. The horse reached forward, pulled himself out onto the hay bales, and climbed out of the trailer. Except for some minor abrasions, he was uninjured. He was a little stiff and sore for a few days, but made a full recovery.

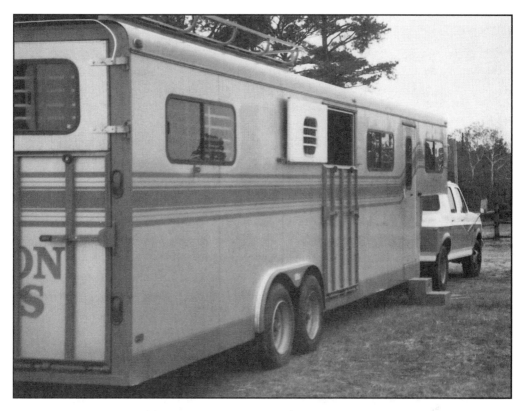

This centerload trailer has a long ramp with a non-slip mat. The top door cover has a hold-back, which keeps it neatly out of the way. There is an identical ramp on the other side, and the back horses can be loaded from the rear.

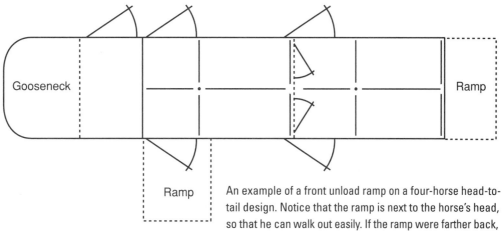

An example of a front unload ramp on a four-horse head-to-tail design. Notice that the ramp is next to the horse's head, so that he can walk out easily. If the ramp were farther back, the horse would have to bend very sharply to get out.

Ramps on the front and side can be a real benefit, but then again, it depends on the ramp. All the rear-loading ramp warnings apply here, and there are a few other precautions to consider:

- Larger trailers are often higher off the ground than two-horse trailers, and sometimes the ramps are too steep. The longer the ramp, the better. A steep ramp can be intimidating, and sometimes horses don't want to walk down them, they would rather jump! Any ramp, steep or not, can be slippery, so make sure the surface covering will not let your horse slide down the ramp. Walk down the ramp yourself. If you have any trouble at all, you can be sure your horse will also.

- Ramps that are placed at the horse's shoulder rather than at the head make it difficult for the horse to find the middle of the ramp easily, since he has to make quite a bend to get out. The horse should be able to walk out without the danger of stepping off the ramp or bumping his sides on the doorway or any other part of the trailer.

- Many side ramps come in a standard width of 4 feet, but a 5-foot width can be a better option for safe unloading.

This ramp is so heavy that a winch must be used to lift it. This is an example of a poorly designed ramp.

Some ramps have sides, usually made of plywood, that fold up, which create a barrier to keep the horse on the ramp. While a good idea, sometimes they make the ramp too heavy. Sides should be solid and sturdy. They should not shake when the horse steps on the ramp—it's scary!

Because front and side ramps are usually longer and wider, they also tend to be heavier. Some are so heavy it takes a weight lifter to raise them. Take heart, they don't have to be so cumbersome. It may take a little extra shopping, but it is possible to find spring-assisted fold-down ramps that lift easily, and slide-out ramps that can be pulled in and out by one person. Before buying a trailer with a side or front ramp, make sure you can lift it easily, without risk of back injury. For anyone physically challenged or unable to lift a ramp for other reasons, electric lifts are available.

5

Interior Features and Options

Once the horse is loaded, he has to stay in his trailer until he reaches his destination. The interior of the trailer can make a big difference in his comfort level, and subsequently, his stress level. Sometimes he will be traveling alone, and sometimes he will have company, making it necessary to separate the horses from each other. For the horse and handler there are many choices of interior features, some better than others.

Dividers

Most trailers are built to haul two or more horses, therefore, dividers are installed to separate and protect the horses from each other.

Horses are valuable animals, both monetarily and as pets. We want to protect them from harming each other while traveling together, and we also want to be able to handle and control each of them separately. Dividers help accomplish these goals. Dividers also protect the horse from the emotional stress of being threatened by another horse.

There are many types of dividers, posts, and bars. This one has a partial center divider with a shoulder divider, no rear center post, and safety catches that hold the butt and breast bars until a hand is free to put the pin in the latch. When the butt bars are down, the divider swings over to give the first horse the entire width of the trailer to walk into.

However, unsuitable dividers can cause problems for the horse. Horses can injure themselves by hitting a divider when loading or unloading. Inappropriate pins and latches holding the divider in place can cut or puncture. Scrambling and other problems can be minimized by choosing the proper divider.

CENTER DIVIDER

Many older trailers come equipped with a full divider, and full dividers are available on every style of trailer today.

A full divider extends to the floor, completely separating the horses from each other so that they can't kick or step on each other. Some people believe that a full divider will help the horse keep his balance.

However, a full divider does not meet the criteria we have established for choosing a horse trailer because the horse does not have enough room to spread his legs for balance. If you look at used trailers with full center dividers, you will be hard-pressed to find one that is not scratched and dented on the sidewalls with hoof marks from scrambling horses. When the horse is restricted from spreading his legs, he has no choice but to scramble around to keep from falling down. He'll even try to climb the walls. He ends up leaning on the divider, and many people who have seen this happen have the mistaken impression that the horse needs the full divider to keep his balance. In fact, a horse that has been hauled this way may also believe he needs the divider for balance. In addition, he may be a nervous hauler because his trips have been rather traumatic. Now and then, it takes some time for a horse to unlearn this behavior when he is later hauled in a less restrictive trailer, but often, the scrambling problem goes away the first time he has enough room to stand on his own. This can be quickly accomplished for one horse in a two-horse trailer by removing the divider or moving it at an angle, latched to the side, to give the horse more room. (Make sure there is a butt bar or chain behind him.)

A different style of divider with no center post. The butt bar takes two hands to clip the pin. The horse can easily push back out before the handler has a chance to catch the clip. (The sidewalls are lined with a smooth gel-coat fiberglass.)

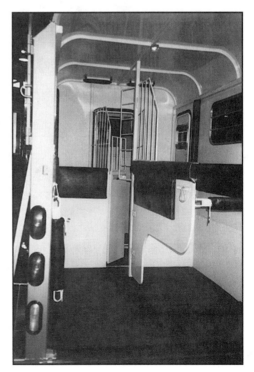

A partial divider is more commonly used today. It separates the horses from each other, but it does not reach all the way to the floor, thus increasing the legroom and giving more floor space than the full divider provides. Partial dividers can be any size or configuration. Some almost reach the floor, and some are only poles. The best ones have padding and leave enough room at the bottom to allow the horses freedom to move. A divider too close to the floor can trap a leg if a horse falls down, no matter what you have done to prevent it. A center divider should be high enough to reach the horse's shoulders. A divider that is too low will not accomplish the intended purpose, and one that is too high may allow the horse to get under it.

This trailer has a rear center post that does not remove. A center post can become a real hazard, and when it cannot pop out easily, the trailer must be torn apart in an emergency. This post is probably part of the structure of the trailer. If it were cut out, the trailer may lose the integrity of the frame.

Some people are still convinced that horses will kick or step on each other if the divider does not go all the way to the floor. Although anything is possible, this seldom happens. Adding more legroom reduces enough stress to the horse to outweigh this minor concern except in rare cases. If the horse's legs and hooves are protected with shipping boots or bandages, injury should not be a problem in most instances.

A good safety feature is a partial divider that comes up off the hinges if the horse falls under it and pushes back up. We heard of a horse that was fatally injured by

This slant divider has a removable solid lower divider, which restricts the ability of the horse to spread his legs for balance. This is an expensive option that probably does more harm than good, unless there is a special reason to separate one horse from another.

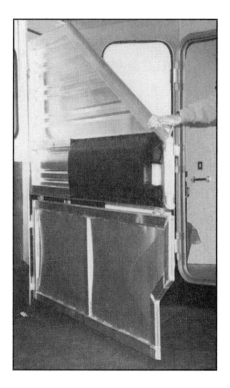

falling under a partial center divider and getting stuck. Although this is highly unusual, anything is possible where horses are concerned.

Horses usually have enough to think about in the trailer, so kicking each other is not usually a problem. That's not to say it can't happen, but it is not a problem when the horses are separated by a partial divider instead of a full divider. If a horse is a confirmed kicker, it's better that he be hauled alone, or if that is not possible, a loosely attached rubber divider can be used.

A swinging rubber divider is a rubber mat that hangs from a partial center divider. The mat allows a horse to spread his legs because it gives way when a horse pushes against it, and it protects the horses from each other by absorbing a blow. Such a divider should only be used as a last resort because the horse doesn't need a mat swinging into his legs while he is traveling unless there is a good reason for it. The swinging divider will be less likely to swing on its own if it is long enough to set on the floor or, even better, to wedge into the slat between the two floor mats. It is also possible to loosely attach the rubber divider all the way down, giving it enough play for the horse to be able to push it over a little. A rubber mat that hangs by clips or snaps can be easily removed when not needed. If the stalls

Most horses don't need to be separated by such a fortress. The usable stall space in this trailer is made even smaller by the front manger, the wheel wells, and the restricting full divider. Notice that there is a vent for each horse in the roof. This provides good ventilation.

A partial center post rests on the floor to give the divider stability. These divider hinges are not strong enough to hang the divider without it. This trailer is built extra tall and wide, but the dividers have not been built extra strong for the size of horses for which it is designed. Since this is a steel trailer, there should be some sort of lining on the sidewalls to protect the surface from scraping.

are spacious, 3 ¹/₂ feet to 4 feet wide or more, a solid center or slant divider may be acceptable for an unusual situation.

A shoulder divider is an extension of the center divider. Different manufacturers design them differently, but usually a shoulder divider makes the center divider higher in the front than in the back, therefore, separating the horses more completely from the shoulders forward. The shoulder divider also keeps the horse(s) from reaching behind the front center post over the center divider, often getting his head and neck stuck. A shoulder divider is a good feature with no real disadvantages.

HEAD DIVIDERS

Head dividers are used to separate the horses at their heads. Some head dividers are solid, some are bars, some are stationary, and some are removable. Manger-type trailers are likely to have stationary head dividers that are welded at the bottom to the manger. If this is the case, there should be a feed door on both sides so you can reach each horse and add hay from either side. Newer manger trailers are more likely to have a removable or swinging head divider. Walk-through trailers are made more effective by a swinging head divider because it allows a person to walk from one side to the other if necessary, or to get into the trailer on an empty side to reach the horse on the other side.

Head dividers keep the horses from interfering in each other's space—a good idea, since fights can start that way. Solid dividers keep the horses from seeing each other. Some horses may be better off without direct threats from another horse. Conversely, some horses may be better off if they can look at their traveling companion for reassurance. Bar dividers not only accomplish this, but also allow more airflow within the trailer.

The choice of bar dividers or solid dividers is a personal one, but whichever you choose, it should be removable. Safety is always increased when parts of a trailer come apart when you want them to, especially in an emergency. It also makes the trailer more convenient to use.

A few things to watch out for:

- The head divider in a walk-through trailer should be low enough so that a horse cannot get his head under it trying to reach the other side. If he doesn't break his neck, he can lift the divider right off the hinges. It should be high enough so that he can't get his head over it.

- If the head divider swings or is removable, it can rattle at the latches and be very noisy when the trailer is moving. Rubber grommets or tape can eliminate the noise. Make sure the latches will not come undone while the horse is in the trailer. A floppy head divider can really cause a nervous horse to freak.

- Some head dividers, especially aluminum ones, vibrate and make a lot of noise even if they are stationary. Horses don't need the extra stress of constant noise around their heads. Before you buy a trailer, jump around in it and shake it up to test for noises that could disturb a horse.

If the head divider is removable, know how to work it and make sure you can lift it off without help.

Interior dividers are generally constructed of the same material as the trailer. Steel trailers will usually have steel dividers, and aluminum trailers will have aluminum ones. Sometimes the center dividers will be made of plywood. Whatever the construction material, the dividers and the hinges that hold them in place should

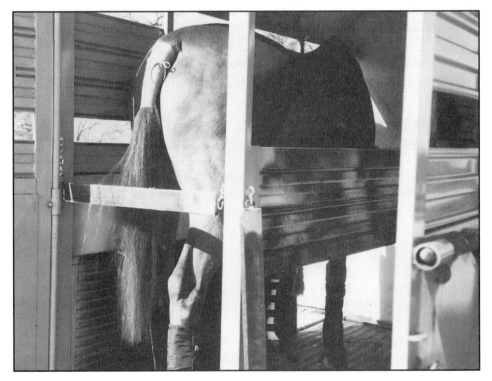

There is no shoulder divider on this trailer and the horse can easily get his head over to the other side of the front center post. However, the divider itself is very strong, which it should be for such a large horse. The divider comes out easily by pulling pins and the rear center post can be removed quickly.

be strong enough to hold up to the largest, strongest horse you will be hauling. The divider needs to be strong enough to protect the horse in an accident or to hold up if the horse is misbehaving in any way. If the horse accidentally breaks the divider, he may learn that he is able to do it and may deliberately continue the behavior in the future. If he acts up and nothing breaks, he will learn that it cannot be broken, and he probably won't do it again. The dividers must be removable by quick-release so that a horse that is really in trouble can be rescued when *you* make the decision, not before. Some slantload trailers have a latch that can be unfastened from outside the trailer.

Flimsy dividers will cost you money in the long run because of repairs, and your horse can suffer some major and costly injuries. Aluminum dividers can bend and rip apart, causing sharp edges, and wooden dividers can splinter and crack.

An example of a full center divider made of a soft plastic. If the horse needs to spread his legs, there is enough for him to do so. Unfortunately, the flimsy frame of this divider is not strong enough to hold up to any kind of mild abuse. This particular trailer has been recently repaired. It was broken when an average-size horse pushed back and the divider was pulled out of the floor. After the broken divider lifted up, the horse got stuck under the butt bar. It took a while to undo the latch to free him because the pressure on the latch kept the quick-release from working. He was lucky enough to escape with minor injuries.

Butt Bars and Chains

Butt bars or chains, breast bars or doors are trailer devices that hold the horse in place until you are ready to deal with him. When the ramp is down or the back doors are open, the butt bars or chains keep the horse from coming out until you are ready. They keep the first horse in the trailer until the other horse is loaded and you can close the doors or ramp. Breast bars or doors work the same way, by controlling the horse from walking forward until you want him to.

Butt bars are just that, bars made of metal that close behind the horse. They have many functions.

The minute the horse gets into the trailer, before he is tied, the butt bar should be put up behind him so he can't back out. This allows the handler to take the time to tie the horse and to close the back ramp or doors. If there is another horse to be loaded, the butt bar keeps the first horse in place so he doesn't interfere with the process.

An example of a full center divider. The stall is a full 3' wide so the particular Thoroughbred who rides in this trailer has adequate room. It would be better if the divider were pushed over to the diagonal, and there would still be enough room for the hay and buckets. The photo doesn't show it, but the sidewall of the trailer is scraped from the previous owner's horse. Notice that the hay net is tied in a very good position, high enough to be safe from the horse's legs and not too high over the horse's head.

When it is time to unload the horse, the butt bar keeps the horse in place until it is time to deal with him. When the ramp or doors are opened, the butt bar keeps the horse from rushing out. The butt bars allow the handler to control the horses individually, unloading one horse at a time. A word of caution: The horse should always be untied before the butt bar is taken down. If the horse hits against the tie when he is backing out, he may panic and pull back. The result could be a broken tie or halter and the horse being flung out of the trailer.

The butt bar also works as a safety buffer between the horse and the ramp or back doors. If he can't lean on the back doors or ramp, he won't be putting undue pressure where it doesn't belong. The back doors are not built to hold the weight of a leaning horse, and yes, horses have fallen out of their trailers onto the high-way from breaking out the back doors.

The butt bar should be low enough that the horse cannot get under it. It's possible for a horse to break his back or pelvis if he gets stuck under the bar. It's incredible how much a horse can lower his hindquarters when he wants to, but once he's stuck, he never thinks about lowering himself to get out of the mess he's gotten into. If the butt bar is attached in such a way that it has no play in it or if it does not have a quick-release function, the chance of injury increases. If the trailer is not strong enough to handle a horse thrashing about, it will break. In other words, in a situation like this, either the horse or the trailer will have to break. The ideal situation is for the butt bar to be low enough to avoid the problem in the first place, but since anything is possible, working quick-release latches are mandatory. If the butt bar is attached to a center divider that is free of the center post, there will be enough play in the divider to allow the horse to push up the butt bar enough to get himself free. Some trailers have butt bars that are designed to come off the hinges or pins if the horse pushes up from underneath—a simple feature that works very well.

Most trailers have the butt bar set for the average-size horse. Problems start when a trailer has been built for larger horses, and the butt bars have been raised to accommodate horses up to 18 hands. Some trailers have butt bars that are higher than they need to be even for large horses and are downright dangerous for the average or small horse. A trailer that will be used for horses or ponies of different heights should have butt bars that can be raised and lowered or even moved forward. This is easily done by having separate brackets for each passenger.

If the space between the butt bar and the back door or ramp is large enough, it's a nice place for the horse to put his tail, instead of leaning on it or hanging it out the back door. Anybody who has had a horse rub his tail against the door will appreciate how frustrating it can be to arrive at a show with a tail of broken, fuzzy hairs. Not only is this a cosmetic problem, but the tail can be permanently damaged if the horse leans on it for too long a time.

Since the horse should be able to support himself on the butt bar, it should be round, smooth, and/or padded. Although padding is nice, it also gets manure on it and is a little harder to keep clean. A big fat bar without padding can be comfortable for the horse, and easier to maintain.

Some older aluminum butt bars will cause gray and Palomino horses to have green hindquarters from leaning on them. This is a good case for padding if you haul light-colored horses in an aluminum trailer. One more tip about aluminum bars: They need to be fatter than steel bars if equal strength is desired.

Properly working butt bars are very important for safe trailering. Horses very often walk into the trailer, only to back right out. If the butt bar has not been fastened, the horse cannot be kept in and the person who is trying to latch it can be pushed aside and may get hurt. If the butt bar has a safety catch that will hold it in place until the pin has been dropped in or another type of latch has been secured, the horse can back up against it all he wants without endangering anyone. When arriving at the destination, some horses will bump against the bar when the doors are opened or the ramp is taken down. Any latch that allows the handler to keep the horse in place while he takes the time needed to secure or unsecure the butt bar, and open and close the doors or ramp, will increase the safety and ease of using the trailer. (Remember, the butt bar must be attached before the horse is tied and the horse must be untied before the butt bar is taken down.)

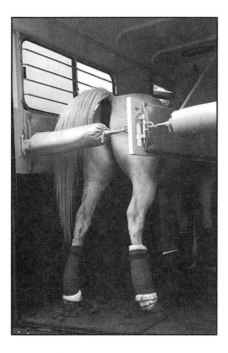

This butt bar fits into a safety slot that holds it until the pin is dropped in. The horse cannot push it out before the handler is ready. Both sides of the butt bar have quick-releases. The breast bars in the front have the same feature.

We have previously mentioned moving a center divider over to the side or removing it altogether to give a horse more floor space. In most standard horse trailers, this will make it impossible to have a butt bar across the back because most butt bars only cover one stall and attach to the center divider. A solution is to have a special butt bar made that is long enough to go across the back of the whole trailer. It can be attached to the same brackets that hold the normal butt bars in place on the trailer sides. A butt bar like this can be special-ordered on most new trailers.

Another idea is to attach the two butt bars together with a custom-made link in the middle.

Butt chains serve the same purpose as butt bars, but because they are usually thin, they can be painful to the horse when he pushes on them. Also they are easy to break and can chafe or cut a horse unnecessarily. Chains are often covered with a rubber hose for these reasons. Butt chains are better than nothing, but butt bars are a better choice, especially for the large or strong horse. If the trailer does not have a rear center post to attach the center divider, butt bars must do the job. One solid butt bar can hold the divider in place when one horse has been loaded and the other one is still outside. If chains are used, they are too flexible and one horse can push back on the chain, squeezing himself with the center divider unless the other chain is attached on the other side to hold the divider. Some trailers have a bar on one side and a chain on the other. We think two bars are best.

BREAST BARS AND DOORS

Breast bars, or chest bars, are used in walk-throughs to hold the horse at the chest to keep him from walking more forward than he should, such as out the door or into the aisleway in a centerload. The horse may use the breast bar for support when he is traveling.

All the same criteria for butt bars apply to breast bars. They must be comfortable for the horse, which is why padding is more important for breast bars than butt bars, because the chest area is more vulnerable. They must have quick release latches so that they can be undone should the horse go over the bar. On some trailers, however, the quick-release function will not work if the weight of a horse is on the bar, but some manufacturers have designed a latch that can still be released quickly in that circumstance. An accident like this is not usually injurious to the horse if he can be removed from the situation easily.

Breast bars enable the handler to walk in the trailer and walk out the door. If the handler is limber, he can scoot under the bar while it is still raised, eliminating the need to pick up the bar before the horse tries to walk out too. If the handler takes the breast bar down, walks through, and lifts the bar up in front of the horse, it should have a safety catch that will hold the bar in place until two hands are free to latch it. The walk-out door is the safety exit for the handler. It should not be closed while the handler is loading a horse by walking inside with him.

Because the horse needs to stretch his head and neck down, the breast bar should allow him to do it. It should not be so high that it causes pressure on the neck. Adjustable breast bars are available for hauling different-size horses.

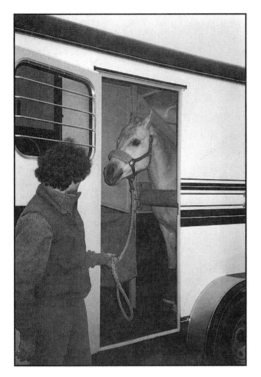

This breast bar is too high for this mare. It is pushing against her windpipe when she leans over it to eat hay. It can be lowered by installing extra brackets below the existing ones.

When hauling a horse in a walk-through, his head must be tied so that he does not get it under the breast bar. Otherwise, a serious injury can be the result, a broken neck being the worst, a broken trailer the least. Quick release again becomes important.

Breast doors serve the same purpose as breast bars. They work on hinges that hang down when not latched. Some have spring latches that make them very easy to work. The handler can walk through and slam the door behind him, automatically latching the door without further adjusting. Not many trailers have this type of door, but they should. It is a very good feature as long as there is a quick release latch.

Lower breast doors are doors under the breast bar. For the person concerned that the horse will paw things stored on the floor of the head area, breast doors will separate the stall area from the head area. Like mangers, lower breast doors restrict the forward movement the horse needs for balance. For those who believe they need them, be sure the doors are removable by quick release. Hinges should not stick out when the doors are not being used. If storing hay, buckets, and other items is a problem under the head area, store them somewhere else and forget about lower breast doors.

A breast door like this makes it very easy for the handler to walk through and slam it shut behind him. The pin gives the door a quick-release function.

This spring-loaded latch on the breast door slams shut leaving hands free.

Tie Rings

All trailers are equipped with interior tie rings in the head area to tie the horse. Any rigid tie ring that protrudes from the wall is a potential hazard. Since horses have such strange vision, they are prone to run into things humans may think are obvious. How many times have statements like these been heard? "That stupid horse! Look what he did! He just tore his eyelid off. He knew that thing was there. He's been hauled in this trailer for years!"

The horse isn't stupid, it's that he has been put into an environment, not of his own volition, that has hazards he is not instinctively aware of. Tie rings that protrude into the safety zone of a horse trailer are not necessary. It is very easy, and no more expensive, for a manufacturer to install a tie ring that lies flat. A very good tie ring is the folding D-ring, which hangs flat against the wall, or is set into it by a hinge so that it can swivel open when in use.

The better trailers have several tie rings in each separate head area to allow a choice. For example, tie rings on each side make it possible to cross-tie a horse, and tie rings on the front offer a different option. All tie rings should be high

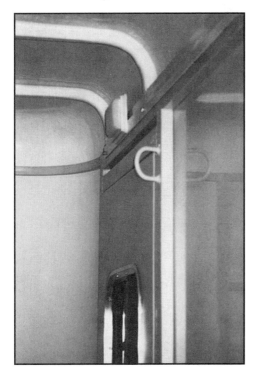

This tie ring is an unnecessary, dangerous protrusion in the horse area.

enough that the trailer tie or lead rope will not hang low enough for the horse to get tangled. For more information about tying a horse in a trailer see chapter 15, "Driving Tips and Horse Safety."

Tie rings should be strong enough to hold up to the abuse the horse being hauled may inflict. They should also be bolted or welded onto the framing of the trailer or welded onto a steel wall. Some trailers have tie rings that are bolted into a ply-wood, or aluminum wall. This type of anchorage is not recommended.

Tie rings are also used to tie up hay nets in walk-through trailers.

It may be flat, but it wouldn't take much for a horse to pull this tie ring out of the wall.

Hay Bags and Mangers

Feeding hay in a walk-through can be a messy job. The majority of walk-through trailers require a hay net to be tied up on a tie ring on the front wall or on the center post right next to the horse's head. In order to keep a horse from getting tangled in the hay net, it must be tied securely enough not to slip down and high over the head so there is no chance of a horse getting a leg into it even if he rears. A horse can be permanently injured by a run-in with a hay net, and every time he takes a bite of hay, dust, mold, and debris fly out and he has no choice but to breathe them in. Debris can also get into the horse's eye, causing irritation or injury.

Although a walk-through type trailer allows the horse to lower his head and cough out debris, it is better if he doesn't have to. The problem can be solved by solid hay "bags" that are hooked into place, usually from the breast bar and the front wall, lower than the horses head. The horse must reach down to eat the hay, so the air is kept free of debris. Manufacturers use different materials for the bags; canvas or cordura are the most common. Hay bags can also be used on slantload trailers.

Because hay bags are solid material, the horse cannot get a foot tangled in it like a hay net. Should a fractious horse go up and into it, it will tear apart or break off the hooks, saving the horse from serious injury. Hay bags that are too low can cause a problem: A horse can easily put a foot into it. Hay bags that are deep should have ventilation holes in the side away from the horse, to inhibit the buildup of mold-causing moisture and help keep the air clean when the horse reaches down into the bag to eat.

Hay bags also help keep hay off the floor of the trailer, but don't count on that too much. Horses like to push the hay out as they sift through it. It's probably horse humor. They like to see their human friends pick it up.

Mangers are the alternative method of providing hay space in a horse trailer. The first manger trailers were built for cowboys who had the old type of Quarter Horse and who needed a space for western saddles. These horses weren't too big and decades ago there sure wasn't a lot of knowledge about traveling stress on the horse. The logical conclusion then was to build a utilitarian trailer with a manger so that a tack compartment could be put in the space underneath. That way, the horse could have his hay, and the saddles could be stored in an easy to reach, lockable place without adding extra length to the trailer. There are still quite a few of those original old trailers being used today. Many were only 6 feet tall and 5 feet wide and most of them only had 8 feet of overall stall length with only 2 feet designated for the head area in the manger!

Nowadays manger trailers are bigger and better than the earlier ones. Later model horse trailers are mostly 7 feet tall and 5 $\frac{1}{2}$ to 6 feet wide. Stock and stock combos can still be found with 6 $\frac{1}{2}$ foot heights, extra height being optional.

Manger trailers restrict the horse's front leg area. If the horse tries to push his legs forward for balance, he runs into the wall in front of him. This is probably the reason that some horses jump up into the manger. They have nowhere else to go when they feel so restricted. Also, as we've discussed, the horse's respiratory system can be compromised by the small hay area.

An early 1970s manger model. Even though this steel trailer has been maintained well enough to stay structurally sound, it doesn't meet our criteria for room, light, and ventilation. Also, there is no escape door on either side for a handler to exit.

If you absolutely must have a manger trailer, a few things can improve the situation:

- The edges of the manger should be smooth and without a lip around it. It is quite common for a lip to be built to keep the hay from falling out, but the horse can get stuck on this lip if he does go up into the manger. If there is no lip for him to get caught on, a horse can slide back out of the manger more easily.

- It is also easier to keep the manger clean when the edge is smooth, both on the inside of the trailer and around the feed door. Hay, saliva, and all that other stuff horses snort out can be really damaging to the trailer itself. Leaving it there it can cause rust or corrosion around the seams and in the manger itself. It's so much easier to whisk out dirt and moisture when there is no lip to thwart your efforts, and it can even be easily hosed out to wash it clean.

- Chest padding under the manger helps to buffer the impact of the horse hitting against the front wall with his chest. The thicker the better.

- Manger trailers that have no dressing room often have one feed door in the front of the nose that services both mangers. A better arrangement is a feed door on each side so each horse can be attended to individually. Dressing room models will always have a feed door on each side.

Since the manger does not allow the handler to walk all the way through the trailer when he needs to enter the trailer with the horse, escape doors are usually put in the stall area as an exit route. Usually these doors are small and the handler must squeeze through and step on the fender to get out. There is no breast bar to contain the horse, so it is not unheard of for an unruly horse to also try to squeeze out this door, an action that can cause serious injuries. When purchasing a manger trailer, pay careful attention to these doors and ask these questions:

- Are there escape doors? A trailer with no escape doors can make it very frustrating to load an unwilling horse because the handler can only enter the trailer on the empty side of the center divider unless he wants to get stuck in there with the horse. The horse may not understand why he is to go into his designated side of the trailer when his handler is walking into the other side. The handler will not be able to walk into the trailer at all

The doorway between these mangers takes at least 1' from the width of each manger. At least the bar dividers allow light and air to enter, somewhat alleviating the effect of a smaller head area. The chest padding in this trailer is very nice, but there is a big lip around the manger. A horse could easily get stuck if he happened to jump up into it. The lip also makes it hard to clean out the manger.

Bad to the Bone

Bad to the Bone was a Standardbred race horse with a promising career before him, but there was one big problem. Bad to the Bone could not get to the local racetrack in good enough shape to run the race. He threw such a fit in the trailer every time he was taken to the track and hurt himself just badly enough that his owner would to have to scratch him from the race. He did the same thing when they took him back home.

On one last attempt to get Bad to the Bone to the track, he not only hurt himself again, but he did enough damage to the trailer that his owner, Mr. Owens, had to get a new one. When Mr. Owens came into our dealership, he was a very frustrated man. He really had high hopes for this horse, but even if he was going to have to give up on Bad to the Bone, he still had other horses to transport. He brought the damaged trailer in for trade. It was a very small two horse manger model that was only six feet tall and five feet wide. Bad to the Bone had not been the only source of destruction. It had had years of hard use, and should have been taken off the road long before.

Tom suggested to Mr. Owens that if his horse had more room in a trailer, he might get over his transport problem. Mr. Owens was skeptical, but he took Tom's advice and purchased a steel two-horse walk-through that was 7 feet 2 inches tall and 6 feet wide. The horse stall area was 10 feet long. The trailer was equipped with rubber torsion suspension.

One month later, Mr. Owens called Tom to tell him the good news. Bad to the Bone had not only ridden quietly to the track in his new trailer, but he won his first race! Mr. Owens checked in with us periodically after that. He wanted Tom to know that Bad to the Bone continued successfully in his career. Although, as much as Mr. Owens loved his trailer, he didn't give us much referral business. He believed strongly that the trailer was responsible for his horse's success and he didn't want to give up his secret to the competition!

when loading the second horse. A trailer with no doors to open can also cause a loading problem because it will be very dark inside and not very inviting to the horse.

- Are there doors on both sides? A door on one side only is not much better than none at all. Doors on both sides allow for individual attention to each horse.

- How hard will it be for the handler to get out? A door that is too small may be difficult for the handler to exit safely, but a door that is too large may encourage the horse to come through it.

A manger style that was used sparingly in the past has recently been revived. It could be called a "split manger" because the manger is split in the middle of the trailer to make room for an escape door between the mangers. The handler can walk out the middle front of the trailer, or into the dressing room if there is one.

This arrangement seems kind of clever, but upon further inspection, it isn't really that great an idea. It's no more convenient than a walk through trailer for the handler, the horse only gets about half the space of a regular manger, and bars or solid partitions on the inside walls of the mangers further restrict the horse's head space.

Padding

Padding protects the horse from bumps and bruises, making him more comfortable in the trailer. Padding usually consists of foam rubber covered with vinyl or another waterproof and washable material. High density foam will keep its shape longer than a lower quality foam and it will last longer, unless of course, a bored horse decides to chew on it. There should always be padding on the sidewalls where the horse's hips rub the wall and on the center dividers. Padding on breast bars or manger walls will make it more comfortable for the horse when he bumps against it and will also protect him from unsightly marks on his chest, especially if he is a leaner. Butt bar padding is more of a personal choice. If the butt bar is round, fat, and smooth, padding is probably not necessary, unless you prefer to have it. Since manure always lands on the butt bar, it is easier to clean the smooth metal than the padding. If the butt bar is narrow, padding will greatly increase the horse's comfort. Aluminum butt bars can discolor light-colored horses, so padding may be desired for Palominos and grays. Butt chains should always be covered with something such as a rubber hose to protect the horse from the chain.

Mats

All horse trailers should have mats on the floor in the horse area. Good mats prevent slipping, and help to absorb road shock, therefore protecting the horse's legs and hooves from stress. They also add years to the trailer by not allowing urine and manure to come in contact with the trailer floor. Poor quality mats can cause problems of their own.

There are many different kinds of mats on the market. Most of them are not made specifically for horses, but have been adapted for use in horse trailers.

For many years the most common horse trailer mat was a very heavy mat made of old tire strips that were woven together with wire. Mats like this are still being used today, but they have become outdated, and with good reason. They do provide a fairly non-slip surface but the benefits end there. Urine and manure fall right through to the floor, causing wood rot or aluminum corrosion if the mats are not removed after each use and the floor cleaned. Manure collects in the spaces between the tire strips, making the mats slippery and very hard to clean. As if this isn't enough, as the mats get older, the wire comes loose as the mats come apart, creating sharp protrusions that can cut horses' hooves. People get cut too, trying to move the mats around.

Many manufacturers use mats made of conveyer belt material, which are hard, thin, and may contain bits and pieces of steel. Even if they are ribbed, because they are so hard and thin, they are still slippery, especially when wet. For the same reason, they offer very little cushioning. They also curl up in the corners, causing horses and humans alike to trip over them. Sometimes the manufacturer will tack them permanently to the floor to prevent curling, but this makes it next to impossible to check the floor of the trailer if the mats cannot be easily lifted. Mats like these are also very dangerous on a ramp, but because they are fairly light, you will find them used quite frequently for this purpose. These mats are easy to clean, however, but this is not reason enough to compensate for the problems they may cause. A better use for these mats is to line the sidewalls of the trailer with them because they are strong and tend not to rip if a horse tries to scramble up the wall.

Another commonly used mat is a pressed rubber mat that is $1/2$-inch thick. These mats are usually cut to fit each individual stall lengthwise. They are solid, so they protect the floor. They are soft enough that the horse's hooves will sink into them and they will not slip even when wet. There is some cushioning quality to them, and they are light enough that one person can move one easily. These mats are also good for sidewall lining, although they may tear apart if a horse gets a toe hold on

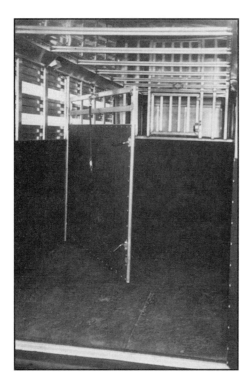

This stock trailer is nicely built with sidewall lining and $^{3}/_{4}$" stall mats that completely cover the wood floor. Stall mats can be installed like this in any size trailer.

one. (Even then, it is better to have a mat tear than an injured horse or damaged trailer. The mat can be easily replaced.) They easily sweep clean and can be hosed even cleaner. Several manufacturers make these mats, which can vary in quality. These mats may break when folded over for removal, or tear apart at the edges from the concussion of horseshoes. Even the lower quality mats of this type are better than the hard slick ones. However, these are not good mats for a ramp. Even though they are not slippery on a flat surface, when the surface is slanted, they can turn the ramp into a slide.

The best and, of course, the most expensive type of mat for a horse trailer is the $^{3}/_{4}$-inch stall mat that is made specifically for horse use. These mats are made of pure pressed rubber shavings and have no other material to contaminate the quality. They have a pebble surface on the top and grooves in the underside. The grooves on the underside allow ventilation for the trailer floor and help keep the mat in place. The mats are soft enough for the horse to sink into the rubber, enabling him to "grab" onto the mat for solid footing. The thick, solid rubber provides a shock absorbing cushion that protects the horse's hooves and legs better than any other mat. If the trailer has drop-leaf suspension, these mats help absorb the floor shock, and the horse that is riding on rubber torsion and stall mats is just about riding on air! Stall mats are made to be put into horse barns, so they come in 4-foot × 6-foot pieces and each one weighs about 90 pounds—too heavy to curl at the edges. They are best installed in a horse trailer widthwise and cut to fit the floor exactly. However, keep in mind that the weight of the mats adds extra weight to the trailer.

Even though these mats are more expensive, they add so much protection to the trailer and to the stress reduction of the horse that they pay for themselves in the long run. There are a few competing brands which all seem alike, but there is some difference in quality. You can tell the best ones by the warranty. A few have a five-year warranty, and at least one company guarantees its mats for ten years. Stall mats are much too heavy to be used for ramp mats. Warning: When wet, these mats may be slippery for foals because a youngster may be too light for its hooves to "grab" the mat.

Note: Mats should be easy enough to pull out of the trailer without breaking your back! A one-piece mat that covers the entire trailer floor is awkward and requires a lot of effort to remove it.

If you have solid mats in the trailer, you should take them out occasionally, check and wash the floor, and let it dry before putting the mats back in. If you are not going to use the trailer for some time, put the mats up against the sides so the floor can breathe.

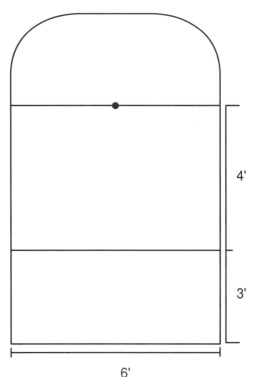

A suggestion for cutting 4' × 6' stall mats to fit a 6' × 7' stall area. The rear mat gets dirtier than the front mat and needs to be removed more frequently for cleaning. Put the 3' mat in the rear because it is easier and lighter to pull out.

4'

3'

6'

SIDEWALL AND BACK DOOR LININGS

Mats are not only used for the trailer floor, but also to line the sidewalls and back doors. Lining the stall walls with mats protects the trailer from damage from horses' hooves and protects horses from harming themselves on the metal surfaces. Horses being hauled in manger trailers can benefit from mats on the manger wall to protect their front legs. Some mats are bolted on, some riveted, and some are glued to the walls. There are many ways to attach the mats and manufacturers use different methods for different materials.

Since the horse will not be standing or walking on the mat, it is not so crucial to choose a mat for shock reduction. The manufacturer probably knows what is best for his type of trailer, but assess the mats for quality and potential problems. Check for smooth edges—you don't want waves or wrinkles that could be caught by a horse's hoof. Ask the dealer how expensive it would be to replace a damaged rubber lining in case you need to do so in the future.

Lining the interior sidewalls and back doors in the horse area can also be done by using other materials besides rubber mats. "Kick plates" can be made of aluminum, steel, stainless steel, fiberglass, or FRP (Fiberglass Reinforced Product). Some new materials can be glued or even sprayed on. All of these materials are acceptable to protect the interior wall of the trailer from damage by the horse. They also strengthen the wall to guard against a horse kicking through it. Many trailers are manufactured without sidewall linings, and those trailers show kick marks and scrapes that fester into rust or corrosion problems later. When the paint and rust protection is scraped off a steel trailer, rust sets in and the deterioration process starts. Aluminum trailers don't have the rust problem; however the metal is softer and dents more easily, so a horse can kick a hole through a sidewall or back door. If the sidewall material is smooth, slick, and dent-resistant, such as fiberglass, the horse will simply slide off without hurting himself or the trailer. There should be no protruding bolts or screws that could cut a horse.

Sidewall protection is a personal choice. Most materials are satisfactory if they are installed properly, but we prefer mats because they provide a softer cushion, especially on the back doors, to protect the horse if he kicks. If mats are damaged, they can be more easily replaced. Mats also absorb noise and make the trailer quieter for the horse's benefit. Our least favorite material is plywood. It is better than nothing but can break under the stress of a kick or trailer accident. If it does, it can splinter, causing injury to the horse. A horse can also wear holes through it over time by scrambling or pawing against the walls.

6

Controlling the Interior Environment

Get in your prospective trailer and close the doors and windows. Is it quiet? Is it too hot? Too drafty? Is it dark? Can you change the environment for the better? Can you open vents and windows if it is too hot? Can you easily keep the drafts out without limiting ventilation? Do you care? If you do, the following features can help you accomplish environmental control.

Insulation

Insulation has been available in horse trailers for at least twenty years. Many horse trailers that have dual-wall construction have an insulating material between the walls. At least one manufacturer used to spray a foam insulating material usually used in refrigerators onto the ceiling of the trailer. There are also construction materials, such as FRP, among others, that have insulating properties in themselves. Whatever method or material is used, insulation has many benefits for the horse.

Insulation keeps the outside out and the inside in. An insulated trailer will be cooler in the summer and warmer in the winter. Outside noise will be deadened, and the horse will be more protected from highway sounds. All these factors have a beneficial effect on the horse.

Materials that are most commonly used for insulation include, but are not limited to, Styrofoam, wood, Fiberglass Reinforced Product (FRP), and refrigerator insulation foam. Each product has its own properties, and each is used in a different way.

Some horse trailers are built with dual-wall construction—an exterior wall and a separate interior wall, quite often made of different materials. It is easy to enclose Styrofoam sheets or other material between these walls. This is a very neat and effective way to insulate the trailer because the material is out of sight and does not need any maintenance. This insulation has a good R-factor—it varies between manufacturers—and is a good sound insulator. This insulation is usually installed on the sidewalls only, but some trailers are also insulated in the roof.

Only one major manufacturer has ever used refrigerator foam insulation, and they don't do it anymore. However, there are still many of those older trailers out there because they were very well constructed and have had a very long life span. The foam was sprayed on the interior roof only and was not very pretty. However, it was quite effective. The insulation on the ceiling kept the heat of the sun from entering the trailer, therefore, keeping the trailer very cool. The sound-deadening properties were also good. The older the trailer, the better this insulation has held up over the years, because as the company changed hands in the 1980s there was no one who could learn to run the machine as well as the original owners. In later models, the insulation had some bubbling problems, and the new management discontinued the process after a few years.

FRP is constructed of layers of wood glued together between exterior sheets of fiberglass. This product is used for trailer sidewalls and has its own insulating properties.

When a trailer is built with "dual-wall" construction, a layer of Styrofoam can fit between the inner wall and the outer skin. In this case, the inner wall is galvanealed steel, and the outer wall is aluminum. Large windows and roof vents improve ventilation, and a white roof and white exterior walls reflect heat.

Wood is also an insulating material, adding some protection without a lot of expense. The best use of wood as an insulator is in the floor of the trailer. The wood insulates the trailer from the heat of the road. Aluminum has very few insulating properties, and aluminum floors, which have become a new trend, allow the road heat to come up through the floor, building up into the environment of the trailer.

The benefits of an insulated trailer can be neutralized if the trailer is not managed a little differently from a trailer that is not insulated. Insulation will allow heat to build up inside the trailer from the body heat of the horses that are being hauled in it unless it can escape through a vent or window. If the trailer is highly insulated and fairly airtight, it can be a mistake to close the windows and vents in cold weather because the environment can become hot, steamy, and damaging to the horse's respiratory system. Even if the weather is very cold, it is better to open the vents and some windows, and then blanket the horse accordingly.

In hot weather, the horses will be much more comfortable in an insulated trailer. The heat will be kept outside, and the vents, windows, and doors will allow a nice airflow to keep them happy. For climates of extreme temperatures, hot or cold, insulation is highly recommended.

Insulation absorbs noise and reduces stress by improving the sound quality of the trailer interior. A quiet trailer ride produces a quiet horse—usually.

Windows and Vents

Whatever style trailer you choose, the ventilation system should be adequate enough to provide the horse with the cleanest environment possible. Vents have traditionally been used to accomplish this purpose, but they cannot do the job alone. Older trailers generally have little circular vents in the nose of the unit that can be opened and closed by turning the circle to open small slats. Although these are better than nothing, they don't do the kind of job that is required to keep the air quality clean. This type of vent is still used today, usually in trailers that are inexpensive. The effectiveness of these small vents depends on the design of the overall trailer. A small, enclosed trailer will depend on these vents entirely to control the interior environment, but this is too much to ask of such a small vent. If the trailer has extra windows, roof vents, or the open slats of a stock trailer, these circular vents can serve a useful purpose as extra ventilation.

Roof vents are not always installed in horse trailers, but they are very important in controlling the air quality and the temperature of the interior. Horses generate quite a bit of body heat while they are enclosed in the trailer. Roof vents allow the interior air—and heat—to escape out the top of the trailer through the roof. Some trailers have one vent for every two horses, but a vent overhead each horse in the trailer is a much better option.

There are different types of roof vents, but the most efficient ones are two-directional. When the weather is hot and the windows of the trailer are opened, the vent can be opened to allow the air to blow into the trailer. When it is raining or the weather is cold and the trailer has been more closed up, the vent can be reversed so that the interior heat can escape up and out without raining in or blowing directly onto the horse. Types of directional vents are dual-action scoop vents that can be made of steel or aluminum. Aluminum is best for longer appearance life. Dome ventilators are square-type vents, which lift by a handle and have a screen. Some are also available with electric exhaust. The problem with these vents is that they stick up even when closed and can be easily lopped off the roof by low branches.

Windows come in all shapes and sizes. Through light and temperature control, windows can be used to solve many trailering problems simply.

From the horse's point of view, a dark trailer is very intimidating. When the trailer is equipped with windows that allow a good amount of light to enter, the trailer

A two-directional roof vent. Aluminum vents like this keep their appearance longer than steel ones, but either are effective for ventilation.

becomes more inviting. Everyone who has ever loaded a green horse has had the experience of the horse's walking into the trailer only to rush back out before the butt bar can be closed. This happens when, because of his equine vision, the horse hits a blind spot after he passes the side window where there is light and gets to the dark space between that window and the feed door window. His natural instinct is to get away from this dark space. This is also the main reason that horses will more readily enter a stock trailer. The side slats of the stock trailer are open all the way to the front, giving the trailer a more open appearance. Although it is not usually standard, there are enclosed horse trailers that have optional extra side windows available so the horse sees light all the way to the front.

Windows not only add stress-reducing light to the trailer, but also add more ventilation control. Windows that can be opened and closed according to the weather make traveling adjustments easy. Again, trailers that are fully insulated need the windows to be opened to keep heat from building up inside, even in colder weather. Trailers that are not insulated are not airtight and do not build up so much heat inside, so it is sometimes more necessary to close the windows in inclement weather. Horses are cold-weather animals, and it is easy for them to get too hot inside a trailer. They are likely to get sick if they get too hot, sweat, and then have cold air blow directly on them. If the weather is cold enough to put a blanket on your horse when he's not in the trailer, keep the blanket on him and keep the vents and windows open enough to allow airflow. How and when to blanket, and how and when to open windows and vents is a judgment call. More information on this subject is in chapter 15, "Driving Tips and Horse Safety."

Windows can be made of Plexiglas, glass, or tempered safety glass. Bus-type windows are most common. Windows should open and close from the outside of the trailer so that you don't have to squeeze into the trailer with the horse to close a window after the horse is loaded. Bar guards on the inside of the window protect the horse from the window in case he should bang his head into it or rear up and put a foot through the window. Bars should not have any sharp edges or stick out into the trailer where they could become a hazard; the best ones are round and recessed into or placed flat against the window opening. Bars should be spaced closely so that a horse can not get a hoof stuck in it. It doesn't happen very often, but horses actually can get their legs up that high. (Double-check the spacing if you will be hauling foals and other small-type horses.)

Windows should be sealed around the frame to keep excess moisture out of the inner walls and to keep leakage at a minimum. There are a number of ways to seal a window frame, and most are effective if they are done properly. Some manufacturers caulk around the windows, and some use a closed cell tape, and there are

Both windows are protected by adequate bar guards. The round bar (left) guards are somewhat better because they are smooth and have no sharp edges. The flat bar guards have sharp edges, and it is easy to see where a horse has banged his head against the bar guard and bent the aluminum. The horse that did this also suffered a cut on his face.

other methods as well. By checking the quality of the window seals, you can get a good idea about the quality of the trailer.

At first thought, screens appear to be a fancy item for a horse trailer. However, screens have a useful purpose because they keep outside debris from blowing into a moving trailer. We have personally seen two separate instances of trailers stopped on the side of the highway, a fire having occurred in the hay manger because someone threw a cigarette out the window and it blew into the trailer. In one instance, the driver of the trailer had thrown out the cigarette, and in the other, a passing motorist was responsible. Only one horse was injured among the four horses involved, but these were unnecessary accidents. A less dramatic, but equally serious, issue is that of eye injuries from foreign material flying into the trailer.

It is a shame that we have to worry about such things, but screens also protect horses from people who might slip something harmful, intentionally or otherwise, into the trailer when the horses are left alone in a parking lot, rest area, or other stopping place. A naive horse lover could also get accidentally bitten by placing a well-meaning hand into the trailer.

Screens also discourage wasps and bees from making nests in the trailer when it is stored with the windows open.

Interior Colors

When Tom and I were just beginning our trailer business, the sales manager of our main manufacturer told us that the airlines had done a study on horses and the stress-reducing qualities of colors. He said that this study concluded that pink had a calming effect on horses. Now, I understand horses don't see colors very well, and I never saw this in print, but it sounded like a pretty good story. I know that pink has a calming effect on humans, but I had my doubts about horses.

However, this reported study also concluded that the second most effective color was light gray. This makes more sense. "Nobody would buy a pink trailer," our sales manager said, "so that is why we painted the interiors of our trailers light gray."

I was intrigued by this color effect, so over the years I made it a point to learn about how horses were affected by the interiors of the trailers. By using my own horses and by helping customers solve problems, I found that interior colors make an incredible amount of difference in the attitude of horses.

My horses have been hauled in just about every size, type, and color of trailer known. I have had the same four horses for twelve years, two of them for twenty.

After all these years, I know them very well. They are all good loaders and haulers, but they didn't start out that way. They started out in a small, manger, step-up trailer that was painted maroon inside, and through the years, they progressed to an extra-large, warmblood-type trailer that has extra windows and a light gray interior. Since I am a horse trailer dealer, I have had access to trade-ins, new models from every manufacturer, and prototypes of trailers we have designed ourselves to use in my experiments. As experienced as my horses are, when I ask them to go into a trailer that is painted a dark color inside, each one will still slightly balk at first. When they are loaded into a light-colored interior, no matter what size or style, they walk in by themselves.

I experimented further by hauling other horses that had problems loading. Tom and I have been giving clinics for years, and we have been able to load dyed-in-the-wool problem loaders into our light-colored interior trailers on the first try. Our most difficult horse was brought to us because it usually took the owners at least two hours to load him every time they took him somewhere. He didn't go all the way into our trailer the first try, but he did on the second try. Once he was in there he was perfectly relaxed and started eating hay.

A dark interior is not very inviting. Some horses will not load into a trailer like this. (One horse alone should be hauled on the left side, not on the right side as was done here, unless for some reason a particular horse does not haul well on the left.)

Many of our customers with problem loaders were dumbfounded when they tried their new trailers for the first time at home and the horses loaded easily. (After they got used to the smell of the new mats.) The excited phone calls from our new believers have been one of the more rewarding aspects of the trailer business.

Light-colored interiors make sense when you consider the horse's vision. Horses have very good night vision, but their eyes take longer than ours to adjust to light changes. A dark trailer looks like a dark hollow cave to a horse. There may be a mountain lion in there!

Light gray is probably calming because it is light, but not glaring. White is a good color, too. A trailer with a light-colored interior and lots of windows is very inviting to the horse.

Once a customer bought a used trailer from us that was painted dark blue inside. During our conversation, we told her the "pink" theory. A month later she brought the trailer by our lot to show us her new paint job. She had changed the interior from blue to pink. And you know what? She said her horse loved it!

Exterior Colors

It looks so good to have a matching truck and trailer. Our personality shows through our choice of color and design. Fancy trailers have a look of success and prosperity, intimidating the competition as we arrive on the show grounds. So far we have been looking at the trailer from the horse's point of view, but the exterior doesn't matter to him. He doesn't care what color it is, right? Wrong!

Of course he doesn't care what it actually looks like, but he does care how it makes him feel. Dark exterior colors absorb light and make the surface hot. Light colors, white being the best, reflect light and make the surface cool. If the trailer is not insulated, the hot metal greatly affects the temperature in the interior. Insulation helps protect the inside wall from the outside wall, but still, the temperature will be compromised. Lighter exterior colors will be much appreciated by the horses that are being hauled, especially when the weather is hot. Fancy-colored striping can satisfy the craving for a trailer that matches the truck.

A light-colored roof is extremely important, whatever the color of the rest of the trailer. White is more light reflective than any other color, including bare aluminum. Most new trailers have light-colored roofs, but not all, so be discriminating. When buying a used trailer, you will have to shop carefully to find a white roof. Some trailers have a color stripe around the top edge, but the roof itself is white even though you can't see it from the ground.

Interior Lighting

Lights inside the trailer can be very convenient for loading on those dark mornings when you are leaving for the horse show. They are also great for packing the trailer the night before, but interior lighting is good for the horse, too. Some nervous horses worry about passing traffic lights when they are being hauled at night. By turning on the inside lights, the outside lights become less disturbing. Interior lighting makes it easy to check on the horses at night, and if you have a trailer with no dressing room, you can probably look in the rearview mirror to keep an eye on them through the front trailer window while you are driving. There are no disadvantages to interior lighting.

Interior lamps should be flat against the interior wall or ceiling where a horse can't bump into them. A light for each door is the most convenient, since you don't have to walk all the way around to the other side when you need a light on the side without the light. A very few trailers are equipped with a switch on the outside so you can turn on the lights without getting into the trailer.

Some trailers are wired so that the headlights of the tow vehicle must be on for the lights to work inside the trailer. This can be annoying. It is better when the interior lights are "hot wired" so that they can be turned on separately from the vehicle. However, even with the hot wire, the trailer must be plugged into the tow vehicle for the lights to work. If the lights in the trailer are accidentally left on, like in the daytime when it is easy not to notice, they can drain the power from the tow vehicle battery. Some manufacturers install an optional battery in the trailer that can connect to the interior lights, and the trailer does not need to be plugged into anything to use the lights. There are different types of batteries that can be used for this purpose. Marine or camper batteries are the usual, and some types can be recharged while the tow vehicle is running.

Exterior Load Lights and Floodlights

Exterior loading lights or floodlights can be installed on the rear entry, side doors and ramps, the front nose, or anywhere else you want. They can be used for loading and packing at night, and for handling emergencies on a dark highway, such as changing a tire.

There isn't a lot to say about exterior lighting, except that it is more convenient to have the lights hot-wired and have a separate on-off switch, and, better yet, on a separate battery. In an emergency, the tow vehicle may be the one that has the problem. If its battery is dead, you won't have lights. If it isn't dead, it will surely run down if the tow vehicle isn't running and you need the trailer lights for any length of time.

Interior Fans and Other Fancy Stuff

Interior fans are a luxury most people can't, or won't, afford. However, for those who can and will, oscillating interior fans may improve the airflow in the horse trailer. They are probably superfluous in a two-horse trailer, but when the trailer is carrying four horses or more, all producing body heat and warm breath, oscillating fans can be a bonus to the horse's comfort. They are most useful if you get stuck in traffic on a hot day. For those living in warmer climates, fans could be very important. They must be located high enough to be out of harm's way, and bars or screens should protect them from the horses, and vice versa.

For the truly opulent trailer, air-conditioning can be installed in the horse area. However, air-conditioning is a luxury that may not be worth the expense. Again, this type of climate control is best for those who have a large trailer with multiple horses and haul for long distances in extreme temperatures. Just like people, horses may get too used to perfect temperatures and become unable to endure normal temperature environments.

Closed-circuit TV cameras can be installed in the horse area so that the driver can monitor the horses. Cameras can also be attached to the rear of the trailer, enabling the driver to see what is behind him, an advantage for backing a really large trailer. Pretty fancy! You can do without it, but if you can afford it, go for it!

If you can't see inside the trailer, intercom systems can let you hear what's going on back there. You can have one unit in the truck and another in the trailer. It can be left on so you can hear any trouble, and if you have a groom riding in the back (not in a tag-a-long, it's illegal), you can have a two-way conversation while you are on the road. Intercoms can be a real advantage in large trailers carrying multiple horses for long distances.

7

Exterior Features and Options

Fenders cover the wheels and protect the trailer from gravel, mud, and road debris. Fenders can be constructed of the same material as the body of the trailer or made of a different material. Most newer trailers have "tear-drop" fenders, which curve downward in the middle of the two tires. These give better protection and look better.

No matter what material the fenders are made of, they must not have sharp edges or points that can injure a horse. Run your finger along the edge to check for potential problems. The edges on steel or aluminum fenders should be rolled or covered with an edging material. Some fenders are made of fiberglass, which is softer than metal, so the edges do not cut quite as easily.

If horses are going to be tied to the outside over the fender when the trailer is parked, the fender will take a lot of abuse. Be prepared to deal with dented, bent, and chipped fenders. Horses paw and kick, and we have even seen horses stand with both front feet on the fender. Steel and aluminum fenders may be bent and folded by an impact, creating sharp points that were not in the original design. A bent fender can rub on the tires, causing major tire damage. Chipped paint and torn edges can start a future rust problem for steel. Fiberglass fenders will more likely tear from stress, making them unsightly but not dangerous.

A fiberglass fender with very nice trim on the edges.

Fenders also get crushed when the driver takes a corner too closely. This can be a big problem with goosenecks trailers, since they tend to cut the corners more sharply.

If the fender is part of the trailer, repairs will have to be made at the body shop unless you can do that kind of work yourself. Our favorite type of fender is attached to the trailer body by bolts, and if desired, the entire fender can be popped off and replaced by a whole new fender—already painted to match—ordered directly from the manufacturer. Fiberglass is a good material for fenders because it does not rust, is soft enough to tear instead of cutting the horse, is easy to repair, and is lightweight.

A beautiful, molded fiberglass fender with a rolled edge. The shape of this fender is innovative and appears to be safe for horses tied to the side by the sturdy-looking tie rings. Since there is no gravel guard, the finish may be subjected to pitting.

Manufacturers are always looking for new materials and designs for fenders. Sleek new fenders are being developed to improve appearance and create a space-age look. New is not always better, so ask questions to ensure that any new designs or materials will be a safe alternative that will be easy to repair if damaged.

Gravel Guards

When gravel and other junk from the road are thrown against the fenders and trailer nose, they play havoc with the finish of the trailer. Steel components suffer the most insidious damage, because when the paint or other rust protection has been chipped off, it makes it possible for rust to start. Other materials such as aluminum or fiberglass may also suffer from the pelting, and the damaged finish will spoil the looks of the trailer. This is why gravel guards are essential.

Gravel guards are made of several different materials. The most inexpensive is an antiskid tape that is glued onto the trailer surface. This does the job of protecting the trailer, but in hot weather it can shrink and come unglued, becoming wavy and unsightly. Aluminum is a better material, although it is more expensive. A lot of older trailers and some new ones have gravel guards made of sheets of extruded aluminum with a border riveted around the edges. This kind of thin aluminum sheeting can dent easily, and sometimes the rivets around the border come out after a time. They do a good job of protecting the fender, however, and most last the life of the trailer with a small amount of maintenance. Anodized aluminum is somewhat better than extruded, but the most impact-resistant material used for gravel guards is diamond plate aluminum. Diamond plate is very shiny and hard enough to withstand dents from flying gravel. It keeps its appearance for the life of the trailer and works well as an entire fender, not just as a gravel guard.

Gravel guards can be placed anywhere there is a need, but the most common places are on the front of the fenders, the entire top fender surface, the lower nose of the trailer, the running boards, and the front gooseneck wall.

A fiberglass fender with a gravel guard of aluminum sheeting attached with rivets on the surrounding aluminum border.

This anti-skid tape has slipped and buckled on the fiberglass fender of a trailer less than two years old.

Running Boards and Steps

While we're on the subject of diamond plate aluminum, it makes for wonderful running boards and steps. Running boards are not always installed on trailers, but they are nice to have because they are very convenient for standing on to look into the trailer or for stepping in and out. They also improve the looks of the trailer and add more protection from road debris. Some running boards are constructed of the same material as the trailer. A steel trailer will have steel running boards, for example, but it is better if the running boards are made of a material that is rust-free and impact-resistant. Running boards experience the same problems as fenders because they stick out enough to get abuse from horses and driving accidents.

The running board on this steel trailer protects the fender from road debris and provides a nice step. The aluminum guards provide a non-slip surface and protection for the running-board finish.

If the trailer does not have running boards, it is a good idea to at least have steps to get in and out of the trailer, especially in dressing rooms and living quarters. Steps that lift and slide up under the trailer and out of the way when not in use are the most convenient.

All steps and running boards should have a non-slip surface. The "diamond" pattern on diamond aluminum provides traction. Other types should have a nonskid tape or corrugated rubber to eliminate the danger of sliding off.

Exterior Tie Rings (Horse and Hay)

It is often necessary to tie the horse outside the trailer. This is probably not the safest thing to do, but there is not always an alternative. If the fenders and running boards are not sharp and the framing and back gussets (if present) do not have sharp edges, the horse will most likely be all right. But be careful.

Tie rings are usually attached to the frame on the back of the trailer or on the side of the trailer over the fender. Both places have advantages and disadvantages, depending on the trailer.

If the tie rings are placed on the back corners, two horses, each tied on either side, can see each other and will sometimes be happier and, therefore, more calm. Some trailers have sharp corners at the bottom that can cut a horse's leg, and some have reinforcing bars on the gussets that can be just far enough apart to get a hoof caught.

If the horses are tied on the side of the trailer, they must contend with the fender. If the fender is not sharp, the horse will probably fare pretty well, but the fender is in danger of getting damaged by the horse. If two horses are together, each tied to a side, they may get upset if they cannot see each other and make life miserable for everybody.

It would be very dangerous to tie a horse next to a fender like this. The sharp edges have been made even worse by the bending of the fender. A license plate installed in the bracket would present a hazard in this location. Also, a horse's hoof could easily break the light.

If there is only one tie ring for each horse, it will be necessary to tie a hay net to the same tie ring that the horse is tied to, which is too low. Sometimes there will be a door hinge to tie it up higher, but it is a simple and inexpensive option to have extra tie rings installed up over the horse's tie rings. This way, the hay net can be tied high enough to be out of harm's way. This also keeps the hay net off the fender where it can scratch the finish. For those who do not like to hang a hay net on the side of the trailer because of the scratching problem, an enclosed canvas hay bag is a soft alternative and less hazardous to the horse than a net made of rope or nylon.

Tie rings should be strong enough to hold the strongest horse that will be tied to it. (I know, we keep repeating that, but it is important.) Tie rings on the gusset will usually be welded on steel. If they are thick enough they are strong, but will usually get chipped and a little rusty. Stainless steel is also strong but can eventually chip and rust—more of an appearance problem than anything else. Many manufacturers are now using cast aluminum because it never rusts, and if they are thick, they will probably be strong enough to hold up to most horses, although we have seen large horses snap them.

Tie rings that are put on the side should be bolted into the frame of the trailer, which is stronger than the sidewall. If you will be tying your horse to the trailer, check your prospective trailer for anything that may be dangerous to him. Feel underneath the trailer in the place where he will be tied and be sure there is nothing he could get cut or caught on if he starts to paw. License plates are very often attached where they are a potential menace.

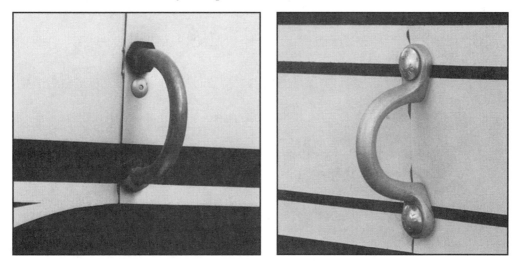

Both of these tie rings are bolted into the frame of the trailer. The ring on the left is stainless steel. However, the bolts are not and they have rusted, which is more of an appearance problem than a structural one. The ring on the right is cast aluminum, and the fasteners are stainless steel. No rust problem here.

Door Latches

Since there are many different kinds of doors on so many different kinds of horse trailers, naturally there must be many different kinds of latches to open and close them.

The simpler the latch for a rear door, the better. Rear door latches should never stick out the sides where a horse could run into it if he decides he doesn't want to go in the trailer but would rather go off the side. Latch arms that stick out should fold down to get out of the way. Sometimes the latches are attached to the center post where they pose a hazard if they do not fold down. Quite often, the latches are supposed to fold down, but they rust and become set in place if they are not maintained with a lubricant.

If the door latch is the kind that uses a pin to keep it closed, the pin should be held on by a cable or chain so that it does not get lost. Make sure that the pin clasps securely and will not come out while you are traveling down the road.

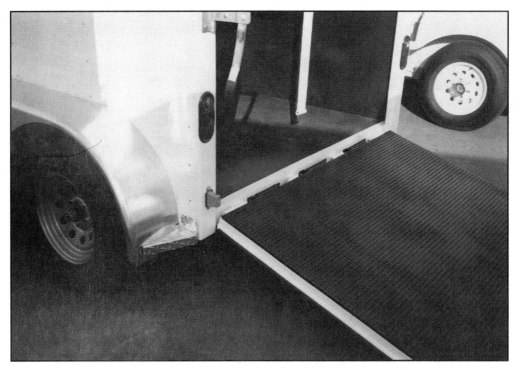

These rear ramp latches are a hazard because they do not fold flat. Notice the license plate lamp on the lower left. It won't last long because a horse is going to knock it off once this new trailer gets used.

Secure and simple. Not much can go wrong with this escape door latch.

Some stock-type trailers have latches that are so wonderfully simple, no parts need maintenance. However, avoid pins and latches that can stick out and be hazardous to the horse.

Door latches become more varied when we get to the dressing rooms, tack compartments, and living quarters. Higher quality trailers have higher quality latches on the doors. Dressing rooms and tack compartments should be lockable to protect valuable belongings, but it is possible to lock the horse doors, too. Lockable paddle latches and camper door latches with dead-bolt locks are usually standard on horse trailers today. Dead-bolt locks give better protection against professional thieves.

Locking the horse in the trailer may or may not be a good thing. If the horse can open the door from the inside, he may get out of the trailer while it is moving. This is usually not a problem if there is a bar to keep the horse from coming out the door. It would be a good idea to lock the horse in at a rest stop to keep strangers out. The problem arises in an accident or other emergency where someone without a key needs to get into the trailer. It's possible that the driver could be injured or incapacitated and someone else would need to care for the horses. Whatever. If the door

A locking paddle latch with a separate dead-bolt lock.

This latch is protected from horse lips by a metal guard.

latch is such that the horse could get it undone, a bar guard should protect it on the inside from horse lips. Beware of locks that do not unlock from the inside without a key. It is very possible to lock yourself inside without thinking!

When there are multiple doors on a horse trailer, there will be multiple locks, and sometimes that means multiple keys. When manufacturers use latches that can only be locked by one key number for security, each lock must have a separate key. One of our trailer lines had six separate sets of keys for each trailer. Each of three doors had one latch with two locks—one regular lock and one dead-bolt. It was rather embarrassing to hand each new customer a bag of keys for the new trailer!

We like latches that make life simple. Doors that quietly slam shut and stay shut are a pleasure to use. Simple latches that need no maintenance will last for the life of the trailer. Some aluminum arm-type latches may not be strong enough on a rear horse door. Beware of any latches that are sharp or stick out into the horse's space.

Roof Rack and Ladder

For people who do a lot of traveling with horses, a roof rack and ladder on the top of the trailer can be a great help. Storing hay out of the way of the interior gives more storage space for other equipment and keeps the hay out of the horse area where it can contaminate the environment. Luggage and even carts can be carried on the roof.

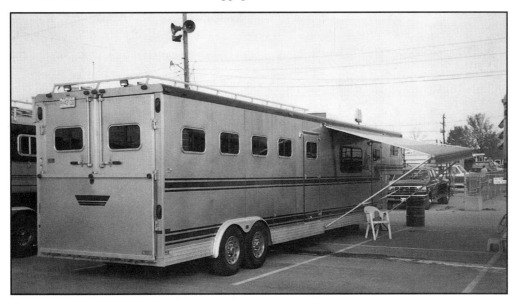

A trailer carrying a lot of horses plus living quarters needs this extra hay and luggage space on the roof.

Roof racks can be made of aluminum or steel. Many older trailers have rusty steel roof racks and rust stains dripping down over the trailer body. Galvanealed and stainless steel are being used more frequently now, so rust is no longer a problem. Depending on the quality, aluminum may also be acceptable. We have seen many older aluminum roof racks that are bent or broken from the weight of the hay. This should not be a problem on a later model trailer of good quality.

Roof racks must be bolted into the roof of the trailer, which is a disadvantage. Anytime the integrity of the roof is penetrated, there is a potential for leaks.

Water Tanks

James Hamilton, D.V.M., coauthor of *Hawkins Guide: Equine Emergencies on the Road*, recommends that as much as 20 gallons of water should be a part of every emergency kit carried on the horse trailer. He maintains that in an accident with injuries, water would be needed to care for wounds. In the case of a long, unexpected lay-up, water would be needed for the horses to drink or for bathing a stressed horse to keep his temperature stable.

In addition to emergency use, it is always nice to be able to carry the horse's own water with you when you take him on a trip. Horses more readily drink water that is familiar smelling and tasting. If you have water with you, you don't have to go looking for it when you get to your destination. You will be prepared when the horse show organizer forgets to order the water truck, or when the campground has only one inaccessible water spigot.

You can always carry water in a jug, but by installing a water tank on the trailer, you can save valuable space. If the tank is on the outside, the water is easy to reach and you don't have to lift, carry, and pour. You can fill the tank from a hose, and let it drain out the bottom into your bucket. Water tanks can be installed on the side of the trailer or under the gooseneck if you have one. They can also be installed inside somewhere out of the way, such as under a bench seat in the dressing room.

Water tanks are available in sizes up to 30 gallons and can be made of steel, plastic, PVC, or a number of other materials. They should be installed so that they are convenient to fill and to empty completely in an uncomplicated manner.

Note: All the features discussed in this and the previous chapters are intended to reduce the risk of injury or stress. No amount of planning can guarantee that a horse or handler will not suffer injury or other ill effects from traveling in a horse trailer. The best you can do is to make the trailer as safe as possible so that any unforeseen predicament can be minimized.

8

Mechanical Parts

Couplers

The coupler is a device that connects the trailer to the hitch ball on the tow vehicle. There are many different couplers, and when you choose your trailer, you will usually not have much choice about the coupler that the manufacturer has chosen to use. No matter what the construction material is of the trailer, the coupler assembly must be made of steel. No other material is strong enough to safely carry the load of a horse trailer.

Almost all older tag-a-long trailers have a "bull-dog" coupler, which has jaws that open and close over the ball and a collar that is pushed forward to keep the jaws closed. There is usually a safety pin that fits into a hole behind the collar to keep it in place. If there isn't a safety pin, do not even consider using this coupler.

Bulldog couplers are pretty standard and are safe to use if they are in good condition. If the working parts start to corrode or jam, the coupler can become dangerous. The collar can become ineffective, and the jaws can come undone. Also, if the parts are not working properly, the coupler can stick shut and you may have to pound it with a hammer to get it off.

A bulldog-type coupler. This is a typical system on an older trailer. It does the job, but there are better components available today. Notice that the trailer tongue is very short, the jack is greasy to handle because the gears are not enclosed, and there is no breakaway emergency brake.

Some newer tag-a-long trailers have a drop down coupler that works more simply. A lever atop the coupler is pulled up to open the enclosed coupler assembly. The trailer is jacked down onto the ball, and the lever is snapped shut. Done! When it is time to uncouple, the lever is lifted to release the ball, and the trailer can be jacked up. This is our favorite coupler for a tag-a-long because it is very safe and easy to use.

Gooseneck couplers have the same basic system with a lot of variations. Many are similar to the tag-a-long bulldog types. Jaws open and close and a collar or pin system keeps them closed over the ball. Many people like the open jaws because

This drop-down coupler is connected properly. The safety chains are crossed underneath, and the break-away brake cable is attached to a substantial part other than the hitch. The jack is enclosed to contain the grease and to keep fingers away from the gears. Notice the diamond plate aluminum guard on the tongue. It will protect the appearance of the tongue for the life of the trailer.

you can look out the back window of the truck and see where to back the ball in the bed into the open jaws. The downside of this type of coupler is that you have to get into the bed of the truck to close or open the coupler every time you use the trailer. It is very inconvenient, not to mention dirty, to have to crawl under the gooseneck every time you go somewhere with your horse.

There is also variation of the drop-down hitch for goosenecks. You have to be a little more accurate to back the ball under the coupler, but you don't have to get into the bed to hook up. Just jack the trailer down onto the ball. A lever automatically lifts to open the enclosed socket and as it goes over the ball, the lever goes back down, locking the system onto the ball. The best part is a long cable that attaches to the lever. When you want to unhook, just pull the cable from the outside as you are jacking up the trailer and it releases the coupler without having to get into the truck bed. This is our favorite type of gooseneck coupler.

Manufacturers are using different and new systems all the time. Sometimes they will use a coupler because they believe it is the best one, and sometimes they will use the one they can get for the best price. Because the coupler is the most important safety link in the entire trailer, pay attention to it when you are buying your trailer.

The coupler is one of the components of the trailer that is used to determine the gross vehicle weight rating (GVWR), which is the amount specified by the manufacturer as the maximum loaded weight of a vehicle. This will be covered in more detail in chapter 9, "Capacity," and chapter 14, "Tow Vehicles and Hitches," but be aware that there is a rating on the coupler, and this rating is very important.

Most tag-a-long trailers have couplers that fit onto a 2-inch hitch ball. Usually a 2-inch coupler is rated at 5,000 pounds, but some can be rated higher. If this is the case, the ball and hitch must also have a matching higher rating. This rating is marked or stamped on the coupler, the ball, the ball mount, and the hitch. If the coupler is rated at 5,000 pounds, the trailer must not weigh more than 5,000 pounds when fully loaded (gross vehicle weight—GVW) or it will not be safe—the coupler could break. Trailers that will weigh more than 5,000 pounds, fully loaded, must have a heavier duty coupler that is rated to do the job. Sometimes there will be a 2 $5/16$-inch coupler on trailers that weigh more than 5,000 pounds, fully loaded. "Fully loaded" means the weight of the entire trailer plus the weight of the horses

This type of gooseneck hitch makes it easy to back the truck ball into the socket, but it is necessary to get into the bed of the truck to close it. The height of this trailer can be adjusted by sliding the coupler up or down the outer tube.

Another style gooseneck coupler with safety
cables and an emergency breakaway brake cable.

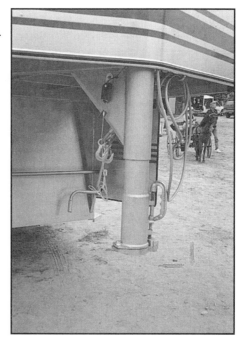

A mini-fifth-wheel kingpin. This type of coupler slides into the wheel that is installed in the truck bed.

that will be hauled in it and all the equipment: water, hay, mats, and anything else you have on board. It is not hard to reach 5,000 pounds or more in a two-horse trailer.

Warning: Even though a ball may be 2 inches or $2^5/_{16}$ inches, the ratings can be anywhere from 2,000 pounds to 10,000 pounds. Make sure the ball is rated to match or exceed the coupler rating. Also, if the trailer is equipped with a $2^5/_{16}$-inch coupler, make sure that the manufacturer has placed a plainly visible sticker on the coupler that warns anyone who may use this trailer that a $2^5/_{16}$-inch ball is required.

Tag-a-long trailer couplers also have a rating for the tongue weight of the trailer. This is the amount of weight the coupler can carry from the downward pressure of the trailer onto the trailer hitch. On trailers that weigh over 2,000 pounds, loaded, the tongue weight should be 10 to 15 percent of the trailer weight. For example, a coupler that is rated at 5,000 pounds should have a tongue weight rating of at least 500 pounds. A gooseneck trailer coupler should have a tongue weight rating of 25 percent of the trailer weight. It is not safe or legal to haul a trailer that does not have a coupler rated to pull or carry the load. However, there is no downside to being overrated.

Since couplers have moving parts, and they take a lot of wear and tear from use, check over the coupler on any trailer you buy. Even a new one can be defective. Make sure all moving parts are working easily. Look and feel inside a used coupler and check that the ball socket has not been worn larger than it should be. A quick check is to hook up the trailer to the tow vehicle and close the coupler. Slowly lift the trailer with the jack. The coupler should hold enough to slightly lift the tow vehicle by the hitch. You don't have to put a lot of strain on it, but it should give you a good idea how secure the coupler is. If you have any questions or doubts about the coupler, have a mechanic or body shop check it for you. The coupler can be replaced if there is any doubt about its safety.

After you have bought your trailer, do not take the coupler for granted. Check it periodically and keep it lightly lubricated. If you have any trouble with it that makes you uncomfortable, have a qualified person check it.

Jacks

Jacks lift the trailer up and down so that you can hitch and unhitch to the tow vehicle. There are many styles and brands of jacks, but they all work pretty much the same way. The differences are related more to ease of use and maintenance.

Tag-a-long trailers usually have the jack located on the tongue of the trailer behind the coupler. A handle can be on the top or the side of the jack that turns to lift the trailer by a gear and post or tube. Some jacks have a castor wheel as a rest, and others have a foot plate. Trailers that have the castor wheel can be rolled a short distance—sometimes it will do it when you don't want it to—and the foot plate is more stationary and does not sink into mud or sand. The wheel or foot plate must lift up and out of the way when the trailer is hitched to the vehicle. It makes it easy if the wheel or plate is removable. Actually you can take it off and leave it off, then stand the jack tube on a block. A few trailers have a swing-a-way swivel jack that swings up and out of the way.

Most gooseneck trailers have drop-leg jack stands. The jack stand drops down out of the tube and secures with a pin to lengthen the leg and reduce the jacking effort. Some goosenecks can be very heavy and have dual jack stands to stabilize the load. Special gearing can make jacking easier, and 2-speed jacks are available. It is also possible to have an electric jack if it's too much of an effort to hitch up the trailer.

A typical gooseneck jack. Some heavy goosenecks have two of these jacks to stabilize the trailer.

Jacks are rather boring to talk about, and there's not much to say except that a good jack can take a lot of grief out of the whole trailering experience.

The best jacks for tag-a-long trailers have tubes that enclose the gears and stay clean on the outside. Jacks with exposed posts and gears are sure to get grease on your white breeches or best jeans, no matter how much you try to avoid it. Also, by having the jack installed in the center of the tongue instead of up near the coupler, the jack will not get in the way of the open tailgate of the tow vehicle.

The most common damage to a tag-a-long jack is caused by driving with it still down. If the jack is welded onto the tongue, it will be more difficult and expensive to replace when it is damaged. It is also possible to damage a jack by forcing it to lift higher than its intended limit. Nowadays many jacks are bolted in place, and a new jack can be put in quickly just by rebolting.

Gooseneck jacks do not have to be hard to work, but many are. Before you buy a gooseneck make sure that you can jack the trailer up alone.

Jacks will have a much longer life if they are regularly lubricated. Grease should be applied to the gears, and a lightweight oil can be applied to the jack handle. An enclosed jack may make it easy to forget that you have to maintain it, but if you have one like this, remember there are gears inside and you have to take off the top and check it every once in a while.

Safety Chains

Safety chains for tag-a-long trailers are required in almost every state for noncommercial trailers. Those few states that do not require safety chains as of this writing highly recommend them and will probably pass laws to require them. For vehicles classified as commercial, safety chains are required for all tag-a-long trailers, according to Federal Motor Carrier Safety Regulations. As of now, 29 states require safety chains on ball hitch gooseneck trailers. Interestingly, many law enforcement officers and trailer manufacturers are also not aware of this. Safety chains are not required on mini-fifth-wheel gooseneck trailers.

Safety chains do work effectively if the trailer breaks away from the tow vehicle and must be rated to hold the weight of the trailer, or they will be useless if they are called into service. Many trailers on the road do not have safety chains, but it is not an expensive undertaking to have them installed.

Safety chains should not be hooked over the ball of the hitch or attached to the slide-in ball mount or any other removable part of the tow vehicle. Should the trailer become unattached, it's possible that the ball or the slide-in mount is the part that has failed and will go with the trailer. The chains should be attached to the main part of the hitch itself or to the frame of the tow vehicle—a part that could support the weight of the trailer if need be. Gooseneck safety chains need special brackets as part of the hitch ball assembly, or welded or bolted through the truck bed onto the frame.

For a tag-a-long trailer, the chains must be crossed underneath the hitch assembly and attached with closable hooks or chain links that have at least the same strength as the chain. (The chain is only as strong as its weakest link.) If the trailer should come unattached, the chain will act as a safety net, catching the trailer tongue and keeping it off the ground. The chains should not drag on the ground, but they should be long enough to let the trailer turn without interference. Chains can be bolted, welded, or both, onto the trailer. Whatever method is used, the attachment should be strong enough to match the rating of the chains and coupler.

Note: Some manufacturers use cables instead of chains. These are acceptable as long as they are properly rated.

Brakes

Brake requirements vary from state to state, but most states require trailer brakes on at least two wheels (one axle) for trailers under 3,000 pounds GVW, and brakes on all wheels (two axles) over 3,000 pounds GVW. Most horse trailers fall into the over 3,000 pounds GVW category. In the few states where brakes are not required, they are strongly recommended. Those particular states have laws that require the combination to stop by X number of feet from a speed of X many miles per hour without sway, even though they do not specify by what means you should do so. (The specifics vary among states.) The United States Department of Transportation (USDOT) requires brakes on all wheels for commercial vehicles.

These laws have been enacted for a good reason. If you don't have functioning four-wheel brakes on your horse trailer, you are flirting with disaster and needlessly risking your life and that of your horses, not to mention other innocent people on the road. Horse trailers are different from other trailers because the cargo is large, alive, and unpredictable; therefore, it is more important that the brakes be adequate to handle unexpected situations than on a boat or camper trailer.

For the last few years, the majority of horse trailer manufacturers have been complying with the USDOT standards and building their trailers with four-wheel brakes. This is not always the case with livestock trailers or horse trailers that are produced in states that do not require brakes. Some new trailers only have two-wheel brakes, and many used trailers that are still on the road are not up to standard.

Brakes should be synchronized so that the trailer brakes activate just slightly before the brakes of the tow vehicle. When the brakes are adjusted properly, the trailer does not push the tow vehicle from behind when decelerating. In a situation where the trailer does not have brakes, the combination can lose control when stopping, because the trailer becomes a "tail wagging the dog." Jackknifing and turning over can result from inadequate braking power.

Electric brakes are the brakes of choice for horse trailers. A controller box, installed near the driver in the tow vehicle, sends electrical current through the electromagnets in the brakes. The controller is activated when the vehicle brake pedal is pushed. Increasing the current flow to the electromagnet causes the magnet to grip the armature surface of the brake drum more firmly. This results in increasing the pressure against the shoes and brake drums until the desired stop is accomplished.

There are several advantages to electric brakes. They can be manually adjusted to provide the correct braking capability for varying road and load conditions. They can be modulated to provide more or less braking force, thus easing the brake load on the tow vehicle. They have very little lag time from the moment the tow vehicles brakes are actuated until the trailer brakes are actuated. In an emergency, they can provide some braking independent of the tow vehicle.

If the trailer should start to sway while the combination is on the road. The driver can reach down to the brake controller and activate the trailer brakes without stepping on the vehicle brake pedal. This should straighten out the trailer without suddenly slowing down and losing control of the tow vehicle.

For many years, surge brakes were commonly used on horse trailers. This system uses a specially designed trailer-hitch coupler that has a hydraulic cylinder built in. There is no need for a controller box in the tow vehicle. When the tow vehicle decelerates, the trailer applies a pushing force against the hitch. The force actuates the surge hitch hydraulic cylinder, transferring high-pressure brake fluid to the wheel cylinder. The trailer brakes are then activated.

Surge brakes can have some problems. If the brake is not working properly, the trailer may lose its backing ability because every time the tow vehicle is pushed into the trailer, it activates the brake. A friend of ours who had an old trailer with surge brakes had to carry a screwdriver in her truck. Every time she wanted to back the trailer, she had to get out and stick the screwdriver into the surge brake mechanism so that it would not activate and the trailer would move backward!

An electric brake controller allows the driver to activate the trailer brakes from the driver's seat. This is also the instrument to synchronize the trailer brakes with the tow vehicle brakes.

Even though it is less expensive to do without the controller in the truck, you lose the ability to brake the trailer from the driver's seat without braking the tow vehicle. Surge brakes may make it more complicated to use a weight distribution hitch.

Vacuum/hydraulic and air/hydraulic brakes are also available for horse trailers, but they are usually reserved for larger units and cost extra. These systems require more specialized installation throughout the trailer and tow vehicle.

Brakes should be inspected, adjusted, and maintained. Adjustment intervals are after the first 200 miles, and every 3,000 miles thereafter. More information is in chapter 16, "Operation and Service."

Emergency Breakaway Brake

Most states require trailers to be equipped with an emergency breakaway brake. Also, the USDOT requires all commercial trailers to be so equipped as part of the Federal Motor Carrier Safety Regulations. Emergency breakaway brakes activate the trailer brakes if the trailer comes off the tow vehicle. The system should be equipped with a charged battery that can hold the brakes for at least 15 minutes.

This is usually accomplished by attaching a cable to the tow vehicle that connects to a pin on the trailer. If the trailer breaks away from the tow vehicle, the pin is pulled and the battery is invoked to activate the trailer brakes.

Breakaway brakes are standard in new horse trailers. Some manufacturers do not offer it as a standard feature if the regulations in their particular state do not require it, but it is always an option. The breakaway brake can also be installed in an existing trailer.

The breakaway battery will only be effective, and legal, if it is in working condition and the cable is attached to a part of the tow vehicle that does not come away with the trailer. It should not be wound around the ball or attached to the slide-in ball mount.

The battery is usually housed in a plastic holder on the tongue of the trailer. Some trailers have it installed in the interior of the trailer or under a gooseneck, where it is out of the weather. The battery should be a 12-volt motorcycle battery, but it looks like the size of a 9-volt double-lantern battery, so don't be confused and buy the wrong one. It is difficult to find the 12-volt battery, and it sometimes must be special ordered at an auto supply store. Check the battery at least twice a year, and replace it each new season. Rechargeable batteries are now available. You can check the battery by pulling out the pin and moving the trailer forward slightly. If the brakes have activated, the battery is working, but you can't really tell if it is fully charged without a battery tester.

Note: If you accidentally pull the cable out of the breakaway switch, the battery will burn out in a short time. Put the pin back in immediately and you may save the battery for another, more important, time. If it has been activated for more than a few minutes, the battery will probably need to be replaced or recharged.

The breakaway switch can be used for another emergency. Sometimes it may become necessary to unhitch the trailer in less than ideal situations, such as a vehicle breakdown on the expressway with the horses in the trailer. The breakaway switch pin can be pulled out to activate the brakes to ensure that the trailer does not roll away for at least enough time (less than 15 minutes for a fully charged battery) to rehitch to another vehicle. You must also securely chock the wheels in all directions—you can't be too careful. It is always dangerous to unhitch a trailer with the horses inside and the practice is never recommended, but sometimes there may be no choice if it would be even more dangerous to unload the horses. This is an absolute last-resort procedure and must be done only on level ground.

Note: If you must unhitch in such a dangerous situation, unhook the safety chains last to test that the trailer is secure enough to stay where it is when the hitch is uncoupled. Rehitch to another vehicle immediately!

Rubber Torsion Suspension—I'm a Believer

We had been in the trailer business about two years when our manufacturer added rubber torsion suspension as an optional feature to the trailers we were selling. I usually hauled with a rather fancy "demo" trailer that had all the features and options possible so customers could see what was available. This was my first demo equipped with the newly available rubber torsion suspension as well as a 20-gallon water tank installed on the trailer exterior.

One of my horses had always been a nervous hauler. Even though he was eager to load, he was usually wringing wet when I got to my destination, even on short trips. He was always hauled in a nice trailer, and I am a very careful driver, so I was puzzled about his reaction. The first trip in the new trailer with the rubber torsion was an eye-opener for me. He arrived at the show as dry as when we left home. His attitude was so great at the show that he won all his classes for the first time. Well, that's a great story, but not the one I started out to tell.

Back to the new demo with the water tank. Tom and I enjoyed horse camping with our horsemen's club each month, and we were going to the late summer outing with my new trailer. I filled my water tank before we left, and we set off to the campground. It was nice to be able to have water so close to the horses all weekend, but I had to take the screw cap off the top of the tank so the water would drain out of the faucet at the bottom. I laid it on the fender.

After a wonderful weekend, we drove the 26 miles of country roads home on Sunday night. During the ride, I suddenly remembered that I had not put the screw cap back on the water tank. "I'll never see that again!" I told Tom.

It was dark when we pulled in the driveway. We were tired, so I unloaded the horses, put them away, and left the trailer cleanup for the morning, knowing my daughter was going to use the rig to haul her furniture to college the next day. Since my daughter was eager to leave, she took it upon herself to clean the trailer and take out the dividers so she could load up to go. As planned, she and her friend left that afternoon and drove the 175 miles to the university. It was mostly highway driving, but many miles were under construction

continues

and very bumpy. She unloaded the trailer and her friend drove it home to me the next day.

The trailer was still hooked to the truck the next morning when I had a slight emergency with one of my horses, and he had to go to the vet. I put the dividers back into the trailer, loaded my horse, and drove another 25 miles of country back roads to the vet clinic. After some minor treatment, he was again loaded onto the trailer and we drove home. By this time, the trailer was badly in need of a good cleaning, so I put the afternoon aside for the job.

I was almost finished scrubbing when something caught my eye. Laying on the edge of the fender, underneath the water tank, was the screw cap. It had been there all the time. It sure made a believer out of me! Since then, I have never owned a trailer that didn't have rubber torsion suspension, and my horses really appreciate the smooth ride.

Suspension and Axles

The horse trailer rides on its suspension system. The choice of the components used to make up this system can make a difference in the price of the trailer, but these differences affect the safety, ease, and cost of maintenance, and most decidedly, the stress factor to the horses being hauled in the trailer.

With few exceptions and with good reason, horse trailers are built with tandem wheels, in other words, two axles and four wheels. By using two axles, the trailer can be placed and balanced to determine the tongue weight of the trailer. Two axles distribute the weight of the trailer more evenly. If there is only one axle, the weight must be distributed between the axle and the tongue, therefore, increasing the tongue weight to unacceptable levels. For maximum tow stability, the tongue weight of a tag-a-long trailer should be 10 to 15 percent of the GVW and 25 percent of the GVW for gooseneck trailers. Some hitch installers say that keeping the tongue weight on the higher side will make for better tracking.

For the best tow, the axles are placed to balance the trailer when it is loaded with horses, accounting for the weight distribution of the horses. Differences in overall length or numbers of horses being hauled will determine if the axles are placed in the middle of the trailer or farther back.

Having two axles and four wheels also provides the security of having three tires left if one tire is damaged. Some people think that having only one axle on a trailer will create better maneuverability, but this is a bad idea for tag-a-long trailers. The tongue weight is compromised, a flat tire can be disastrous, and furthermore, it is illegal in most states. Some larger gooseneck trailers have one heavy-duty axle at the rear, but the tow vehicle must be adequate to handle the increased tongue weight. Single-axle trailers will bounce over bumps more than a double-axle trailer will because it cannot "walk" over the bump. This option is not good for the average person.

Long tag-a-long trailers, a four-horse, for example, may have a triple axle, with three wheels on each side, to further distribute the weight and keep a lighter tongue weight. (This makes the trailer less maneuverable, but may be desired in some instances, such as towing with a motor home.)

Axles are used according to capacity. For example, if the manufacturer wants to build a two-horse trailer that will weigh 5,000 pounds, fully loaded, including the weight of the trailer and all equipment, he will install two axles with 2,500 pounds capacity each. Using two 3,500-pound axles will result in a capacity of 7,000 pounds, and so on. See chapter 9, "Capacity," for more information.

For many, many years, horse trailers have been built with leaf-spring suspension. By looking under the trailer it is possible to see the leaf springs between the wheels. These springs are curved together in layers and absorb the shock of the road, determining the smoothness of the ride. Although many trailers on the road have leaf-spring suspension, how these trailers actually ride varies. If the manufacturer has installed a heavier duty axle than required, the ride can be very bouncy because the weight of the trailer and load is not heavy enough to keep it "down" on the road. Even with the correctly rated axle, many of these trailers are very bouncy when empty or with one horse but ride smoother when fully loaded. If the manufacturer has been overcautious enough to install a heavy-duty axle for extra safety, the ride may never be smooth even when the trailer is loaded to the maximum. In general, the heavier the trailer, the smoother the ride will be on leaf-spring suspension. A smooth ride is not only important for the well-being of the horse, but also for the driver.

When the trailer is being pulled, each wheel will individually drop down into potholes in the road, creating even more bounce. If your tow vehicle is bouncing you around while on a rough road, you can be sure the trailer is making life pretty miserable for the horses. If the tire goes flat, the wheel will also drop down with the tire, making it difficult to drive the trailer safely until the tire is changed or reinflated.

Leaf-spring suspension is visible by looking between the tires. (This trailer has mismatched tires that can cause towing problems.)

Leaf-spring suspension also requires regular maintenance. The leaf springs can slip out of place, and bolts and other parts can break or wear, creating a dangerous situation. It is easy to check the springs though, because they are clearly visible by looking under the trailer. If there is any question about the leaf springs of a trailer you are considering, have a mechanic look at them for you before you buy it. If there is a problem, get an estimate for repair. Make sure that it will not cost more to fix it than the value of the trailer permits.

The most important improvement in the trailer industry today is the increased use of rubber torsion suspension. This is a torsion arm-type suspension that is completely self-contained within the axle tube. It attaches directly to the trailer frame, using brackets that are an integral part of the axle assembly. This axle provides improved suspension relative to leaf-spring axles through the unique arrangement of a steel torsion bar surrounded by four natural rubber cords, which are encased in the main structural member of the axle beam. The wheel and hub spindle is attached to a lever, called the torsion arm, which is fastened to the rubber-encased bar. As load is applied, the bar rotates, causing a rolling-compressive resistance in the rubber cords. This action provides the same functions as conventional spring axles with several operating advantages, including independent suspension.

So what does this mean? First and foremost, it means a better ride for the horse. It has been said that rubber torsion axles absorb as much as 98 percent of the road

Rubber torsion axles can be seen only by getting under the trailer. On this quality aluminum trailer, these axles are attached by a steel subframe system.

shock. This means less stress on the horse's legs while the trailer is moving and a smoother, quieter ride all around. A smooth ride also means better road handling and stability. Put a bucket on the trailer floor, and it will be in the same place when you get to your destination.

The second, but also foremost, reason to have rubber torsion suspension is safety. The same feature that gives a smooth ride is also responsible for increasing the safety of using the trailer.

Each axle is attached separately to the bottom of the trailer. When the trailer is pulled over a hole in the road, the wheel that is passing over the hole does not drop into it, and the trailer is supported on the other three wheels. As the first wheel passes over the hole, it catches solid ground and supports the following wheel while it is being pulled over the hole. This feature makes it possible to pull the trailer for a time without one of the wheels! If a flat tire cannot be changed at the site—if no spare tire is available or if stranded on the expressway—the flat tire can be removed and you can drive the trailer without it until you can get off the road or to a service station. The remaining three wheels and the trailer tongue can support the trailer in an emergency.

This feature also makes it easy to change the tire. Roll the good tire onto a block of wood, a trailer jack, or a nearby rock, and the bad tire will be lifted off the ground.

Except for periodic inspection of the fasteners used to attach the axle to the vehicle frame, no other suspension maintenance is required on rubber torsion axles. They are, of course, subject to the maintenance and inspection procedures regarding brakes, hubs, bearing, seals, and tires.

For either suspension system to work properly, it is important that the trailer be level, with equal weight riding on each axle. Safety hazards such as swaying, uneven tire and coupler wear, unsuitable tongue weight, and other problems can be caused by unequal axle weight. The horse riding in the trailer will be subject to added stress since he will always be fighting the upward or downward tilt of the trailer. His unsteady balance may also change the balance of the trailer.

The rubber torsion suspension "walks" over the holes in the road.

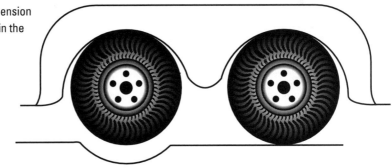

Even being this little off level can cause a problem. More weight is on the rear axle than on the front axle because the tongue is too high.

Safety and Rubber Torsion Suspension

Mary Jo had a very fancy two-horse gooseneck trailer with 12-foot living quarters and separate tack area. She was driving this very long trailer to the barn to get ready to leave the next day for a weekend horse show. Even though she had driven this winding road every day for several months, she was not as careful as she should have been when she drove over the bridge that took a gentle turn to the right, then to the left. She thought she had felt a bump, so when she arrived at the barn, she checked the trailer. The left fender was bent. She had caught it on the guard rail on the bridge. It was dark and it didn't look too bad, so she manually straightened it so it looked a little better, and went on about her packing.

The next morning she loaded her horse and took off to the horse show, which was about 90 miles away. She had gone about 75 miles on the expressway when a car came up beside her, the driver honking and pointing to her trailer. Panicked, she immediately pulled over to the emergency lane, fearing the worst. When she jumped out of the car, she couldn't believe her eyes. The bent fender had shredded the front tire on the trailer. It was completely flat, and the still partially attached tread had been beating the fender, damaging it even more. She had to have been driving that way for a while but had not even noticed a change in the way the trailer handled because the trailer was equipped with rubber torsion suspension.

Mary Jo did not feel safe changing the tire on the expressway, so she drove the rig a few more miles to the next exit, where she found a service station to help her change the tire and take off the fender. She made it to the horse show on time and repaired the trailer the next Monday.

Hubs, Drums, and Bearings

The mechanical parts of the trailer that need regular maintenance are the brake drums and bearings in the hubs. For information about these parts, see chapter 16, "Operation and Service."

Wheels and Spares

When you buy a new trailer, you will be limited to the wheels that the manufacturer offers. The quality of the wheels will be reflected in the price of the trailer. Most manufacturers offer an upgrade for extra money. If the wheel is properly rated for the weight of the trailer, the safety of the wheel is probably not as much concern as the appearance, but it is a good idea to ask the dealer about the wheels and other mechanical parts so you know what maintenance is required. Some painted steel wheels will chip and eventually look rusty when the paint comes off, but higher quality painted steel wheels can keep their appearance for a long time. Since the early 1990s, wheels have been double-painted, using a process called E Coat, which keeps the rust to a minimum. Aluminum or stainless-steel wheels are more expensive but look good for the life of the trailer. Hubcaps can dress up the look of trailer and can be replaced when they have lost their original luster.

Replacement wheels can be tricky, so when buying a used trailer, find out if the original wheels have been replaced. Many bolt circle dimensions are available, and some vary by so little that it might be possible to attach a wheel that does not match the axle hub. Make sure that the wheels have enough load-carrying capacity and pressure rating to match the maximum load of the tire and trailer. For more detailed important information about wheels, see chapter 16, "Operation and Service."

The same holds true for a spare wheel. If the spare did not come as original equipment from the manufacturer, make sure it is a match.

Tires

Most older trailers and many new ones have bias tires, but radials have become standard on many new trailers, and soon will replace bias tires on vehicles. Bias tires actually track better on the road, but radials give a smoother ride and get about 30 percent more mileage. Radials are more pliable and don't get that flat spot on the bottom in cold weather. Tires that are marked ST are Special Trailer tires. The only difference is that the rating on an ST tire is exactly what is marked on the tire, whereas a passenger vehicle tire must have 10 percent of the rating deducted from the marked rating to determine the actual rating if it is used on a truck, bus, or trailer. (This practice is the result of a law from the 1960s, when tires on new cars were cheap and not good enough to be taken off a car and put onto a truck, bus, or trailer.)

The most common problem with horse trailer tires is dry rot from being stored outside in extreme weather before they ever have a chance to wear out from road use. If any uneven wear shows on the tires of a trailer that has been used, there is a problem somewhere that should be corrected. It may be as simple as improper tire pressure or as serious as a bent axle. Tire wear should be checked frequently because once a wear pattern is firmly established in a tire, it is difficult to stop even if the underlying cause is corrected. Improper tire pressure is also responsible for trailer sway. All tires must be the same type. Never put bias tires and radial tires together on the same trailer.

Spare tires should also always match the other tires. Sometimes it is more expensive to buy the tire with the trailer, so an economical alternative is to buy the wheel rim with the trailer, to make sure it matches, and buy your tire somewhere else. People have different preferences for the placement of the spare tire on the trailer, but wherever it is, it should be easy to reach, easy to get off the bracket, and it should not restrict the driver's vision through the rearview mirror. Usually the tire is placed on the right side of the trailer, sometimes referred to as the "ditchside" (this keeps you out of the moving traffic lane in case you have to get to it on the highway), under a gooseneck, or on the nose of the trailer over the tongue. We have even seen them under the tongue. While this seems like a good idea, on investigation, we found it very hard to get to it if it had to be used. (For more information about tires, see chapter 16, "Operation and Service.")

Exterior Lights and Plugs

Through the Federal Motor Carrier Safety Regulations (FMCSR), the USDOT regulates the placement, color, and brightness of the exterior lights and reflectors of all commercial vehicles that cross state lines. Each state also has the power to regulate the vehicles that are registered in the state even if they do not cross state lines. Usually the regulations are the same for all commercial vehicles. Each state also has the power to regulate the light requirements of noncommercial vehicles. In most states, those requirements equal the requirements of commercial vehicles. In a few, mostly agricultural states, the requirements for noncommercial vehicles are not quite as strict.

If a trailer and tow vehicle combination has a GVWR of 10,001 pounds or more, a decision must be made to declare a commercial classification. If the vehicle is being used with the intent to profit, the driver must follow the FMCSR. The intent to profit does not just mean hauling horses for money, but anyone who hauls horses for sale, breeding, showing, race, rodeo, training, and so forth, or runs a commercial stable (a sign on the side is advertising—that means "commercial") is considered commercial by the USDOT if the vehicle crosses state lines. The driver must keep a log book, carry a medical card, and follow other requirements specified by the FMCSR. The vehicle must also meet several requirements, among which is the standardization of exterior lighting. States have similar regulations for commercial vehicles that do not cross state lines.

Running lights, turn signals, brake lights, and reflectors make your trailer more visible on the highway. A well-lit trailer is less likely to be involved in a traffic accident. Therefore, for your safety, any trailer that you consider for purchase should have a lighting package that follows the USDOT requirements, whether you are considered commercial or not. Most new trailers will automatically have lights that follow FMCSR regulations, but trailers just a few years old may not be so equipped. A few companies may still offer the USDOT light package as an option, so ask your dealer about the light package that comes standard with your new trailer. Older trailers may be exempt from some of these requirements.

This is a simplified list of FMCSR requirements for lights and reflectors for trailers over 80 inches wide (items asterisked are required on trailers *under* 80 inches wide):

- Tail lamps*: 2 red—rear, one lamp each side of the vertical centerline at the same height and as far apart as possible.

- Stop lamp*: 2 red—rear, one lamp each side of the vertical centerline at the same height and as far apart as practicable.

- Clearance lamps: 2 amber—one on each side of the front to indicate width, on the same level as high as practicable.

- Clearance lamps: 2 red—one on each side of rear to indicate width, both on the same level as high as practicable.

- Side marker lamp: 2 amber—one on each side at or near midpoint, between front and rear side marker lamps, not less than 15 inches above road surface.

- Reflex reflector: 2 amber—one on each side at or near midpoint between front and rear side reflectors between 15 and 60 inches above road surface.

- Reflex reflector*: 2 red—rear, one on each side of vertical centerline as far apart as practicable.

- Reflex reflector*: 2 red—one on each side (rear), as far to the rear as practicable.

- Reflex reflector*: 2 amber—one on each side (front), as far to the front as practicable.

- License plate lamp*: 1 white—at rear license plate.

- Side marker lamps*: 2 amber—one on each side as far to the front as practicable.

- Side marker lamps*: 2 red—one on each side as far to the rear as practicable.

- Turn signal*: 2 amber or red—rear, one lamp on each side of the vertical centerline as far apart as practicable.

- Identification lamps: 3 red—rear, one as close as practicable to vertical centerline. One on each side with lamp centers spaced not less than 6 inches or more than 12 inches apart.

- Vehicular Hazard Warning Flashing Lamps*: 2 amber, one lamp on each side of vertical centerline as far apart as practicable. 2 amber or red—rear.

A turn-signal and marker lamp on the fender lets you keep track of the trailer at night by looking in your side mirror. It also makes the trailer more visible to other drivers. Notice that this trailer has many deluxe features such as extruded aluminum running boards, gravel guard on the entire fiberglass fender, and fancy aluminum wheels.

According to a new regulation, trailers 80 inches or more in width, with a GVWR of 10,000 pounds or more and manufactured after December 1, 1993, must be equipped with either retroreflective sheeting, reflex reflectors, or a combination of retroreflective sheeting and reflex reflectors. The purpose of this requirement is to mark the length and width and corners of a large trailer in low-light conditions.

A few manufacturers add an extra light on the fender of the trailer that indicates turn signals and marker lights, and it can be added as an option on some trailers. This light enables the driver to keep track of the trailer at night by checking through the side mirrors, and it signals an intended lane change to a vehicle that may be in the next lane but a little too close to see the rear turn signal light. Once a driver has hauled a trailer with this lighting option, it is very hard to do without it. This is a very good feature.

Plugs and Wiring

Your trailer must plug into the tow vehicle for the power to work the brakes and lights. The most frustrating thing about trailer wiring is that there has been no standard in the industry and there are so many different types of plugs and wiring configurations. The problem is worse on used trailers because older trailers had fewer regulations for lighting and braking requirements and manufacturers used a smaller circuit connector plug—whatever was suitable for the trailer they were building. These connectors were hardly ever interchangeable with receptacles for trailers from other manufacturers.

As horse trailers became more sophisticated and more electrical features were incorporated in the design, more sophisticated plugs were required to handle the load. Six-, seven-, and nine-circuit plugs were acquired to handle the electric brakes, "hot" wires, breakaway brake systems, and more extensive lighting required by USDOT.

The industry is finally coming around to standardizing the wiring and the plugs, but a few manufacturers are still holding out. Some plugs have round prongs and some have flat prongs. Some plugs look alike, but are not actually wired the same.

If you only haul one trailer and do not have to interchange the horse trailer with a camper or other kind of trailer, this shouldn't be too much of a problem. If you do have more than one trailer, you can change the wiring to agree, or have an adapter made so that you can interchange the trailers on the same tow vehicle. It can become a problem when you need to use another tow vehicle in an emergency and the lights and brakes will not work.

Most new trailers are equipped with a 7-circuit plug with flat prongs. Very large trailers sometimes need a heavier duty 9-circuit plug. When, and if, all trailers are standardized, it will make it much easier and less expensive for consumers to use the same wiring for multiple trailers.

Wires throughout the trailer should never be exposed where a horse or handler could accidentally come in contact with them. Differences in manufacturing techniques determine the placement of wiring, but overhead wiring is the most common in trailers of good quality. Check that wires could not fall down into the horse area or that they are not placed where a horse could chew on them. Look for exposed wires on the outside where they could be damaged by the elements. Some trailers are equipped with fuses. If so, make sure the fuse box is also protected from the elements and that it is easy to reach.

9

Capacity

The trailer you buy will have a limit to the amount of weight that can be safely hauled in it. You must know that limit so you do not overload it, and you must also know how much the trailer weighs when fully loaded so you may choose the proper tow vehicle to pull it.

The gross vehicle weight rating (GVWR) is the value specified by the manufacturer as the maximum loaded weight of a single vehicle. This includes the weight of the trailer plus everything in it, including horses, mats, tack, water, spare tire, hay, and any equipment. The two main factors used by the manufacturer to determine this rating are axle capacity and coupler capacity, but the whole trailer, in fact, the entire trailer and vehicle combination, can only be rated as high as the capacity of its weakest component.

To determine the GVWR of a trailer with two 2,500-pound axles, add the two together to reach a 5,000-pound axle capacity. If the coupler also has a rating of at least 5,000 pounds, the trailer may be rated with a GVWR of 5,000 pounds. If a trailer has two 3,500-pound axles, but the coupler is still only rated at 5,000 pounds, the trailer cannot be rated more than 5,000 pounds, even though the axle rating would indicate the capacity is 7,000 pounds.

Once the GVWR has been determined, you must stay within that limit to safely use the trailer. Using a trailer with a GVWR of 5,000 pounds as an example, you must make these calculations: If this particular trailer weighs 2,300 pounds, including mats, tires, and so forth, and two horses being hauled in it weigh 1,200 pounds each, it adds up to 4,700 pounds. There is a 300-pound leeway left for equipment and feed. Put two 1,500-pound warmbloods in the same trailer, and the trailer is overloaded by 300 pounds. (Getting a lighter-weight trailer in this particular case is not the idea. The warmbloods need a trailer with a greater capacity and strong frame. The capacity states that the axles and coupler can handle a particular weight. Although trailers with a greater capacity are usually built with a stronger body to handle the greater weight and abuse, it is not a requirement that the trailer walls, frame, etc., be strong enough to stand up to the stress of the horses that are being hauled in it.)

The trailer should have a sticker on it that indicates the manufacturer's GVWR. The GVWR is also printed on the Manufacturer's Certificate of Origin that goes with the trailer.

The gross vehicle weight (GVW) is the actual weight of the trailer, including its full load. The trailer may have a GVWR of 7,000 pounds, but if the actual weight of the trailer with the horses and any equipment, feed, or any other cargo only adds up to 5,500 pounds, the GVW is 5,500 pounds. The tow vehicle that is chosen to pull the trailer must be rated to pull at least the GVW of the trailer, but it is even better if it is rated to pull the GVWR of the trailer. (More about tow vehicles in chapter 14, "Tow Vehicles and Hitches.") Depending on the state in which the trailer is registered, the GVWR, GVW, or the empty weight must be determined to register and license the trailer.

The best way to determine GVW of the trailer is to load the horses and the amount of equipment that is usually carried on board and take it to a scale. In some states, it is necessary to register the trailer by empty weight. This weight should include the mats, tires, and any other standard equipment, including filled permanently installed water and propane tanks. Commercial scales are available at truck stops and gravel yards, and you can weigh your rig for a small fee.

The GCVWR is the rating specified by the vehicle manufacturer that determines the recommended weight of the tow vehicle and the trailer combined. This is an important rating that must be considered when choosing a tow vehicle. More about this in chapter 14, "Tow Vehicles and Hitches."

Measuring the Trailer

Measurement claims are not always as accurate as they should be. If a trailer is touted to be 6 feet wide, does that mean interior or exterior? If the trailer is measured to be 6 feet from the outside of the sidewalls, there will not be a full 6 feet of space in the interior. To get the benefit of the desired width, measure the interior of the trailer from inside the sidewalls. This is also true of the height and length. Interior space is taken up by double or triple sidewalls, dividers, padding, and butt and breast bars. These factors should be considered when deciding how much room your horse actually needs.

Space is one of the three criteria we have used to determine the suitability of the trailer for the stress reduction of the horse. It is necessary to check interior measurements to insure that you are getting what you are paying for. Adequate height is very important and is the measurement that seems to have the most emphasis in buying a trailer, but width and length are just as important to the horse.

HEIGHT

There are few new trailers on the market that are less than 7 feet tall, and nowadays, trailers shorter than that do not have a very high resale value. The term "extra tall" now means more than 7 feet. Trailers measuring 7 feet 4 inches interior height are quite common, and trailers 7 feet 6 inches and more are also easily available.

When measuring the interior height of the trailer you must consider the usable head area of the horse. A trailer that has a flat roof will have the same usable head space from sidewall to sidewall. A trailer with a rounded roof will be shorter on the sides than in the center of the ceiling. If the height measurement is advertised as 7 feet on a rounded roof trailer, that measurement will be taken at the highest point of the ceiling in the middle of the trailer. The headspace for the horse will be considerably shorter on the outside wall of his stall than on the inside. Therefore, the advertised measurement of this trailer is not a truly usable measurement. This is not a bad thing, but this factor should be considered when buying the trailer.

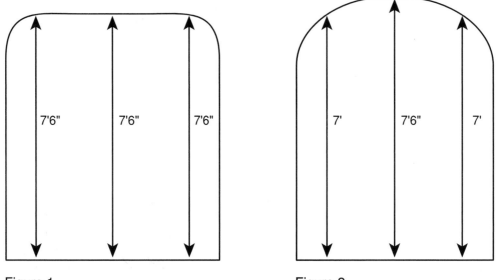

Figure 1   Figure 2

Using a 7'6" tall trailer as an example, it is easy to see that a flat roof gives a more consistent height measurement than a rounded roof. The rounded roof (Figure 2) is 7'6" in the center, but there is not a true 7'6" of usable height for the entire width of the trailer.

One other important measurement when considering the overall usable height of the trailer is the height of the horse's entry opening. Make sure that the door frame is not so low that the horse has to watch his head when he gets in or out. When the horse is stepping into or out of the trailer, his head is at the highest point in the trailering process. This is also the time when he may throw his head up if he resists and backs out. It's great to have an extra tall trailer if you need one, but if your horse hits his head every time he gets in or out because of the shorter doorway, it isn't an effective trailer.

WIDTH

Most straightload horse trailers being built today are built on axles that are 96 inches or less. A trailer can be built with an interior width up to 6 feet without interior wheel wells on a 96-inch axle. The fenders cover the wheels on the outside of the trailer body. If the trailer has an interior width of more than 6 feet, the wheel wells must come inside the trailer to cover the trailer wheels. Using axles that are no wider than 96 inches insures that the overall width of the trailer, including the fenders and gussets, is no wider than 96 inches or 8 feet. An overall width of 8 feet is legal on all roads and highways in the United States.

Most slantload trailers and some extrawide straightload trailers are built on 102-inch axles. These wider axles allow for the interior width to be increased up to 6 feet 9 inches without requiring the wheel wells to come inside. Also, a trailer can be built with an expanded interior width up to 8 feet with less wheel well than the trailer with a 96-inch axle. A slantload trailer can be built on the 96-inch axle, but the stall length will be very short—too short for most horses. A trailer that is built on a 102-inch axle must be considered 102 inches ($8^{1}/_{2}$ feet) in overall width. Trailers that measure $8^{1}/_{2}$ feet are allowed on all expressways and major trucking highways. Some states restrict all other roads to 8 feet of overall width. The loophole is that a vehicle is usually but not always allowed to travel on these restricted roads to get to its destination.

Seven-foot widths are the most common dimensions for slantload trailers. All these are examples of common stall measurements on 96" axles in a 13' space. Figure 1 shows that slanting the dividers at a steeper angle can make the stalls longer, but the corners become very sharp, and the stall is somewhat distorted. It takes just as much overall trailer length to put two horses in this slant as a straightload with a full 10' of stall length and a dressing room. Making the stall wider will help, but then the trailer needs to be even longer to do this. Figure 2 shows that the dividers can be slanted almost straight across to use less trailer length (11'). The stalls are very short. Figure 3 shows that the width can be expanded, but the wheel wells still take up the floor space. Two stalls have lost 1' and the center stall has lost 2' of usable floor space. The amount of wheel well can be reduced by using 102" axles, which is quite common, but the trailer will not be legal on all roads.

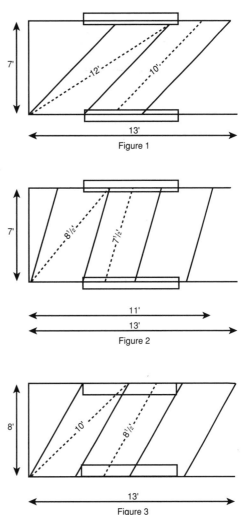

Figure 1

Figure 2

Figure 3

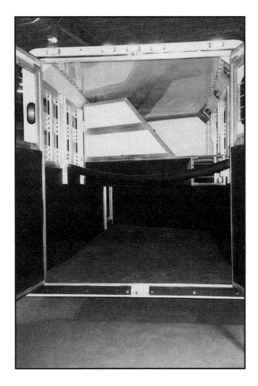

A typical 7' wide trailer on 102" axles. The slight wheel well has been covered by a smooth mat. The stalls measure $8^1/_2$' from center to center. This is a light, roomy trailer for horses under 16h.

When measuring the floor width for the horse stall, the amount of wheel well must be accounted for in your consideration of usable space. When the wheel well is located under the horse's head in a straightload, it is not a problem because it doesn't take up space in the standing area. However, in a slantload, there is the possibility that the horse can stand on it if it is flat on top. A horse standing in a slantload with a wheel well rubbing against his hocks does not have the benefit of the full floor space of his stall. Wheel wells can also take up width in straight load trailers. Always keep in mind that the width of the floor space is more critical to the horse than the upper width of the trailer. He must be able to spread his legs to keep his balance. When horses are hauled in trailers that are too narrow, they learn to scramble. The more width the horse has, the more comfortable he will be.

Wheel wells are not always unsatisfactory as long as the particular horses that are being hauled in the trailer have enough room. Just like saddles, blankets, and horse-shoes, the trailer should be measured to fit the horse. The presence of wheel wells can be made less treacherous by covering them with rubber matting or other material. Slanting the interior wall over the well instead of building the wheel well to be flat on the top makes for a smoother, therefore, safer design.

For stress reduction, each average-size horse should have a minimum stall width of 3 feet in a slantload trailer. The overall usable space of the stall is influenced by the width of the stall as well as by the width of the trailer. The larger horse—over 16 hands—should be hauled in a straightload trailer also with a minimum stall width of 3 feet. Smaller horses can do with less but should not have a full divider to close in the floor space.

LENGTH

The overall length of a tag-a-long trailer includes the tongue and coupler. The overall length of a gooseneck trailer includes the gooseneck. The bed length is the length of the trailer without the tongue or gooseneck: the actual floor of the trailer.

There are also regulations that restrict the overall length of the tow vehicle and trailer combined. Although horse trailers hardly ever reach lengths that exceed the legal limits, it is possible, and every trailer owner should be aware that these laws exist. Restrictions for overall length of the combination of tow vehicle and trailer together vary from 48 feet to 70 feet, depending on the state. A few states have regulations that also restrict the overall length of the trailer alone. More information on this topic can be found in *Hawkins Guide: Horse Trailering on the Road* (Bluegreen Publishing, 1996).

Although width gives the horse a wider base, stall length is also important because the horse needs the full use of his head and neck for balance. Length is also a significant measurement in providing enough headroom to reduce the horse's stress from claustrophobia. An average-size or larger horse requires at least 10 feet of length, and no trailer should have less than 9 feet even for a small horse. Ponies can do with less, but buying a trailer just for ponies reduces the resale market.

In a straightload trailer with stalls 10 feet in length, the headroom in front of the breast bar or manger wall should be at least 3 feet, leaving 7 feet for the horse behind the bar or wall. If you have large horses, be aware that there are few manufacturers that are truly familiar with the needs of large horses. This has resulted in some "large horse" trailers on the market that have the breast bar placed too far forward to make a $7\frac{1}{2}$-foot space for extra body length, but leaving only $2\frac{1}{2}$ feet of head space.

When we expressed concern over this placement at a dealer meeting a few years ago, one of the dealers shouted from the back of the room, "What's the big deal? When a horse hits his nose against the wall once or twice, he won't do it again!" Unfortunately, bumping his nose is exactly what will happen. The idea to give the horse more body area behind the bar may be sound enough, but to take it out of the head area is ridiculous. A large horse may have a longer body than the average horse, but he will also have a longer neck and a bigger head. If the trailer makes an abrupt stop and the horse is pushed up against the breast bar, he will hit his head on the front wall. Seven feet behind the bar or wall should be enough room for almost any horse, but in the case of the really large horse, the stall should be made longer overall, not by taking the length from the head area. There should be enough head space for a horse to stand up to the breast bar or manger wall and not touch the front wall of the trailer with his nose.

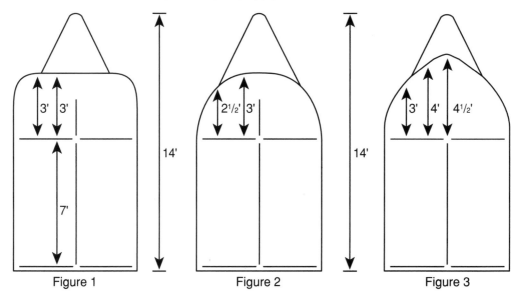

Figure 1   Figure 2   Figure 3

The flat nose (Figure 1) gives a full 3' of headspace for the entire width of the trailer. The rounded nose (Figure 2) takes away head area on the sides. By extending the nose over the tongue, the head area can be expanded to 3' on the sides and 4½' in the middle without increasing the overall length of the trailer.

When considering the usable space for the horse in a slantload trailer, the stall length should be measured from the middle of the stall from sidewall to sidewall, not from corner to corner. If the manufacturer specifies a 10-foot stall on the diagonal, there won't be that much usable space for a horse that actually needs 10 feet, because his nose will have to be stuck in the front corner and his hindquarters in the rear corner. The horse needs full use of his head and neck to retain his balance, and if he is confined in this position, he will not have the ability to easily stand on his own. Also, measure the actual floor space between the wheel wells. Will your horse have enough length to stand comfortably?

When buying a trailer, make sure that there is enough room for your horse to feel unconfined. It is better for the horse to have more room than not enough, so if more than one horse will be traveling in the trailer, buy it for the largest one. Butt and breast bars can be adjusted down and forward to accommodate really small horses or ponies by having additional brackets installed.

EXTERIOR MEASUREMENTS AND LEGAL LIMITS

When you are hauling your trailer, you should know the exterior measurements so you know your legal limits and your clearance limitations. We have already mentioned the restrictions on width and length, but there are also overall height restrictions. Usually it is $13^1/_2$ feet, but it can range from 13 to 15 feet, depending on the state.

The manufacturer has built your trailer to legal requirements unless you have requested otherwise, but before you drive through McDonald's for a breakfast biscuit, know how tall your trailer really is, including opened vents. When you find yourself on a country road with a "low clearance" sign, you will want to know if you can go under it without tearing off your roof. Traveling with a horse trailer often involves driving on country roads and into out-of-the-way gas stations with low-clearance challenges. Be prepared.

10

Construction Materials

Horse trailers can be constructed from a number of materials, used alone or in combination. Many opinions and claims cloud the real issue, which is the safety and well-being of the horse. If we approach the choice of construction materials from this point of view, the final one may be much different from what you would expect.

We have discussed the effects of travel on the horse and have explained that it is possible to reduce stress by choosing the right style of trailer and optional equipment. As we shall see, the choice of construction materials can affect the well-being of your horse.

Until the 1980s most horse trailers were built of steel. Although a few of those trailers are still on the road, many have rusted into oblivion. The problem of rust prompted manufacturers to look for new materials that would produce a longer lasting trailer. In that quest, longer life was not only a factor, but also looks and prestige. The entire horse industry underwent an explosion in the late 1980s, and as horses became more valuable, people were willing to pay more for trailers in which to haul them. The trailer industry became more competitive and more innovative.

Many, many improvements have been made in the last 15 or so years. But it has taken all those years to correct some major problems. Because of innovations in the metal industry, what were once-established facts about construction materials are no longer true. Since there are no regulations protecting the health or safety of the horses, the "testing" of these materials is accomplished by trial and error. Because human injury is not involved, lawsuits do not amount to the millions of dollars that worry the automobile industry. Consequently, there is no crash testing. New ideas are implemented and if there are problems, changes are made after the fact. Accident statistics about horse trailers are virtually nonexistent. Even the insurance industry has not kept records.

Like any good capitalistic enterprise, the trailer industry is motivated by sales. Since the industry must fulfill the wants and needs of its customers, manufacturers build what people buy. The customer is the final regulation, so if horse people demand safety for their horses, they will get it.

Before you buy your horse trailer, make sure you choose the construction that is right for you and your horses. Don't be deceived by misinformation.

Aluminum

Aluminum has burst into the horse trailer marketplace with such force that one would believe it is the perfect choice of materials. Like all materials, aluminum has advantages. But it also has disadvantages.

There are two main advantages of building a trailer entirely of aluminum, including the frame. It makes an attractive-looking trailer, and its resistance to corrosion gives the trailer a long life. Aluminum also weighs less than other materials; however, that may not always be true in some finished trailer weight comparisons, especially on smaller units.

Pure aluminum is not strong enough to be used alone, so the aluminum that is used in the construction of horse trailers is combined with other metals to increase its strength. The result is called an alloy. The two basic types of aluminum alloys are those that are heat-treated and those that are not. Different aluminum alloys contain various combinations of other materials such as silicon, magnesium, copper, and zinc.

The type of alloy determines the strength of the material. If metal is stressed beyond its yield strength (the level beyond which it cannot recover elasticity), the material may change shape, but not break. This means that an overstressed part can no longer be used. The tensile strength is the maximum stress the metal supports before fracture. Fatigue stress is another important factor in determining the choice of a metal for construction. This is the stress that occurs when a material is used again and again. Fatigue failure begins with a crack that grows until the material fails.

Aluminum itself does not score very high in any of these strength tests. The quality of the aluminum depends on the quality of the alloy. The quality and, therefore, the strength of the horse trailer is determined by the manufacturer's choice of alloy. As with any other material, it is more expensive to buy the higher quality aluminum, both for the manufacturer and the consumer, but it is more important for the strength of the trailer that the best aluminum be used in its construction.

Aluminum (as an alloy) may be used with other materials or by itself in the construction of horse trailers. As a rule, aluminum is one-third the strength of steel and 70 percent of the weight of steel. When building an all-aluminum horse trailer, the manufacturer must use quality structural engineering to make the trailer lighter than steel, yet with enough strength to safely hold up to the shifting weight of horses and the pounding of hard road use.

The structure, or frame, of an all-aluminum trailer must meet certain specifications to be strong. The strength of the trailer depends on the integrity of the top rail and bottom rail of a gooseneck trailer and the bottom rail of a tag-a-long trailer. Gussets reinforcing the stress points, the back corners of the trailer and the angle under the gooseneck, are especially important in reducing flexibility in the frame, because too much flexing causes fatigue stress in aluminum. Corner caps, side slats, and the floor may also be part of the structure. New engineering techniques on some trailers make a square or "box" back possible without the use of gussets.

Aluminum can be successfully welded, but the welder must be knowledgeable. Aluminum welds are not as strong as steel welds, so it is important that the manufacturer has considered this. Rivets, bolts, and other fasteners should be stainless or zinc-plated steel, since aluminum fasteners have a tendency to shear. (If you are wondering about electrolysis, this is not a problem with stainless steel against aluminum.)

Most aluminum trailer manufacturers use aluminum extrusions that are built strong enough for the large horse trailers, and then they use those same extrusions for

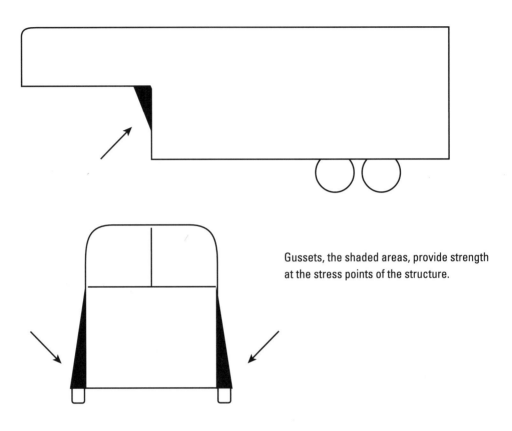

Gussets, the shaded areas, provide strength at the stress points of the structure.

building two-horse trailers. The result is that the two-horse trailers are "over built." Consequently, there is often little or no difference in weight between the smaller all-aluminum trailers and comparable steel or hybrid trailers. The weight difference becomes more apparent as the trailers get larger (four-horse or more).

As the trailer model becomes larger, the frame becomes longer and is subjected to more stress. It's very important to the structural integrity of the trailer that the manufacturer use the proper application of the aluminum alloys, fasteners, and welds. In many quality trailers, steel will be used to reinforce the frame when large doors or openings have compromised the continuity of the frame.

Aluminum trailers also have aluminum floors. Each manufacturer has its own method of building a trailer floor. Some have tongue-in-groove panels, others incorporate the floor into the chassis of the trailer, making it part of the structure. An understructure of cross-support I-beams is usually used, the closer together, the better.

Because aluminum is not strong enough to be used for a coupler or an axle, a method must be devised to join these steel parts of the trailer to the aluminum

An aluminum floor from underneath the trailer. These support beams are 5.3" apart. The highest quality all-aluminum trailers will have support structures under the floor at least this close together.

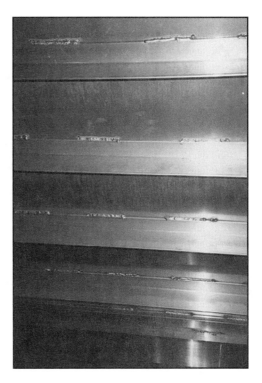

frame. A good-quality aluminum trailer will have a steel "subframe" that accomplishes this. An 8-foot steel subframe bolted and welded onto the aluminum frame will enable the axles to be attached to steel instead of aluminum. A 2-foot steel subframe or a steel drawbar on a tag-a-long trailer enables the coupler to also be attached by this transitional steel method.

Other parts of so-called all-aluminum trailers that may be steel are hinge pins, tie rings, and ramp springs. If steel is used for these parts it should be stainless steel. Ramp springs, however, should be a very low grade of stainless with a high iron content so that the springs maintain elasticity.

So what does this all mean? It means that you depend on the manufacturer to know how to build a safe aluminum trailer. Even though high-grade aluminum is available, the manufacturer must actually use it where it counts. Beware of the cheap all-aluminum trailer, it's probably too good to be true. High-quality aluminum is not always readily available, and it also fluctuates in price. Because aluminum is so much more expensive than other metals used for horse trailers, some manufacturers may cut corners to keep the price of the trailer more in line with what the consumer wants to pay. Usually those corners will not be cut from the structure but will more than likely be cut from the parts that do not support the

This coupler is attached directly onto the aluminum drawbar by only 4 bolts on each side. A stronger method is to use a transitional steel subframe and more bolts. Some manufacturers use as many as 24 bolts on each side.

integrity of the trailer. Dividers, center posts, butt and breast bars, and the fasteners that hold them may be the parts that will most likely be affected.

Although aluminum does not rust, it does corrode in the form of aluminum oxide. This is a reaction from moisture and other elements. After time, natural aluminum (not coated or painted) will take on a spotty or uneven milky appearance from this oxidation often called "pitting." It can be removed by an acid bath. Many manufacturers offer anodized aluminum that is actually a controlled oxidation that produces an even coating over the aluminum. Although it costs a little more, it protects the aluminum longer and gives a nice appearance. Aluminum can also be painted, clear-coated, or finished with a baked-on enamel to protect the appearance.

Electrolysis causes galvanic corrosion when two dissimilar metals touch, such as steel and aluminum, forming an electric current. Competing manufacturers have made an issue out of this, but it takes many years for galvanic corrosion to affect touching dissimilar metals that have any bulk. Besides, most manufacturers that use both aluminum and steel know to separate the metals by Mylar tape or special coatings, which eliminates the problem. Stainless steel is safe to use against aluminum.

If all aluminum trailers never rust and keep their appearance with little maintenance, what are the disadvantages?

Aluminum is more rigid and does not absorb shock and stress as well as steel. If the trailer is not built properly, flexing of the frame can lead to fatigue fractures and eventually failure.

Because aluminum is more brittle, it will not withstand impact as well as steel, and if the trailer is in an accident, damage can be severe and injury to the horse may be increased. If the butt and breast bars, hinges, and dividers are stressed by horses thrown by an impact, they may break easily, even at low speeds. Horses may be injured unnecessarily even if the trailer structure remains intact. (Picture a six-horse slantload trailer in a head-on collision at 30 miles per hour. When six horses are thrown forward at 20 Gs, aluminum hinges and dividers may not keep the horses from piling up on each other.)

Aluminum is not as malleable as steel and if a trailer is structurally damaged it may not be possible to restore it to its original strength. Since each manufacturer uses a different method to build the trailer, parts are custom-made and not always available. The trailer will have to go back to the factory for repair. So buy your trailer from a manufacturer that seems likely to stay in business for a long while. A solid manufacturer will offer a good warranty and have a reputation for honoring it.

For minor repairs, it may be hard to find a body shop that can perform quality aluminum welding. Not all welders can weld aluminum, and when you find one who can, he will be more expensive.

An aluminum trailer floor may suit the structural engineers but has no advantages for the horse. Horse urine can cause oxidation, which can cause aluminum floors to fall through. Most manufacturers deny that this can happen, but a few aluminum trailer manufacturers will admit that it has happened in the past, although they claim that it doesn't happen anymore.

Aluminum floors do not absorb the road shock as well as wood, although rubber torsion and good mats will help counteract the rigidity of the metal. Aluminum is a conductor and may actually conduct heat from the road into the trailer, especially when the trailer is stopped on the road. Because aluminum does not breath, this heat from the road can build up inside the trailer and combine with trapped noxious gasses from urine and manure to create an unhealthy environment.

Some aluminum floors are made with aluminum sheeting that is supported by the underbraces. Even though the floor structure is adequate for the load, the sheeting can be thin enough to buckle under the step of the horse. Horses don't like it when the floor under them moves and makes strange noises.

Aluminum dividers can be noisy unless measures are taken to control the rattling.

The aluminum trailer industry has come a long way since the first aluminum trailer was built. In the beginning, some were built to be too light, and available alloys have not always been as strong as they are today. Aluminum trailers are built much better now and alloys keep improving, but there are a lot of older trailers out there that were built before these problems became apparent. Welds, bolts, frames, and floors may be suffering from fatigue stress on trailers that were not built very well, even though they still look good. If you are buying a used aluminum trailer, check very closely for hairline cracks or other signs of stress. It would be a good idea to have a qualified body shop or even the original manufacturer look it over.

MAINTENANCE

Natural aluminum that is not clear-coated or painted, can be taken through an acid bath. Have it done by someone who knows how to do it, because it is possible to burn the aluminum. Beware of salt because it will damage the finish by pitting. Unless salt exposure is excessive and long-term, it should not cause any structural damage but will make it harder to clean.

It is a misconception that an aluminum trailer does not need maintenance. Just like any other trailer, it must be kept clean and dry to maintain its long life. To prevent floor corrosion, take the mats out of the trailer and wash any urine off the floor with soap and water. Let the floor dry before replacing the mats. Never let moisture collect under the mats. If you use shavings, sweep them out after every use. Keep urine, wet hay, and mucous from collecting in the seams of the trailer.

Steel

Corrosion in the form of rust has been such a problem with steel horse trailers in the past, that the perception of steel as an acceptable building material has been hard to change. But, like the aluminum industry, the steel industry has also been busy improving the quality of its product.

Steel is the most common and affordable metal used today for construction of anything that requires strength—bridges, automobile structures, building structures, and yes, even horse trailers. Different kinds of steels vary in strength and corrosion resistance according to the amount of carbon and by adding other elements to create alloys. By adding such metals as chromium, molybdenum, and nickel, the strength, toughness, and corrosion resistance are improved. Different types of alloys have different applications, and new improved varieties of steel are being developed.

Manufacturing techniques within both the steel industry and the trailer industry have improved the quality of steel horse trailers considerably. The type of steel used and the way that steel is handled when the trailer is being built will determine the quality and price of the trailer.

Rust is the brown-orange material that forms as a result of corrosion on steel. Rust forms on painted steel like this: Moisture penetrates through pores in the paint film or through a scratch. The oxygen in the water combines with the iron in the steel, and a minute amount of iron is dissolved, forming a solution. When there is an imbalance of electrons between the solution and the surrounding steel, it leads to a flow of electrons, or current. As long as the current flows, the steel will deteriorate, and rust will form.

This old trailer is still structurally sound but not for much longer. It has been patched around the manger where rust is very common. Once rust starts, it continues to spread.

When raw steel is shipped to the trailer manufacturer, rust has already started because it has not been protected from the elements. After the trailer has been built, the paint is applied to coat and, hopefully, protect the steel. But, since the rust has already begun, it will continue to spread and the trailer will eventually rust out from under the paint. Many horse trailers have been built with raw steel in the past, and even now, some less expensive brands may be still.

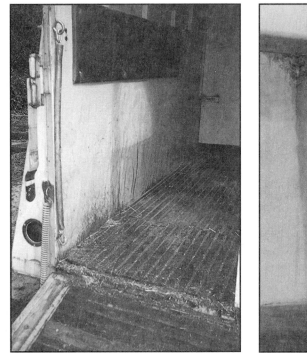

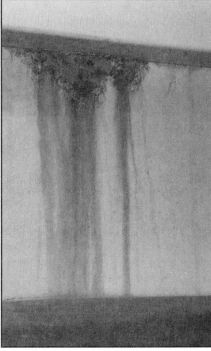

This 8-year-old steel trailer did not start with a good-quality construction or paint coat. No sidewall lining protected the interior walls, and the scrapes have allowed rust to start. The trailer was not well maintained, which further accelerated its destruction.

A closeup of the same trailer. Water has seeped into the trailer from the window above. This rust will continue to spread.

If the trailer manufacturer uses a type of steel called Kote steel, which has been painted at the steel factory before being shipped, the quality of the trailer will be better. This steel has been protected from the elements before it has a chance to corrode. After the trailer has been built and given its final coat of paint and undercoating, it will have a longer lasting life than the first trailer as long as moisture is not allowed to enter under the paint.

Many trailer manufacturers are now using galvanealed steel. This steel has been galvanized by coating it with zinc. The zinc coating gives the steel an electro-chemical resistance to corrosion. When a trailer is properly built with galvanealed steel, rust will not be an issue. Galvanealed steel can be used for the entire trailer or only for parts of the trailer, such as the frame and other structural parts.

The advantages of galvanealed steel can be canceled out if manufacturing techniques damage the surface of the steel while the trailer is being built. When the trailer is welded together, the heat from the process can burn the zinc coating off the steel around the welds. The welds and the area around them should be recoated with paint or undercoating to prevent corrosion where the zinc coating has been removed.

A trailer built of galvanealed steel is far superior to those old rust buckets that always come to mind when considering a steel horse trailer. New processes such as powdered steel and other innovations within the steel industry will continue to make steel a viable material for horse trailers.

The price of steel to the manufacturer is cheaper and more stable than that of aluminum because it is more readily available, and there are enough steel companies vying for the market to create a more competitive environment. Steel has a higher yield strength, tensile strength, fatigue strength, and impact resistance than aluminum for a lot less money.

Another reason that steel has come into disfavor is the fact that it is heavier than aluminum. The weight of steel trailers will differ according to manufacturing techniques and design. It is not fair to put all steel trailers in the same category. As the horse trailers get larger, the weight of an all-steel trailer becomes more significant in comparison to aluminum or hybrid trailers.

This steel trailer is 10 years old, 2 years older than the previously pictured rusted one, but built by a better manufacturer. Even though this was not an expensive trailer, it has a very good paint job, and the owner has cleaned it after every use. There is some surface rust in the interior, but this trailer has many years of use left.

Over the years, we have seen quite a few steel trailers that have been involved in traffic accidents. Most have come off the tow vehicle and have rolled over with horses inside. It is amazing how many horses have been able to walk away with only minor injuries because the trailer has held its shape and the interior dividers have kept them in place—like seat belts. In the cases of major injuries or death that we have seen in steel trailers, inferior workmanship or design has been more responsible than the material of the trailer, except in those instances where the accident is so bad that nothing would have made a difference.

Steel can be welded by any welding shop in the country. Repairs can be made easily and less expensively than aluminum welding. Parts can be more easily obtained, and most body shops can fix a horse trailer that has been wrecked or can paint one that needs painting. Repairs can also be more easily made by do-it-yourselfers.

MAINTENANCE

A steel trailer must be kept clean and dry to increase its life expectancy. By not allowing rust to start, the trailer will maintain its appearance and strength for many years. Clean out any leftover hay, grain, urine, or manure after every use. Do not allow any of these things or any water to collect in seams or under mats. Wash the trailer frequently and dry it before storage. If you can, keep the trailer under roof. If you cover it with a tarp, don't let the tarp touch the roof where moisture will be trapped. Put spacers under the tarp to create an air space so the moisture can evaporate. Just like a car, the trailer will benefit from waxing and polishing, inside as well as outside. Touch up any scratches in the paint. If the trailer has not been undercoated from the factory, have it done immediately after purchase.

It is not so hard to make it part of your routine to clean the trailer out after every use. You will add many years to the life of your trailer. Even the most inexpensive trailer will maintain its usefulness for a long time if you keep it clean and dry.

Fender-Bender Nightmare

In the late 1980s we decided to add a major line of aluminum trailers to our inventory. One of the major manufacturers had assured us that the extra tall, extra wide walk-through model would be suitable for our warmblood market. Since aluminum trailers were becoming very popular, we wanted to be able to meet the growing demand for this type of trailer, and this particular brand was developing a very good reputation.

Before actually stocking these trailers, we custom ordered a few for some customers who were convinced that all aluminum was the wave of the future. One of these customers was a personal friend, Barbara, who raised and competed Hanoverian horses. The trailer she had chosen was a two-horse walk-through tag-a-long trailer that was 7 feet 4 inches tall and 6 feet wide.

Barbara and her friend Peg were on their way to a clinic in Dayton, Ohio, on I-75 in morning rush-hour traffic, with the new trailer. They were hauling two large warmbloods and were properly hitched with a weight distribution system and a very capable tow vehicle. The winter weather had taken a turn for the worse, and the roads were beginning to ice from the freezing rain. The traffic was crawling along at 20 mph when the car in front of Barbara suddenly stopped. When Barbara applied the brakes, the tow vehicle quietly slid off the road, but the trailer jackknifed behind.

Barbara and Peg jumped out to check the horses. The damage was far more than either of them expected. The nose of the trailer had completely caved in where it had jackknifed against the truck. The horses were causing such a commotion inside that Peg unwisely opened the trailer door. Her horse had been thrown forward because the breast bar had broken at the hinges and the tie ring had come out of the wall. He was down on the floor in the nose of the trailer, but when he saw the door open, he jumped up and pushed Peg out of the way, running into the expressway traffic.

Barbara's horse was all right, but his breast bar had broken also. This was not the only damage to the trailer. Both butt bars were broken at the hinges, but even more amazing was the fact that the inner wall had pulled away from the outer wall, and the windows were loosened from the frames.

Peg's horse was caught, but they were all lucky the traffic was moving slowly. He suffered some cuts and bruises and a stifle injury that took some time to heal. Peg's shoulder was dislocated. This was far too much damage for a fender bender! The trailer should have been able to support the horses in such a minor accident.

Hybrids

Since steel and aluminum each have their strong and weak points, one logical conclusion is to use them both, taking advantage of the strength of steel and the lighter-weight, long-lasting, attractive look of aluminum. Incorporate the use of other materials such as fiberglass, Fiberglass Reinforced Product (FRP), and/or wood, and viola!—the close to perfect combination. (Remember, there is no such thing as the perfect horse trailer.)

We have already mentioned that sometimes all-aluminum trailers will have steel pieces reinforcing some of the weaker parts of the frame, but a hybrid trailer is more than that. A hybrid trailer is built on a frame of one material, but the nonstructural parts are built of a different material.

By using the strength of steel in the frame and sometimes an inner wall, the trailer may be built with the same strength benefits as the all-steel trailer. But by using aluminum and/or fiberglass on the exterior, the trailer can be made lighter in weight and will keep its attractive appearance with little maintenance.

A covering of thin sheets of aluminum on the exterior is called aluminum "skin." Aluminum skin can be clear-coated, painted, or have an enamel baked-on surface.

An example of a hybrid trailer. It has a galvanealed steel frame and interior walls, and the exterior is an aluminum skin. The floor is wood, the roof and fenders are fiberglass, and diamond-plate aluminum is used for gravel guards. The weight of this two-horse trailer compares very favorably with an all-aluminum trailer of the same size and is less expensive. (Note: The roof is actually white on top, although there is a dark stripe around the edge.) Older trailers have the same type of construction but were built with steel that was not galvanealed, so rust may be apparent on those models.

The clear coat will protect the aluminum from pitting and oxidizing so it maintains the shiny aluminum look. Some of the first hybrid trailers did not have a protective clear coating on the skin, so they have turned ugly over the years. The preparation at the factory will have a direct effect on the long-lasting look of the finish of any aluminum skin, whether it has been clear-coated or painted. Poor quality paint may chip or come off after a time, and vinyl striping may peel if the surface has not been prepared properly. Baked-on enamel may keep its good-looking appearance longer. Scratches on the paint or enamel covering of aluminum may be unattractive, but corrosion will not occur to spread the damage like rust will on steel. Whatever finish is used, good manufacturing techniques will add years to the original beauty of the trailer.

The space between the outer skin and the inner wall may be used for insulation. Sheets of Styrofoam fit easily between the walls, creating a solid, quiet trailer that has a beneficial effect on the environment of the interior.

A hybrid trailer may be built by incorporating additional materials to take out the weight and contribute to a longer life. Fiberglass can be used for the roof and fenders. Walls can be made of FRP or new space age materials that are becoming available all the time.

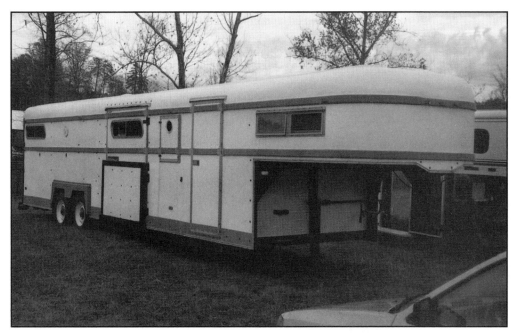

Another hybrid. This one is steel, aluminum, and has a body of fiberglass. Its best feature is the drip moldings over the doors. It should be noted, however, that this trailer is poorly ventilated and the white is beginning to look dull from sun damage.

Some hybrid trailers may have an aluminum frame instead of steel and have fiberglass or FRP walls. There are also hybrid trailers that incorporate a stainless-steel skin instead of an aluminum skin. Stainless steel will not rust and makes a very good skin, although it is heavier than an aluminum skin. Stainless steel is also rather expensive.

Other Materials

FIBERGLASS

Fiberglass is actually a textile that comes on a bolt and must be made into a hard material by adding a liquid resin with a hardener mixed in. When the resin hardens in and on the fiberglass, you have a reinforced plastic. In the process of hardening, these materials bond mechanically and chemically, forming a composite material. The terms "reinforced plastics," "composites," and "fiberglass" can be used interchangeably.

It takes several layers of fiberglass and resin to make a structure. The number of layers will make a difference in the strength and impact resistance. The type of resin will also make a difference. Epoxy resins offer high strength, high adhesion, and impact resistance, but are temperamental to work with. Polyester resins are naturally resistant to ultraviolet light and are used more widely than any other type of resin. The surface can be covered with a gel coat to give it a smooth look.

A fiberglass roof will have a slight cushioning effect if the horse hits its head, because it is rather soft. However, a molded fiberglass roof will not hold up to an accident where the trailer would be turned over, so a frame should reinforce the fiberglass roof to create a roll bar effect. If the fiberglass tears in an accident, the edges will not be as sharp as metal, therefore, less likely to cut a horse. Fenders made of molded fiberglass are also less likely to cause injury to a horse that may be tied to the trailer. If the fender and the horse have a run-in, the fender will more likely suffer the most damage. It is easier and less expensive to repair a fiberglass fender than to repair a horse.

Fiberglass will keep its appearance for many years with little maintenance if it is not subject to a lot of wear and tear. A white fiberglass roof will reflect heat, therefore, creating a cooler trailer environment.

Fiberglass in many different forms can also be used for the entire trailer body. Because we so strongly believe that a horse trailer should have a strong enough body to hold up to wear and tear from the horse and from everyday hauling stress, fiberglass is not our choice as the best material for the body. Not only can the walls be damaged from the horse's kicking, and maybe even kicked through, but damage by being pierced from overhanging branches or other protrusions can be more severe than in metal trailers. Depending on the quality, molded fiberglass can tear rather easily, and it can get a shredded look around the edges as it gets older. These problems can be fixed as they occur, but we believe that there are better choices of materials for the trailer body.

Smooth gel coat sheets of fiberglass can be used to line the inner walls. This type comes in 4-foot × 8-foot sheets that are impact resistant and make for a very nice, easy-to-clean inner lining in the horse area when it is used to cover a more substantial outer wall.

Maintenance

Wash the surface with a mild detergent and water. The fiberglass should be waxed with a wax that is recommended for fiberglass. Tears should be repaired before they become larger.

FIBERGLASS REINFORCED PRODUCT (FRP)

Fiberglass Reinforced Product (FRP) may be described as a "sandwich" of two outer sheets of smooth polyester gel coat fiberglass with 5 to 7 layers of plywood in between. It is glued together by high-tech processes and comes in 4-foot × 8-foot sheets that are usually $3/4$ inch thick. FRP can be used as single-wall construction because it has an attractive finish for the exterior and a smooth finish for the interior of the horse stall. FRP also has insulating properties of its own, so no other insulation needs to be added. FRP may also be called "Fiberglass Reinforced Plastic" or "Fiberglass Reinforced Plywood."

Because FRP is constructed of layers of wood and fiberglass, it is very strong and rather lightweight. Manufacturers of FRP tell us that even though FRP has a good impact resistance rating, the rating does not apply to use with horses because no testing has been done. About five years ago, out of curiosity, we gave a piece of it a sharp blow with a hammer. It broke in half! To give FRP the benefit of the doubt, there are differences in quality among manufacturing techniques and overall it has probably improved since then.

Because FRP is primarily a wood product, moisture is its main enemy. When sheets of FRP are cut for shaping, the new edges must be sealed by the trailer manufacturer so moisture does not creep in and cause the FRP to swell from the inside. All new edges that may be exposed to moisture, around windows and doors, for example, are likely to suffer damage if the manufacturer has not used proper sealing techniques.

Maintenance

FRP needs maintenance to preserve its luster. It should be washed frequently, waxed two times a year, and kept out of the sun to prevent fading. The appearance of the FRP will fade in as little as two years. Waxing will protect it from the UV rays for about five years. After that, the gel coat loses its ability to be buffed. It can be painted, but even then the life span of the FRP itself may be only about ten years. Caulking and other sealing materials should be kept in good condition so moisture cannot invade the integrity of the product to insure the longest possible life. Deep marks in the surface must be repaired professionally to prevent the invasion of moisture.

WOOD

Wood is a porous material and, therefore, "breathes" better than metal, so gasses from urine and manure do not get trapped inside the trailer as much when the floor is wood instead of metal. Also, when wood is used for the floor of the trailer, it more readily absorbs road shock that contributes to less leg and hoof stress than a metal floor.

In the past, 2-inch-thick oak planking was the wood of choice for trailer floors. When the new oak was installed, it would dry and shrink over time, allowing small spaces between the wood planks. These small spaces allow urine to drain out the bottom of the trailer.

Nowadays, most trailer manufacturers use pressure-treated pine flooring, which is less expensive than oak. Pine planks are rated according to the number of knots that are present in the board. The planks with the fewest knots are rated #1 pine, #2 pine has more knots, and #3 and #4 pine have even more knots. Most trailer companies use 2-inch-thick #2 pine. Number 2 pine is not of lesser strength than #1, but only lacks in appearance. Number 3 pine has enough knots to make a difference in the quality and strength.

Pressure treating is a carefully controlled and monitored process involving a series of pressure and vacuum cycles within an enclosed cylinder. During the process, wood preservatives are forced deep into the cellular structure of the wood, forming a chemical barrier against termites and decay. Pressure treatment provides the protection needed to significantly prolong the life of wood products, assuring structural soundness and a long life.

Most wood floors in horse trailers are installed lengthwise in the trailer, not crossways. If the planks span the trailer floor widthwise, the horses could be standing with both front hooves on one board and both back hooves on one board. The horse will, in effect, usually be standing on the same two boards all the time, and the other boards will not be helping to support the weight of the horse in any significant way. If there are two horses standing next to each other, they may both be standing on the same two boards. The boards that are supporting all the weight become weaker much more quickly than the boards that do not support weight. Boards that are installed in this manner are often supported only by the edges with no other support in the middle of the board. If a weak support board falls out, the horse(s) will go with it. Boards are more likely installed crossways in stock trailers. Since cattle and other livestock are usually not tied in place and are free to walk around, they use the floor more evenly.

Figure 1 shows a typical installation of wood planks running lengthwise in the trailer with support beams on 24" centers (dotted lines). Figure 2 shows how two horses can stand on the same two boards all the time when the boards are installed widthwise.

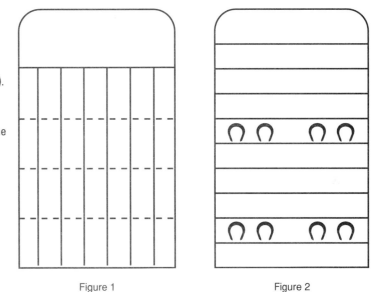

Figure 1   Figure 2

Boards that are installed lengthwise are strong when they are well supported by cross beams underneath at least 24 inches apart. When the floor is supported properly from underneath, the boards alone are not responsible for the load. These beams reduce the span that is supporting the weight, reducing the flex of the board, therefore giving it greater strength.

It is imperative that the floor of the horse trailer be capable of supporting the weight of the load. There is no accident that is as horrible as horses falling through the floor. It happens too many times because people are not careful enough about the condition of the boards, or metal, as the case may be, and the undercarriage that supports it. If there is any question about the soundness of the planks, replace them. If a knife can be easily stuck into the wood and the wood shreds when the knife is turned, the boards are bad. Don't take chances, get rid of them! A high-quality pressure-treated wood floor can last ten years if it is well maintained, but check it frequently so that you are always aware of its condition. A wood floor that is not pressure-treated should be checked earlier and more often, two times a year is not too much. Check the undercarriage as well. Any question of strength needs to be addressed.

Maintenance

Floorboards will last a long time if they are kept clean and dry. If you use shavings, sweep them out after each use, especially in corners and where they have been trapped between the mats and the floor and walls. Use solid floor mats that keep urine and manure from saturating the wood, and turn mats up to the side when the trailer is not in use to allow the floor to breath. Hose the floor frequently, but make sure it is dry before putting the mats over it. Surprisingly, a lot of floor damage comes from underneath the trailer from the salt and other debris that comes up from the road. Undercoating the floor and undercarriage protects them from undue damage.

Plywood is also used for center dividers and sidewall lining and often for floor areas that do not support the horse, such as dressing rooms. (A good reason not to put horses or ponies in dressing rooms.) Plywood dividers and liners can break and splinter on impact, leaving sharp points that can pierce a horse. The impact can come from a horse kicking through it or from a traffic accident. A horse can also splinter plywood dividers with body force by thrashing around in the trailer. Bare, unprotected plywood on the walls or closed ramp can severely injure a horse if he kicks through it. Again, smaller horses may not be as likely to cause major damage, but large horses certainly have the strength and bulk to easily break plywood. Many used trailers with plywood walls will show wear holes from horses constantly pawing.

Note: Many trailers include plywood in the ramp because it is lightweight. The plywood should be covered with a mat or other material to give it extra strength. Sometimes this plywood will collect moisture and rot, so if you have a trailer with plywood in the ramp, check it often.

Warning: It is hard to believe, but a few individuals actually build home-made trailers completely—floor and walls—out of plywood, and make their horses ride in them. A few years ago, one such trailer was brought into a campground where our club was camping for the weekend. The driver (not a member of our club) was completely oblivious to the fact that the horse had fallen through the plywood floor and its legs were dragging on the ground. When he was finally stopped, and the trailer was opened, both of the horse's front legs were torn off below the knees. A vet was not available so a park ranger was called to put the horse out of its misery with his gun, but he refused because of the "liability." One of our club members had to do the job.

It is very difficult to hear stories like this, but sometimes they must be told so that everyone who hauls a horse understands that building a horse trailer is serious business and care must be taken to avoid such horrible incidents.

New Space Age Materials

New materials are being developed every year, and the horse trailer industry is always trying new products in the quest to build a better trailer. "Better" may mean better quality or a trailer that will sell better, two things that do not always have the same meaning. Most of these new materials have been used in other industries like the automobile or boat industry. It seems to us that a lot of these new materials are coming from the boat industry where "lightweight" is the key word instead of the automobile industry where "strength" is just as important as weight.

A different kind of strength is required for a horse trailer than for a boat. Horses are unsteady, unpredictable, abusive, heavy, strong passengers. They are living creatures that can kick through a sidewall, push out a back door, or find any number of other ways to injure themselves or the trailer in a heartbeat. Any new material should be able to hold up to the special needs of hauling horses and should provide a safe mode of transportation that will protect the horses as well as possible in a traffic accident.

Since there is no regulation about which materials may be used, be aware that any new material that is marketed may be just an idea of someone, hopefully an engineer, who believes it will work in a particular application. Because the engineer has been educated to make these decisions, it probably will. However, if you buy such a trailer before its type has been used on the road for a while, you and your horse may be the ones to find out if it does not work. The reputation of the company and the type of warranty provided become even more important when considering a trailer that is made of a new material. Hopefully, any problems that may occur will be minor and will not cause injury to you or to your horse.

Summary

Few subjects about horse trailers cause more arguments than the type of construction material to buy. This subject gets a lot more attention than it deserves, but one thing for sure is that generalities cannot be made. What is true about one steel trailer may not be true for another steel trailer of a different brand. The same goes for aluminum, hybrid, and FRP trailers. There are so many different manufacturers making so many different claims that it is easy to become confused or misled.

Because the industry is making many improvements in manufacturing and the construction materials are also improving every year, it is not feasible to make a decision about a new trailer this year based on what was true just a few years ago. However, even though the quality of trailer construction is making leaps and bounds, the welfare of the horse is not always getting the attention that it should. There are many differences in quality from company to company, and the particular material is not as important as the overall quality of the trailer and the attention that has been paid to the well-being of the equine passengers.

A trailer need not be expensive to be safe, but the wrong trailer is not a good buy at any price. Buy a trailer that suits your needs and that of your horse's. Buy the best trailer you can afford based on the design of the trailer and the quality of the safety features, not only on the type of construction material. Do not sacrifice the health and safety of your horse(s) because you want a trailer made of a particular material because someone else has told you that you should.

If you have horses that are under 16 hands, you have a larger choice of options because most horse trailers, whatever the construction material, are strong enough to deal with the everyday wear and tear of using the trailer. When horses become larger, the strength of the material becomes more important because the larger horses are capable of doing much more damage and will stress the trailer to its limits. The strength of the interior features also becomes very important. It is our recommendation that large horses such as warmbloods and draft horses always be hauled in steel or hybrid trailers. If you are concerned that your horse be protected as well as possible in an accident, we also believe, because of the lack of statistics at this time to prove otherwise, that a trailer with a steel frame will be a better choice.

11

Living Quarters

Do you do a lot of camping or showing? Living quarters installed in a horse trailer can be as simple as a mattress in the gooseneck or as lavish as a living area that rivals the fanciest motor home. Taking your "home away from home" with your horses safely tucked in the back can be a lot of fun and can save on hotel rooms. When you get to your destination, unload the horses, park the trailer, and unhitch your truck. You now have a vehicle to drive around and a place to stay with all the amenities.

History

More than 30 years ago, the first manufacturer to build living quarters in a horse trailer was located in Elkhart, Indiana, the recreational vehicle (RV) capital of the world. Being so close to the RV industry gave it access to parts and technology. Even though this company custom-built living quarters in their horse trailers, they didn't capitalize on the idea. Other companies did, however, sometimes using RV or cargo trailer chassis. These trailers were never successful because they could not hold up to the constant abuse a horse can give.

In the 1980s a manufacturer began producing trailers with living quarters. The idea began to catch on, and this company could hardly keep up with the demand. New businesses began to spring up that specialized in building recreational vehicle interiors into existing horse trailers that were built by someone else. Other horse trailer manufacturers teamed with these "conversion companies," hiring them to build living quarter interiors in their trailers instead of building them in their own plants.

Meanwhile mom-and-pop conversion companies began to proliferate. Quality in most of the industry began to suffer. The decor and design were several years behind that of the RV industry. However, in time, a few companies began to greatly improve their product.

The living quarters idea gained momentum in the 1990s. People liked the economy and convenience of staying in their trailers. Also, using a pickup truck with a trailer was not only cheaper but also more convenient than using a motor home and a trailer.

In 1993, one of the major horse trailer manufacturers outgrew their conversion company and bought its own company in Elkhart. Through an intensive marketing effort, this company increased its production over fivefold, and living quarters became one of the major growth markets of the horse trailer industry.

Appliances

There are a number of reasons to have a professional company build living quarters into your trailer. The first and foremost is that using certain appliances in a space that is not ventilated properly can cause death by carbon monoxide poisoning. Heaters and cooking appliances must be carefully installed to be safe to use. People have died simply by using the wrong heater in a gooseneck trailer and closing the windows while they slept.

That said, what kind of options are available in a living quarters horse trailer? A simple living quarters package may include a sink with a water tank and hand pump, a propane gravity heater that does not have a blower fan, a Porta-potty, and a mattress for sleeping. You can even, instead of a refrigerator, have an icebox that does not need electric or LP gas to keep your food cool. These appliances could be used without electricity, but if you want lights they would have to be run from a battery or plugged into an outlet. This is a weekend type of package because you would have to replenish LP gas, fill the water tank, and recharge the battery after a short time of use. A small package like this may be squeezed into a tag-a-long trailer, but a gooseneck makes a much better unit.

A more complex package can keep you in comfort for a much longer time. The trailer can be plugged into an electrical source, or a recreational battery can take over when an outlet is not available. This battery can be recharged when the unit is plugged into an electrical source, or it can be installed to recharge along with the truck battery. Lights, heater fans, and water pumps, as well as air conditioners and microwaves also need to be powered by electricity. RV-style refrigerators can be switched from electric to LP gas when desired. Cooktops and ovens are usually powered by LP gas.

LP gas tanks can easily be tucked under the gooseneck.

Fresh water can be stored in large tanks, or the unit can be hooked up to an outside water source through a hose that fits into a water line feeding into the trailer. A holding tank stores waste water from the shower and sink, and a separate tank holds "black water" from the toilet. If you are parked at a facility that offers electric, water, and sewer hookups, you can stay indefinitely without having to take the unit elsewhere to empty the holding tanks or to fill the water tanks. It is common to have water and electric hookups available, but not as common to have sewer lines available. In this case, you will have to take the unit to a dumping station to empty the holding tanks when they are full.

Small generators can supply electricity when no other source is available. However, you will need a more powerful generator if you want it to run an air conditioner.

The larger the trailer, the more appliances you can fit into it. A medium-size interior would have room for a microwave, cooktop, bathroom, and so forth, but a large interior may even have room for an 8-cubic-foot refrigerator and a washer and dryer. Televisions, VCRs, and stereo systems can also be installed in a living quarters unit.

RV appliances are very safe and are well proven in the mega-million-dollar recreational vehicle industry. There are a few differences between these appliances and the ones we use in our homes:

- RV microwaves need to be vented out of the front.

- Cooktop ranges and ovens usually have a manual pilot.

- Refrigerators are "two-way" and can be powered by either LP gas or 110v electric. Some refrigerators are manual, others are digital, and they are low-maintenance.

- Furnaces are higher maintenance, but very efficient. Furnaces are usually ducted on the larger units.

- Air conditioners with heat strips are very efficient and low-maintenance.

- Water heaters are usually 6-gallon capacity and are very quick recovery. Better-quality interiors have a remote ignition that eliminates the need to go outside to light the water heater with a match.

- Toilets and showers are water conservative.

- Gas, smoke, and carbon monoxide detectors are invaluable safety precautions.

- An auto stereo is usually better quality than an RV stereo.

Interior Decor

Sleeping and eating areas can be designed to make efficient use of space. A dinette can be converted into extra sleeping space. A sofa can be converted into a bed, although neither a dinette nor a sofa is as comfortable for sleeping as a foam mattress in the gooseneck area.

Cabinetry can be constructed of low-cost, basic materials or of the finest woods and materials. The same can be said of carpeting, linoleum, curtains, and blinds. Efficiency of design will make use of every nook and cranny for storage.

The newest rage for horse trailer living quarters is the "slide-out." This is a 6- to 12-foot expansion room that slides out about 4 feet from the body of the trailer when it is parked, increasing the width of the living space substantially.

A 4-foot slide-out like this adds a lot of room to the living quarters. If the trailer is aluminum, like this one, make sure the frame has been reinforced to accommodate the hole in the continuity of the structure.

Structural Accommodations

When you purchase a new trailer that will be equipped with living quarters, you will be given a choice of floor plans that can be installed, according to the size of the trailer. When the manufacturer knows a living quarters will be added to the trailer, certain adjustments will have to be made at the factory. For example, the roof may have to be reinforced for the air conditioner, and the roof vents framed in. The windows and doors should be installed while the trailer is being built, not added later, and the frame must be designed to accommodate the holding tanks. It is very important that the roof not leak. Once the interior has been finished, a roof leak can be hard to find. A small leak can travel and be hard to stop.

When the trailer is lengthened, the structure is automatically strong enough to contain the weight of the living quarters. However, if there is to be a slide out, the frame must be strengthened because the hole will compromise the continuity of the structure. This is especially important in aluminum trailers.

The average living quarters package adds about 2,800 pounds, empty, to the weight of the trailer.

Maintenance

Maintenance of the living quarters starts by carefully reading all the manuals and taking care of the prescribed service or by getting a recreational vehicle dealer who can do it for you. The most important service is winterization. A poorly winterized trailer can be subjected to a lot of damage or even be ruined.

- Troubleshooting of appliances, especially those that run on LP gas should be done only by an experienced person or technician, since problems can be life-threatening.

- Water system maintenance can be done by anyone who is handy enough to do this work.

- Warranty is usually for one year on the structure. Each individual appliance has its own warranty.

- Most RV dealers can provide information or assistance on an older unit. Larger RV dealers usually carry a large stock of parts to fit older RVs, so they can usually provide help for an older living quarters trailer.

Regulations and Safety Codes

Regulations regarding living quarters are established by individual states; there are no federal regulations. Some states, about eleven of them, are strict and require inspection. These states are called "Plan Approval" states and require specific approval of preengineered floor plans, after which no changes can be made. This certification must be done by an approved engineering firm, of which most are in Elkhart, Indiana.

The Recreational Vehicle Industry Association (RVIA) also makes regulations. This self-regulated industry group makes four to five on-site inspections. A seal is affixed to each coach, but each coach is not inspected. It assumes that all regulations are met in between inspections. While the seal from the RVIA carries some clout with the consumer, the Plan Approval states do not accept it.

All codes of the Plan Approval states are based on the National Electric Code (NEC), which have been in existence for years in the RV industry, but not always in the horse trailer industry. Now that the largest manufacturers have started to comply with the Plan Approval code in order to market in all 50 states, the rest of the industry is beginning to follow their example. The result is an increasing safety factor for all.

What questions should you ask of your trailer dealer to insure that your living quarters conversion meets the code of the Plan Approval states?

- Does the conversion meet code?
- Does the electrical system have ground fault interrupted (GFI) breakers?
- Are the holding tanks and appliances properly vented?
- Are the holding tanks installed in the approved location?
- Is there an escape hatch or window in the gooseneck area?
- Is there a smoke detector?
- Is there an LP gas detector? (This is not required but is a good safety precaution.)
- If there is an onboard generator, is there a carbon dioxide detector?

12

Used Trailers: Buying, Selling, and Trading Up

Shopping for a used trailer can be frustrating. Way back in 1978, before we were in the trailer business, I was sure I could buy a used trailer for around $600 and fix it up. I read some advertisements for trailers in this price range and called to arrange several appointments for the following weekend. That Saturday, after I had dragged Tom, kicking and screaming, from farm to farm, he wearily looked at me and asked, "Why do all of these trailers look like they've been pushed off a cliff?" Lucky for me—and my horses—Tom drove me to a nearby dealer and bought me a new trailer!

Back then, there weren't very many trailers, new or used, to choose from—not like today. Buying a used trailer is a good idea if you can find the right one. If you have some specific needs that require a custom trailer, it may be more difficult to find a used one that meets your demands. But if you can be a bit flexible, you can get more for your money and a "good deal." But remember, the horse still has the same basic needs whether you buy a new trailer or a used one, so all the same criteria for choosing a trailer still apply.

Good used trailers can be hard to come by since people tend to hang onto them until they are ready to go to the junkyard. A few reasons that people sell their trailers follow.

- They are ready to move into a new or bigger one.

- They no longer keep horses.

- Financial problems, caused by a divorce or job loss.

- The trailer is no longer safe enough to use.

If you buy a trailer from someone who is selling for any of the first three reasons, you will probably find a nice trailer if it suits your needs. If you buy one that is no longer safe to use, it will cost you more in the long run to make it safe enough to be road worthy, and it may not be possible to do so.

Someone has tried to fix up this trailer, but nothing can make it worth more than $300 to $500. The structure is in good shape, but it's an example of all that can be wrong with a horse trailer. The back doors are so low that even a small horse can stick out over the back and lean on them. Homemade plywood door covers have been added, but they are very flimsy. No windows or vents in front, step-up, manger, and short escape door all add up to trouble. Road safety is compromised by mismatched tires and no brakes. This trailer is very tall, but it is only 5' wide and 8' long. The best parts of this trailer are the white roof, light interior, and spare tire.

When you look at a used trailer, look it over carefully. If the trailer is a newer model, the owner should have a Certificate of Origin or a Title that should tell you the date of manufacture and the empty weight of the trailer. Sometimes the printed weight is the weight of the standard trailer of that model, not including options. If this particular trailer has more features and options than the standard model, even extra length or height, the manufacturer may not have included them in the weight on the Certificate of Origin. The GVWR is also stated on the Certificate of Origin. This rating will be exact. If the trailer is really old, there may not be any paperwork for it, the company may be out of business, and you may not know the age of the trailer.

Deciding to Buy

If this trailer looks as if it is in good enough condition to warrant your consideration, ask yourself these questions before making your decision:

- Is it the right size for the horse(s)? Will there be enough headroom and legroom for the largest horse that will be hauled in the trailer?

- Are there any protrusions or sharp edges that could injure the horse?

- If there is a ramp, is it steady and not too steep? Is the footing non-slip? Nubby mats may be harder to clean, but non-slip footing is more important than ease of cleaning. Using a little elbow grease is better than having the horse slip and fall to his knees, increasing the chance of injury. The ramp should sit solidly on the ground when down so the horse does not feel it move when he steps on it.

- Are there struts on the ramp? If there are, are they in good condition? If not, how easy will it be to fix them? How easy will it be for the horse to break them again?

- Is the ramp easy enough to lift?

- When the ramp is down, are there any protrusions from the sides of the ramp, such as latches? Are the edges of the ramp smooth? Does the mat curl around the edges, causing a tripping hazard to both horse and handler? Test the soundness of the ramp. Some older ramps were constructed in such a way that water collected in the frame and caused rust to come from the inside. If there is plywood inside the ramp, check for wood rot. Check all ramp hinges and springs. Make sure there are no spring ends sticking up that could injure the horse. Aluminum hinges bear special inspection.

- If the trailer is a step-up, does it sit low enough to the ground to enable the horse to unload easily? Can the horse be turned around to unload or go out a front ramp?

- Are the edges on the bottom step smooth? A rubber bumper is a good safety feature.

The rear entry door should be free of any protrusions that may be a threat to a horse: latches that do not fold down and out of the way; door covers that have sharp corners and edges; door cover hinges that stick out too far. Always consider the worst thing that could happen when you are loading any horse and decide if the trailer would help or hinder the situation.

- Do the butt and breast bars meet your needs? Do they work easily with quick-release latches? Are they strong enough to hold up to your horse(s)?

- Do the escape doors work well enough for you or any other people to use the trailer safely?

If you like the trailer so far, look at the structure very carefully. Look at the frame. If it has a steel frame, is there rust? Slight surface rust may look unsightly but may

Although we don't care for manger trailers, this is a pretty nice one. It should be lighter in color and have larger windows, but structurally it is well put together. It has a very good paint coat and gravel guards to protect it. Rust has begun around the manger, but it would be worth the money to fix it because this trailer will last a long time and hold its value if the rust is stopped.

not affect the soundness of the trailer if the frame is basically solid. Look underneath to check the floor supports. They must be in good condition. Rust that has begun to eat through these or any other parts of the structure or welds is cause for alarm. If the rust is isolated, it may be possible to repair the structure, but enough of the frame must be left to weld on the new parts so they provide the same strength as the original part. If the rust is excessive, the process will continue and will constantly need repair to maintain the safety of the trailer. At some point when rust has taken over enough, repair is not recommended because the trailer will never be safe enough to use.

Rust is rampant on this trailer but it has not yet eaten into the structure. However, if the trailer is not patched and repainted, the rust will soon take over. Even so, the cost of the repairs will not increase the value enough to cover the expense. If a trailer like this can be purchased cheaply enough to fix up for your own use, you may get a few years out of it. But be very careful to monitor the condition and make repairs as needed.

Rust that appears in nonstructural areas can be repaired without actually compromising the strength of the trailer. Manger trailers often have rust around the feed trays, and sometimes rust will start on the sidewalls where horses have been scrambling and have scraped off the paint. Bumped and dented fenders may also show rust. If the rest of the trailer is sound, these rust problems can be dealt with by repainting or replacing them to slow the rust process.

If the trailer has an aluminum frame, check very carefully for signs of fatigue stress. Stress fractures will appear as tiny cracks in the frame and in the welds. They may be in places you can't see. If you question the soundness of the frame, welds, or floor, have an expert check them. You may want to call the original manufacturer for advice before you make the decision to buy the trailer. If the trailer needs repair, it may be necessary to send it to the factory to ensure that it is done properly. You should also check for signs of corrosion, especially on the floor.

The frame of the trailer, steel or aluminum, should not show any signs of bending. A steel frame may be able to be bent back into shape, but it may be difficult to get it to track as well as it did before it was bent. A bent aluminum frame may not be able to be restored to its original strength.

Whether the floor is aluminum or wood, it must be in excellent condition. If there is any sign of corrosion on an aluminum floor, it may be very expensive to fix. If the floor is wood, it can be easily replaced if the undercarriage is sound. Even if the boards look all right, stick a sharp knife blade into the wood. Check any suspicious places and get under the trailer and check the boards from the underside. If the knife can be easily turned and the wood splinters because it is soft, the boards need to be replaced. Pay extra attention to the undercarriage on both steel and aluminum trailers. No matter how good the floor, if the support structure underneath is not acceptable, ask a welder if it can be fixed or if more supports can be added. If not, find another trailer.

The mechanical parts of the trailer also need thorough inspection. Ask the owner to tell you about his maintenance program. If he has been taking care of the trailer, he should be able to tell you when he has had the bearings packed, the tires changed or rotated, the jack greased, and so on. If he can't or won't, look even more closely for potential problems.

You can tell a lot about the trailer by looking at the tires. Uneven wear should alert you to a possible problem. Perhaps the owner has only been guilty of poor maintenance and has not been keeping the proper air pressure in the tires or has put the wrong size or nonmatching tires on the trailer. Either problem can be easily fixed with new tires. A more important reason for uneven wear can be a bent axle or an axle that has been improperly installed. This will cost more money to fix. Gooseneck trailers often show tire and axle damage from excessive turning on a very tight circle. Usually trailer tires do not often show a lot of wear since they more often suffer from dry rot caused by age and exposure than by being driven too many miles.

Old trailers can have axles and leaf springs that are rusted. Leaf springs of any trailer can slip out of place and break. Axles can be bent. You can see these problems by getting under the trailer and taking a good look. If you see anything that does not look right, get an expert to advise you. If the trailer is in otherwise good

This trailer has a bent axle. Notice that the back wheel is out of alignment. It would cost more to fix the axle than the trailer is worth.

condition, it may be possible to have these problems repaired. Rubber torsion axles do not have springs to worry about, but still check for bending.

Most states require brakes on both axles (sometimes referred to as four-wheel brakes), and those that don't now probably will. Since this is a legal as well as a safety requirement, be sure that the trailer meets or exceeds the brake requirements of your state of residence. An older trailer may only have two-wheel brakes, and these should be avoided since the trailer may be obsolete in a few years if it isn't already. Adding brakes to an older trailer will cost much more than the trailer is worth. Some states have "grandfather laws" that exempt trailers of a certain age for meeting the new laws. If this is the case in your state, this trailer may not be illegal, but it will not be as safe.

To check the brakes, ask the seller if you can drive the trailer. If you do not have the proper wiring on your vehicle, ask him if he will let you drive the tow vehicle he has been using. The trailer should not push the tow vehicle at a stop. If the brakes are electric, you will hear a clicking sound in the wheels when the brake pedal is pushed on the tow vehicle. Electric brakes may have to be adjusted to your tow vehicle, so don't worry too much if they grab too soon or activate too late. Sometimes when electric brakes have been parked for a while, especially

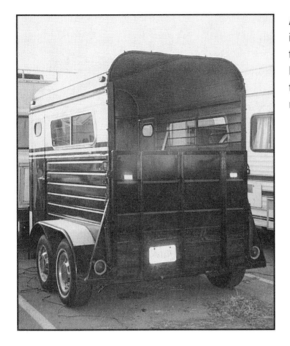

A trailer such as this would be a good buy if the price were fair. So many older trailers are dark and have small windows, but at least this one is lighter on top. This trailer should hold its value if well maintained.

when the weather has been wet, they may grab the first few times they are activated. For a quick check, jack the trailer up and spin the free wheel while someone works the brake controller. Do this for all the wheels in turn. If you have any questions about the brakes, take the trailer to a professional to have them evaluated.

If you will be using the trailer for a commercial enterprise, your trailer must be equipped with an emergency breakaway brake, and most states also require all noncommercial trailers to be so equipped. If this trailer has the breakaway brake installed, check that all the wires are attached. Pull out the pin to check if it is working. If the battery is not charged, this may not tell you anything. If the brakes don't work, have them checked by a professional. It should not be very expensive to fix a breakaway brake, but it may not be cost effective to put one on a trailer that does not have one already installed. Some states also have grandfather laws about this requirement for noncommercial trailers.

The electric system also affects the legality of the trailer. Older trailers are usually grandfathered from the more recent lighting requirements, but make sure all the running lights, turn signals, and brake lights are working, or that the problem can be fixed. Your safety will depend on it. Lamps can be burned out. A simple replacement will fix that problem. Light covers can be missing or cracked, and these are also easy to replace. Faulty wiring can also be fixed, but it may not be worth spending the money on a trailer that is too old. If you see exposed wires that look pieced together, both inside and out, you should suspect a problem. If you are looking at a better trailer that has the wiring installed out of sight, you can be fairly sure that it is in good condition if all the lights and brakes are working. Some of these better trailers have a fuse box. If you suspect an electrical problem, check the fuses. If you cannot do the needed repair work yourself, have a professional give you an estimate.

The coupler should also work properly since it is the part responsible for holding the trailer onto your tow vehicle. Sometimes after a lot of use, the socket will wear out inside and become too big to hold onto the ball safely. Put your hand into the socket and feel for signs of excess wear. Parts should work smoothly, and safety pins should fit easily and securely into place. If the coupler is a bulldog type, the collar should firmly hold the coupler closed, and it should slide open easily— without being hit with a hammer! To test the coupler, hitch it to a tow vehicle and close it over a ball of the correct size. Jack the trailer up enough to put a strain on the coupler. If it does not come off the ball and pulls the tow vehicle up slightly, it is probably working correctly.

The coupler should also be strongly attached to the trailer tongue or to the gooseneck. If there is evidence of structural rust, broken welds, or any other type of

Although this trailer was advertised as having a good ventilation system in its day, there are no windows. Its dark cavelike atmosphere is not very horse-friendly. The awkward little door is the only way out for the handler.

fastener, find out how much it will cost to fix it before you buy the trailer. If the coupler is defective, it can be replaced with a new one. Again, get an estimate.

Properly rated safety chains or cables are required for all tag-a-long trailers and should be in good condition. If you live in one of the 29 states that require ball hitch goosenecks to be equipped with safety chains or cables, you should consider the expense required to install them if the trailer is not so equipped.

Since a horse trailer is essentially a box on wheels, it is possible to fix almost all the above problems, either by yourself or by hiring a professional. The trailer can be completely rebuilt, but if the damage is too severe, it may cost you more money to fix it than if you spend a little more and buy a trailer in better condition. Tires, wood floors, paint, and other parts that need regular maintenance anyway are reasonable expenses when one buys a used trailer. Mechanical parts such as axles, brakes, wheels, and couplers are expensive to repair or replace, which may lead you to think about looking for another trailer. Painting a rusted trailer can be expensive, and many body shops do not want to do it, especially in the interior. (The fumes can be dangerous when painting inside a horse trailer.)

If you have found a trailer in your price range, consider the amount you will have to spend for repairs as part of the cost. If you will be selling the trailer in the future, will the repairs increase the value of the trailer enough for you to get your money back out of it? It is very easy to spend money fixing up a trailer yet not increase its value. For example, if you find a trailer for $1,000 but you need to spend another $500 to $1,000 to fix it, it still may never be worth more than $1,200 when you are ready to trade up. It may have been a better move to find a trailer for $1,500, and even if you have to put in another few hundred, you may be able to increase the value to $2,000. Of course, it depends on the trailer and how good a deal you make. If you find a trailer that is worth more than what you pay for it, you may even be able to make a profit when you sell it. It is impossible for us to make value judgments in this book because so much depends on the condition of the trailer. It is not so much the age of the trailer that determines the price but its condition. A "blue book" does not exist for used trailers, and the ultimate value of a used trailer is how much someone will pay for it.

If the trailer you are considering needs some work, take it to a professional and get an estimate. If the amount of the repair keeps the cost of the trailer within your budget, go for it. You may ask the seller to take less for the trailer to cover or split the extra expense. If the cost of the repairs does not increase the value of the trailer enough to cover the expense, look for a better deal.

If you find a fixer-upper that you like and can afford and if you plan to keep the trailer for yourself and are not interested in getting your money back out of it, it may be a feasible project. If you know what you are doing—really know, not just *think* you know—you may be able to do the work yourself, increase the value of the trailer, and make a tidy profit.

Here are a few things to consider when choosing a body shop. Most large body shops do routine insurance work on automobiles that is paid for on a job basis. If the body shop is fast, a good profit can be made by replacing fenders and hoods, and so forth. Working on a horse trailer is more specialized, so it takes more time and they cannot charge a lot. Consequently, they do not really like to do it. Look for a small independent body shop that may be more willing to take the time, and may even enjoy the work.

You can find used trailers from individuals or from trailer dealers who have taken them in on trade. Everybody wants to make the best deal, both the buyer and the seller. It has been our experience that you can never go wrong by being considerate when dealing with the seller. If you have called to make an appointment to look at a trailer, be thoughtful enough to show up at the agreed time. If you cannot make the appointment or will be late, call and let the seller know. This not only applies to individuals, but to dealers as well. Sometimes people go to a great deal of trouble to meet with you, and it is not fair to take up their time if you are not serious.

Always ask about potential problems in a businesslike manner and discuss them with the seller. Of course, not all sellers are honest about their trailer, but we have found that most people, including dealers, are not trying to put anything over on anybody, and everyone appreciates being treated fairly. In many cases, individuals who are not professional salespeople are not experienced in selling things and can be unsure of how to work with a potential buyer.

Be as truthful with the seller as you would expect the seller to be with you. Don't be afraid to negotiate, but be considerate and the seller will be more willing to work with you. If you like the trailer but feel the price is too high, make a fair offer, especially if the trailer needs some repairs. Some people expect a lower offer and have asked a price higher than they really expect to get. Assuming this is the case, you can negotiate a price somewhere in the middle, or it may still not be low enough for you to buy the trailer. If so, thank the seller for his time and leave your name and telephone number should he change his mind.

A seller may price the trailer at what he thinks is fair, or at the amount he must get, and be unwilling to take less. It becomes a "take it or leave it" decision—you will have to decide if it is worth the price to you.

If you have questions about the trailer, ask the seller if you can have a dealer, body shop, or mechanic inspect it. If you can bring this person to the trailer, it should be a simple request, but if you want to take it off the property before you pay for it, the seller may be wary. Expect to pay a deposit or even to write a check for the entire agreed-on amount, and ask the seller to hold it until you get the inspection done. Also expect to accept responsibility for any damage you may cause while the trailer is in your possession. The seller may be willing to take the trailer to the desired location for you. Whichever method you use, be kind enough to get the inspection done in a timely manner.

If you agree on a price with the seller, it is reasonable for the seller to ask for a deposit to hold the trailer until you pick it up and the balance to be paid when you take it home with you. It will depend on your agreement whether or not this deposit is refundable if you change your mind. Since this deposit is your guarantee that you will, in fact, purchase the trailer, and the seller has agreed to take it off the market, it is not unreasonable to expect that it will not be refundable in whole or in part if you change your mind. The seller may also want the balance to be paid in

Sharing a Ride—Who Is Liable? Two Stories with a Moral

Story 1

The Horsemen's Club had a camping trip every month during the summer. The weekends were always so much fun that everyone wanted to attend. A new member did not have a trailer, and she was generously offered a ride by a couple who had an extra space in their stock-combo trailer. This particular trailer had been modified to accommodate horses, and the full center dividers were kept in place with large pins that stuck out into the horse area at the rear center post. When the horses were being unloaded, the trailer owners unloaded their horse first and the guest horse started to panic. When the butt bar was let down, he rushed out, pushing himself against the center post, which bent from the force. Unfortunately, the sharp pin tore a 10-inch triangle of skin off the horse's hindquarters, exposing the muscle underneath. The veterinarian was called to the campground, and the horse had to be taken to the nearby clinic for treatment. A lengthy recuperation followed.

The weekend was ruined for everyone. Club members took sides, and a burgeoning friendship was destroyed. The owner of the horse blamed the trailer and the couple for her horse's injury, and the owners of the trailer blamed the horse for damaging their trailer. The rift was never settled between them, and the horse was scarred for life. A no-win situation for everyone involved.

Story 2

A young girl asked a friend at the barn to take her horse to a trail ride. Several people from the barn were going, and the number of trailers did not match the number of tow vehicles that were equipped to haul them. It was decided that an El Camino could be used to haul one of the trailers, even though there was no electrical receptacle to hook up the brakes and lights. The trailer was hitched to a ball on the bumper, and no safety chains were used. They were only going a few miles. The young girl believed that the adults knew what they were doing, and since her parents were not horse people, they didn't ask.

As they were driving down the expressway, a tractor trailer rig sped by, almost hitting the horse trailer. One of the horses started to move around when the trailer started to sway from the wind from the large truck. The movement of the horse caused the trailer to continue to sway out of control, and the little truck was not heavy enough to keep itself stable. The bumper flexed, causing the trailer to come off the truck and it careened off the side of the road. The tongue of the trailer dug into the ground and the trailer flipped over the nose, hitting on the top front of the trailer before finally resting on its side.

The trailer was steel and it held up pretty well, considering the force of the impact. The driver's horse survived without injuries, but the young girl's horse was thrown forward and a piece of the torn head divider cut his jugular vein. He bled to death before help could arrive.

Obviously, the trailer was not hitched to the truck correctly. The tow vehicle and the bumper hitch were not rated to tow the weight of the trailer. The accident might have been prevented if the trailer brakes were working. (When a trailer starts to sway, lightly activating the brakes from the hand control instead of the vehicle brake can straighten out a sway while continuing the forward motion of the tow vehicle.) One would think that the driver would have received a citation for illegal towing—he was clearly in violation of the state code—but the police officer at the scene was only concerned that no humans were hurt. He did not even ask about how the trailer was connected. The driver was glad that the trailer came off so he did not lose control of his truck. He never realized that his truck was not capable of the job and that his carelessness caused the accident. The young girl was devastated that her horse was killed. The horse was not a monetarily valuable horse. The parents were not wealthy, but they pursued legal action against the driver.

cash, certified check, or cashier's check especially if you take the trailer that day. When you take possession of the trailer, be sure you have all the paperwork that goes with it. In states that require the trailer to have a title, the title must be signed over to you and notarized. Some states require the Certificate of Origin to be signed over and notarized. There will be a serial number on the title or Certificate of Origin. Make sure that it matches the number that is stamped on the trailer. It should be printed on the manufacturer's sticker that is usually on the inside of one of the doors, and it should be stamped into the frame of the trailer, usually on the tongue. If there is a lien on the trailer, it will be noted on the CO. Make sure that the lien will be paid off before the trailer is turned over to you. A few states do not require either a title or Certificate of Origin, and if there is no Certificate of Origin available, a Bill of Sale can be used instead. When you get your license plate, you will probably have to pay state sales tax on the amount of the sale.

Selling

If it is time for you to move up to a newer trailer, you can trade your present one in to a dealer, or you may get a better price by selling it yourself. Selling a used trailer is not hard especially if it is in good condition. The most difficult thing you have to decide is how much to ask for it. A common mistake is to believe the trailer is worth more than it really is. You know how much you paid for it, and you want to get as much as you can. You don't want to let it go for too little, but if you ask too much, you may be afraid no one will buy it.

If you bought the trailer used, it is fairly easy to determine the price. How much did you pay for it? If it is still in the same condition that it was when you bought it and you didn't pay too much for it, it may still be worth the same amount. If you did some work on it and it is in better condition than when you bought it, you may be able to get more for it. Do not expect to get everything you put into it, but if you have really improved the trailer, it should be worth a little more. You have to consider that it is now older than when you bought it.

If you were going to buy this trailer today, how much would *you* be willing to pay for it? Be objective, look at the trailer as if you have never seen it before. Some trailers hold their value better than others. Trailers under 7 feet tall or less than $5^1/_2$ feet wide have a more limited market and, therefore, a lower resale value. Trailers 7 or more feet tall and 6 feet wide usually sell very quickly and, therefore, maintain a higher resale value. The better condition the trailer, the more quickly it will be snapped up. There are not many good used trailers, and usually the good ones get sold from friend to friend as soon as they become available. This is a good incentive to take care of your trailer while you have it. Keep in mind that you can always take less for it, but once you have quoted a price, you cannot ask more!

If you have a newer trailer, you can call the dealer you bought it from or the manufacturer who built it and ask him for an estimate of the value. The estimate from the dealer who sold it to you may be high, however, since he has a personal reason to believe the trailer has kept its value, or he actually may be afraid to tell you that it is not worth as much as you would like it to be. (Dealers are human, too.)

Advertise in your local newspaper, club newsletters, tack shops, local stables, and on the Internet. If you have a particularly large or specialized trailer, advertise in national magazines such as *The Chronicle of the Horse, The Quarter Horse Journal,* or other breed magazines. When someone calls you about your advertisement, give a true description of the trailer, including an accurate representation of the condition. Don't waste your time or the time of the prospective buyer by portraying the trailer to be other than it is. If you have misrepresented the trailer, the person won't buy it anyway when he comes to look at it.

When you sell your trailer, keep in mind that the new buyers will be putting their horses in this trailer and if you know of any reason why the trailer may not be safe, you should not hide this fact. Your trailer may be the best this person can afford, and he or she may be very excited about the prospect of buying a "new" horse trailer and miss something important or may not be knowledgeable enough to see the problem. By making any problems known, you are giving the buyer the chance to have the trailer repaired before putting himself or his horses at risk. If you have priced the trailer fairly, with the problem in mind, you will not lose the sale. You may want to have the problem fixed before you sell the trailer, but you may not get your money back out of it. It is sometimes better to tell the buyer and let him get it fixed. You also may protect yourself from a lawsuit if you are honest about the condition of the trailer. You may want to put the problem in writing and have a waiver of liability drawn up by a lawyer and signed by the buyer. "Buyer beware" has no place in this situation, where injury or death of people or horses may be caused by deception.

We have advised the buyer to be considerate of the seller, and the reverse is also true. Treat the buyer just as you would want to be treated if you were buying the trailer. Don't take it personally if he points out problems. Answer his questions as truthfully as you would want someone to answer yours. Any problems can be worked out when people are courteous to each other. Sometimes buyers believe that they can bully you into thinking your trailer is not worth what you are asking, and they can get belligerent or rude. Don't take it personally, but you don't have to deal with him if you don't want to. Just smile and thank him for coming as you walk him to his car. If you are selling a good product, another buyer will come along.

If the prospective buyer offers you less money than you want, don't be offended even if it is a very low offer. If you don't want to take the offer, just say no. If you are prepared to take less, make a counter offer. If you truly believe that the trailer is worth what you are asking and you must have that amount, just explain that you could not take any less. The buyer will have to make the final decision. If you think you may consider his offer later, after you have shown it to more people, take his name and number and tell him you will call him back if you do not receive a better offer.

If your trailer does not sell as quickly as you want it to, you may be asking too much money for it. It is only realistic to acknowledge that the trailer is only worth what someone will pay for it. Consider taking less money and assume the loss especially if you must put more money into it to continue using it. If you don't need to sell it right away and it isn't costing you any money, keep it until someone pays you the price you need. If you are going to get a new trailer from a dealer, trade in the used one and let the dealer worry about selling it. You will save sales tax on the new trailer if you pay for part of it with your trade. In states where sales tax is high, this can be a substantial savings.

When you finally make a deal and sell your trailer, be prepared to supply the new buyer with the necessary paperwork. The title or Certificate of Origin must be signed over and notarized. If there is no paperwork with the trailer, you must have a Bill of Sale drawn up. If you need help to do this, call your local license plate office and they will tell you what you need to do. The buyer will probably pay state sales tax when he gets his new license plates, but you do not have to worry about that. Unless you live in one of the few states that keeps the license plate with the vehicle and transfers the plate to the new owner, do not let your license plate go home with the trailer. You do not want the new owner to drive around with a license plate that is still registered to you. If the buyer can't drive the trailer home without a license plate, you can deliver it to him. You can either ask him to reimburse you for gas, or you may include delivery as part of the deal. If you have the keys and the manuals that came with the trailer, turn them over to the new owner.

The buyer may want to have a professional look over the trailer before he makes a decision. If he can bring this person to the trailer, this should not be a problem. If he would like to take it to a dealer or body shop, you may feel apprehensive about letting the trailer leave before the buyer has actually purchased it. There are a few different ways you can handle this. You can haul the trailer there yourself. Or you can ask the buyer for a check that you will hold until he returns the trailer. This check can be a deposit for a partial amount of the trailer or the amount of the trailer in full, whichever you prefer. If you let this person drive the trailer, make an agreement of responsibility, in writing, for repairs in the event the trailer is damaged while it is not under your control. If you do not know the person, ask for identification in the form of a driver's license, and make sure it agrees with the name on the check. Make sure you have his name and address before you let the trailer go. It would be wise to restrict the distance you will allow the trailer to be taken. There should be a qualified professional somewhere locally.

If the buyer agrees to the price but wants you to hold the trailer for him, ask for a deposit, to be applied to the purchase price, to insure his commitment since you may have to turn down other buyers before he comes back to pick up the trailer. If the trailer is under $2,000, a $50 deposit may be enough to seal the deal, but that is your decision. You may want a larger deposit if the trailer is more expensive. You may agree to give him back his deposit if he changes his mind, but it would be reasonable to keep the deposit, in whole or in part, to reimburse you for the risk of turning down other prospective buyers. Ask for cash or check, but when he pays for the trailer in full, you should ask for cash or a certified bank check. Tell him in advance that you will expect this type of payment so that he knows to get the bank check before he arrives to pick up the trailer. You should make your payment expectations very clear to the buyer before you accept the deposit. If he pays for the trailer with a check other than a guaranteed one, you can hold the trailer until the check clears.

When to Trade Up

How do you know when it is time to sell your trailer and get a newer one? Usually it is obvious that the trailer no longer suits your needs. If it is no longer safe, if you need a bigger one, or if you would like to have a dressing room, you need to start shopping. However, some people will keep a trailer forever, and pour way too much money into it to keep it safe. Perhaps you are lucky enough and skilled enough to be able to do the work yourself, and it may be the most economical plan.

There is a point when no matter how much money you put into the trailer, it will not increase in value, and you will not recoup the money and effort you put into it when you sell it. This is when it may be cheaper to sell the trailer or to trade it and get a newer one.

13

Buying a New Trailer

While we were preparing to write this book, Tom and I visited a major horse show to collect information on all the horse trailer models and innovations that were coming onto the market for the new year. I visited sales booths and talked to dealers and manufacturers. All the manufacturers and engineers that I spoke with were helpful and eager to talk about the construction of their trailers. They were proud of their trailers and pointed out that they offered many models and styles from which to choose. As I walked through the sales booths, I picked up brochures from 21 different companies so I could be well informed about the current trends.

It had been a long time since I read a brochure from other trailer companies, and when I read them all, I noticed something quite interesting. Every brochure described the benefits of the construction material, the engineering concepts, the competitive price, the choice of models, the growth of the company, the warranty guaranties, and offers of financing. But out of 21 brochures, only 3 mentioned anything about a horse! Of these three brochures, one included the phrase, "engineered to be horse-friendly." However, it did not explain *how* it was horse-friendly. Only two companies claimed to have included features that contributed to stress-free travel for the horse. Both offered only straightload trailers.

Because of the fierce competition in the trailer industry, improvements in construction materials, structural integrity, design, and road safety have improved so much that any trailer you buy from a reputable company should be structurally sound. However, the manufacturers have spent so much time and effort competing with each other about the choice of construction materials—the steel versus aluminum controversy—that they seem to have forgotten the one factor that is the most important in the equation—the horse.

Back to the horse show. Tom and I spent two days looking over every trailer on display. The manufacturers had put their best specimens on display, and some were so lavish that they took your breath away. Gorgeous living quarters and slantloads were the emphasis at this show. Every trailer had more "eye appeal" than ever before. People were buying, buying, buying.

But even though these models were so impressive, improvements to the horse areas of many of these trailers were lacking. I did not see one slantload on display that was equipped with a front unload ramp, even up to six-horse capacity. Step-ups on some of these trailers were as high as 21 inches off the ground—they should be called "jump-ups"—and rear tack compartments in the slantloads prohibited turning the horses around to unload headfirst. A few of these slantloads had rear ramps, but some were so steep and slippery that it was hard even for people to walk down them without slipping. We saw drop-down feed doors that could be opened by the horses from the inside, sharp bar guards, small windows, and very dark interiors. Quite a few of these trailers had very poor ventilation. Straightload trailers had some problems, too. License plates and lights were sticking out next to the rear ramp, slippery ramps, weak butt and breast bars, and door cover hinges were sticking out too far on the sides. One of the silliest things we saw was a trailer built specifically for large horses that only had 2 feet of head area!

There were also many trailers on display that were quite satisfactory—trailers that were built by companies that have been paying attention to the growing market of concerned horse owners. It helps when the management of the company is

There is no reason for the window frame in the back door to drop down when the window can be opened. This silly option actually costs extra!

personally familiar with the needs of horses, but that is not always necessary if building a quality trailer is a primary concern.

One of the first horse trailer manufacturers, a family-owned business, was building horse trailers for 30 years before anybody in the family ever owned a horse. Another major trailer manufacturer does not want horse people working for his company even today. This is not to say that these manufacturers cannot build a good product, in fact, they do. There can be design flaws, however, that only horse people would care about or notice, such as the ones we have discussed throughout this book. Of course, these companies are extreme examples and many other manufacturers do own or have owned horses, but usually are acquainted with one specific breed or discipline. For example, those who own Quarter Horses do not always understand how much bigger and stronger warmbloods really are, even though they say, and believe, they do. The majority of trailer manufacturers and dealers are men, the majority of horse owners are women. Men and women can have very different views and needs when it comes to trailering horses. Men don't worry too much about things like heavy ramps and mechanical service. They are usually not as emotionally involved with their horses. Women, on the other hand, want to be able to work the trailer easily, and they don't want to worry about the

Mounting the spare tire like this keeps it out of the way, but who would want to crawl under the trailer to get it off?

mechanics. They are also more likely to think of their horses as pets. Still, the views and needs of all horses are the same, no matter what breed.

So what can you expect from trailer manufacturers? We know that foremost they want to sell trailers. They put a great deal of effort into supplying the customer with the trailer he asks for. The problem is that the customer hasn't always had enough good information available to know what to ask for. When the buying public asks for trailers that are truly horse-friendly, the manufacturers will comply. Personally, we would like to see the manufacturers take more interest in developing their trailers to improve the environment for the horse.

Recently horse trailer manufacturers formed an organization called the National Association for Trailer Manufacturers (NATM). Most dealers and manufacturers feel that this organization has been responsible for many improvements and for establishing standards within the industry. Member companies display a sticker on the trailer to show that it conforms to NATM standards, which deal mostly with construction quality and standardization of plugs and wiring, etc. So far, there has not been much emphasis on horse welfare and stress reduction.

Dealers

Most manufacturers have a network of dealers to sell their trailers. It is not unusual for a horse trailer dealer to carry only one brand of trailer, but there are many larger dealers who offer a choice of several brands. Unlike trailer manufacturers, trailer dealers are usually involved with horses in one way or another. Even if they do not currently own horses, they usually like to talk with horse people and enjoy the camaraderie of the equine environment. Some dealers tend to deal mainly with customers within their own discipline because they have similar views and interests. Dealers who are active in the Quarter Horse disciplines will be major dealers among the Quarter Horse crowd, for example, but they are not so specialized that they do not know about other disciplines. As one horse trailer dealer said, "Horses are like music, a universal language!"

On the other hand, it has been said that if you put ten horse people in a room, you will have ten different points of view. Since most trailer dealers are horse people, too, the same thing can be said about them! No qualifications are required to be a dealer other than to buy a prescribed number of trailers from the manufacturer, so as you shop for a trailer, you will find many different levels of expertise. There is absolutely no correlation between knowledge and expertise and the size of the dealership. It will be your job to decide who is giving you the best advice, both about the trailer and about what is best for you and your horse.

In most cases, a dealer chooses the manufacturers he wishes to represent because he believes that the trailer is good enough to sell to other people. Also important to the dealer is how well the manufacturer treats him. If the manufacturer stands behind the trailer, he feels confident in selling the trailers to others. If the manufacturer honors the warranty, delivers the trailer on time, and protects his territory, his business will be more successful. This is very important, because a trailer dealership, small or large, is a business, and the dealer must make enough money to make it worthwhile, or even possible, to continue.

You should expect a dealership to sell you the trailer you need. If you have questions, you should be able to get answers. Even if you do not have a dealer close by, it should be possible to work with a dealer over a long distance. Since any body shop can fix your trailer, it is not necessary to live close to the dealer from which you buy because warranty work can be done near your home at your convenience. A dealer can reimburse you for warranty work even if he is ten states away.

When you buy a trailer from a dealer, he should stand behind you if you have problems and should represent you in any disagreements with the manufacturer. If he takes care of you after you buy a trailer from him, it's likely that you will refer business to him in return.

Compared with an automobile dealership, a horse trailer dealership is small potatoes indeed! Even the largest new trailer dealership cannot compare with a small new car dealership. The smaller sales volume of horse trailers may prohibit the kind of service you can expect and receive from your car dealer. When you take your trailer in for repairs, it may take longer than it does for your car. Parts may not always be stocked and may have to be ordered from the factory. Major repairs may even have to be handled by the original manufacturer.

The dealer is dependent on the manufacturer to reimburse him for warranty work, and sometimes the manufacturer just won't do it. In this case, the cost of repairs may have to come out of the dealer's pocket, and he may not be willing to fix something that you think he should. Also, he probably won't be able to give you a "loaner" while yours is in the shop. Determine whether the dealer is trying to help you or if he is just ignoring your requests before you lose your patience.

Survey Results

We sent questionnaires to all the major horse trailer manufacturers and most horse trailer dealers throughout the United States in order to give them an opportunity to input information for this book. Most of these questions were concerned with the industry itself, not technical questions about trailers. Even though the response was not as good as we had hoped it would be, those that did return the questionnaire were important manufacturers and dealers and they represented a cross section of the industry.

The manufacturers who returned questionnaires represented the entire range of horse trailer manufacturing companies. The smallest manufacturer built on the average 75 trailers a year and the largest company built 4,800 trailers a year. The majority of these companies had been in business more than 20 years, not all of them under the present ownership. The youngest company was 11 years old.

Only one company that responded had researched the safety of construction materials in horse trailers, and it was a large company with its own research and development department.

When asked if their companies had ever participated in any research about the safety of horses and handlers in the use of a horse trailer, horse trailer accidents, or stress and injury reduction to the horse, all either left the question unanswered or responded "no."

Only one company kept statistics about how well their own trailers held up in accidents, but they were not willing to share the results with us.

Every manufacturer that responded said that their companies were always trying to improve their products and would consider using other materials to build their trailers if something better came along.

When asked to evaluate the reasons why their customers would buy a certain trailer, the #1 reason stated was the safety of the horse. Construction material, looks and prestige, and number of horses to haul were all tied for second place. Few manufacturers felt that the safety of the handler and whether the trailer was legally equipped were as important to their customers.

The manufacturers overwhelmingly agreed that the horse trailer industry is building better trailers today, and all agreed that the main reasons for this are customer demand and competition within the industry. Other reasons, divided among the respondents, were better construction materials available, more information available, more concerned customers, more informed dealers, and more affluent customers.

The manufacturers also were very positive about the NATM but felt that it may not be as effective now as it will be in the future.

Horse trailer dealers were also sent a similar questionnaire. Of those who responded, the smallest dealer sold 12 to 15 trailers a year and the largest dealer sold, on the average, 400 trailers a year, an unusually large dealer. The average number of trailers sold by the respondents was under 100 trailers a year. The youngest company was 4 years old, and the oldest had been in business for 36 years. The average number of brands that was sold per dealer was 4, although half of them sold only one or two different brands. Only the largest dealer who responded also sold other types of trailers such as cargo, car haulers, and trucks.

All the respondents take used trailers in on trade except one, but all sell used trailers. Three-fourths of the dealers refurbish trailers, and one-fourth sell them as is. All the dealers who responded have a service department either on the premises or provide service by an independent service company to handle repairs and warranty work.

When asked about experience with horses, more than half had horses at the present time, and the rest had owned horses in the past. All were involved in the western discipline except for one who participated in dressage, combined training, and driving. All had been involved with horses for 30 years or more. Those who did not still own horses were still active by judging or boarding.

All of the dealers sold trailers to people in cross disciplines, and all agreed that there is a difference in preference accordingly. They said that western people prefer step-ups and slantloads, whereas English people prefer ramps and straightloads. All want extra height and width and low maintenance. One dealer mentioned that customers want lighter weight trailers for smaller vehicles.

When asked what percentage of their customers are somewhat informed about horse trailers, they all answered between 30 percent and 50 percent; however, when asked what percentage of customers are informed with the wrong information, one answered 40 percent and the rest answered 50 percent or more!

The dealers felt that their customers were looking for information on the following subjects about trailering. Information about tow vehicles was the most popular answer. Mechanics and maintenance of horse trailers and construction materials tied for second. On the average, the dealers felt that legal equipment, road safety, and horse safety and stress reduction were of the least concern to their customers. (A few dealers chose these last three subjects as important to their customers, but the majority did not.)

Has your dealership ever participated in any research about the safety of construction materials used in building horse trailers? Only two answered yes. Both keep information about problems and make suggestions to manufacturers to fix them. They all were rather divided about participating in research about the safety of horses and handlers in the use of a horse trailer. Not all answered, but some had discussed safety and stress concerns with veterinarians. None were familiar with any independent research done about safety or stress reductions. None kept records about horse trailer accidents.

All respondents acquired their knowledge from their own years of experience or from the trailer manufacturers. When asked if they had acquired their information from the manufacturer, had they ever questioned the accuracy of information, one-half said yes. One-half of those respondents said they received satisfactory answers from the manufacturer.

Why have they chosen to represent the brands they carry? Each dealer said their trailer(s) was the best quality for the money. The next most popular answers were the warranty from the manufacturer and good resale value. The dealers all felt that a good relationship with the manufacturer was important to help them run a good business and to better help the retail customer.

One-half the respondents said they must spruce up or dealer prep the trailers before they are delivered to their customers because sometimes the trailer has a few problems and they must be checked over. The other half said they do not dealer prep the trailers.

We gave the dealers an opportunity to make some feelings known about the business. We asked them what they thought is the best thing about being a horse trailer dealer. More than half said that being around horse people was the best thing. They liked to be able to help people and inform them about horse trailers. Profit was also mentioned. One dealer said, "It's a living."

What is the worst thing about being a horse trailer dealer? This question brought some similar interesting comments. "People want to buy at a low cost. They think we make more money than we do!" was a frequent theme. "People call for directions and don't show up, and they call for quick pricing without seeing the trailer or talking at length about their options and needs," were also major complaints. Problems with the manufacturer about warranty was another common issue.

What about the guy who said the best thing about being a dealer was, "It's a living"? His answer to the worst thing? "Horse People!"

Sixty percent of the dealers who responded to the questionnaire do not like the current trend of "downsizing" tow vehicles and lighter-weight trailers because they do not think it is safe. Only one dealer was positive about downsizing.

We asked the dealers what they thought of the NATM. Their comments were not nearly as positive as the manufacturers' were. None of them knew much about it other than the trailer they sold had an NATM sticker on it.

How to Get the Best Deal

As you have probably gathered by now, buying a new trailer can be rather confusing. If you are like most horse people, it can also be very exciting. If you have read this book up to this point, you probably have a really good idea about what kind of trailer you want to buy if you didn't before.

The first thing you have to do is to find someone to sell you this trailer. Because trailer dealers range in size so greatly and because there are not horse trailer dealers in every town, this is not always easy to do. There may be a dealer close to you, but he may not have the trailer you need. Manufacturers advertise in national horse magazines, put up sales booths at major horse shows, and allow their dealers to work in the booth. Dealers advertise also, but not all can afford to put large ads in national magazines. Most dealers put smaller ads in the classified sections of the magazines and advertise in their local newspaper because it is more cost effective to do it this way. Many dealers also put up sales booths at horse shows and support local clubs by advertising in newsletters and horse show programs. Some dealers will speak at club meetings for the chance to talk about trailers.

If you cannot find a dealer through any of the above avenues, you can call the manufacturer and ask them to recommend a dealer in your area. There is a tendency for people to believe that they can get a better deal by buying directly from the manufacturer. Although some manufacturers have allowed this misconception to continue, it is hardly ever the case. Most manufacturers have given protected areas for their dealers and if you live in one of those areas, the manufacturer will refer you to the dealer in your area. If you still want to buy from the manufacturer, chances are the manufacturer will charge you the same price and will give the profit to the dealer anyway. If you go to another area to buy from another dealer who carries the same trailer, that's your business and the sale belongs to the dealer who has sold you the trailer. Manufacturers used to be rather guilty of selling around a dealer, but the dealers complained enough that they don't do it so much anymore. However, if there is no dealer in your area, the manufacturer may be willing to sell you the trailer at a retail price. Still, the price may not be any better than a dealer can do for you.

There are advantages to buying the trailer from a dealer instead of a manufacturer. If you need warranty work, the dealer will be much more willing to get it fixed for you since you bought it from him. It's easier to get work done locally instead of taking it all the way back to the manufacturer. If the manufacturer balks at paying for warranty work, the dealer can have more "pull" with the company and fight for you. If you have bought the trailer from the dealer, he will have more interest in keeping you happy because he wants you to come back when you are ready for a new trailer, and he also wants you to refer your friends to him.

The right dealer also will take more time with you to make sure that the trailer you buy meets your needs. If he doesn't, look for another dealer. It is not always necessary to buy a trailer from a dealer that is close to you if he does not have the trailer you want, or he isn't working with you as well as you think he should. It is possible to buy from a dealer in another part of the country as long as you know he can help you with your trailer after it has been delivered. You can get warranty work done at local businesses and send the bill to the dealer if the work has been prearranged. He will still be able to intercede for you with the manufacturer, even over a long distance.

The dealer should be willing to answer all your questions. If you feel you are getting satisfactory answers and you like the trailer he is selling, ask him for a price quotation. Some trailer companies have complicated price lists that only the dealer can figure out. Because there are so many styles and options, building a custom trailer can be an ordeal. The dealer must be able to advise you on all those technical things, like light packages and axle capacity, for example, that you may not think about. Because of the plethora of options and features, it is very hard to price compare the trailer with another brand, or even the same trailer from another dealer.

While you are shopping for your trailer, you may want to call around to compare prices. In our survey responses, if you remember, the dealers complained of customers calling to get quick pricing without taking the time to go over the trailer or the options available. The reason for this is that you may get different opinions and advice from different dealers, even on the same trailer brand, and you are doing yourself, and the dealer, a disservice by not listening to what each dealer has to offer. You may have been given the wrong advice at some point, and it is a very good idea to listen to what another dealer has to say. It may become confusing to get too many different points of view, but when you finally do get the answers that are right for you, you will probably know it in your heart. In the long run, you will feel more comfortable dealing with this dealer because you know you have bought the right trailer.

The wrong trailer is not a deal at any price, so even though you want to get the most for your money, make sure it meets the needs of the horses that will be traveling the trailer. If the trailer does not fulfill the requirements that we have set forth, consider another brand of trailer. If the trailer does meet those standards, but the construction material has made the trailer too expensive, consider another trailer of a different, less costly construction material that also meets those same standards of safety for the horse. Don't put too much emphasis on the weight of the trailer. In a two-horse trailer, the weight differences between trailers of different materials do not have to be so significant, depending of course, on the manufacturing techniques. As the trailer gets larger, the weight differences become more significant, but you still have to have a heavier vehicle to pull a large trailer anyway. Gas mileage may be affected, but the difference in the price of an all-aluminum trailer over a hybrid or steel trailer may be so great that if you don't haul a lot of miles you may never make up for the difference in what you save in gas.

The ability and willingness of a trailer dealer to "deal" will depend on the dealer. When you pay for your trailer, you are also paying for the advice and expertise of the dealer and the manufacturer. The dealer has to pay for advertising, a location, utilities, and all the other expenses of doing business and hope there is enough left over for the family. He also has to pay for the trailers when they are delivered to him. A small dealer may not have as much overhead, and therefore may be more willing to take less for the trailer, but then a large dealer may sell in large enough volume that he can also afford to take less. Some dealers expect to negotiate a sale and others believe that the trailer is priced fairly and are not as willing to take less for it. Only you can decide if the trailer is worth what the dealer is asking and how much you are willing, or able, to pay.

If you expect a trailer dealer to be fair with you, it is only reasonable for you to be fair in return. If you decide to shop for a better deal after you have spent time with a particular dealer, don't be afraid to let him know. If you find a better deal somewhere else, get it in writing, and give the first dealer a chance to talk it over with you. Conversely, when you talk to the other dealers, tell them where else you have been looking. (All dealers know that customers shop around. It's no big secret.) You may not be comparing apples to apples, and the dealers may be able to explain the reasons for differences in prices. You also give him the chance to match a price or at least have the opportunity to turn down the sale. I admit that I am talking as a dealer now, but it can be frustrating to take a lot of time and energy to educate someone on what trailer they need and then have them buy it from someone else without the chance to at least talk it over. (I'll get off my soapbox now.)

Sometimes the best deals are trailers that have been on the lot for a while. If the trailer has not sold because there is something wrong with it, it will not be a good deal no matter how cheap it is, but often a trailer doesn't sell for a number of reasons that are just circumstantial. It might be painted a color that has been hard to match to a tow vehicle, or it may be rather specialized and the right customer has not come along. There could be many such reasons that the dealer may be willing to take a lower price to move it off the lot. Sometimes a dealer has been using a trailer personally, and even though it has been slightly used, it still comes with all the warranty that applies to a new trailer. If you find such a trailer that is right for you, take advantage of the opportunity.

Most new trailers are built when ordered. If you decide to buy a trailer that is not on the lot, be prepared to wait for it. Certain times of the year are very busy and it may take longer than usual to build your trailer. Standard models may take less time than custom orders. November, December, and January are slower times in the trailer industry and you may get your trailer very quickly and maybe even for a better price. If you wait until spring, you may have to wait longer.

Whatever trailer that you buy, and whoever you buy it from, make sure that the horses have enough room and light, that the ventilation is good, and that the trailer is strong enough, inside and out, to handle the largest and strongest horse that will be hauled in it. By getting the trailer that is right for you and your horses, you will get the best deal.

Financing and Leasing

Not everybody has the cash to put out for an expensive new trailer. Most new trailer dealers now are able to offer financing for your trailer, new or used. There are financing companies that specialize in horse trailer financing, and some large manufacturers offer financing through their own credit companies. Your dealer will be able to help you get a loan if you need one. If you have credit with a local bank or credit union, you may also be able to finance your trailer through your personal resources.

If you are paying cash or have arranged your own financing, expect to pay the dealer COD with cash or a guaranteed bank check.

For those who use the horse trailer in a commercial business, leasing a trailer may be more advantageous than purchasing one. There are tax advantages that may make leasing an attractive option. Your accountant can advise you if this plan would meet your needs. Your trailer dealer may put you in touch with an independent leasing company who will allow you to choose the trailer that will fit your needs. The leasing company will buy the trailer and lease it back to you. At the end of the leasing period, the trailer may be turned back to the leasing company or may be purchased for an amount that had been agreed upon at the beginning of the lease. If the leasing company is unfamiliar with horse trailers, it may balk about taking on the risk. In order to help make the lease look attractive to the leasing company, the dealer or manufacturer may agree to buy the trailer from the leasing company at the end of your lease. This, in effect, takes the risk away from the leasing company.

Tow Vehicles and Hitches

Selecting a tow vehicle can be a confusing prospect especially since there are now so many different vehicles on the market in addition to full-size pickup trucks that are being used to pull horse trailers. Some who haul a two-horse trailer want to "downsize" from a pickup truck and pull the horse trailer with a dual-purpose vehicle. Sometimes the circumstances permit this option, but a lot of factors must be considered before doing so.

Towing puts extra demands on a vehicle. The engine, transmission, rear axle, and tires must work harder to handle the extra weight and the drag of the trailer. The engine is required to operate at higher speeds and generates extra heat that must be diffused. The vehicle must be stable enough to support the load and keep the entire combination under control without exceeding the capacity of the engine and other components.

Some of the following terms have already been discussed in chapter 9, "Capacity," but they bear repeating because they will help you understand the entire picture.

Definitions

Curb Weight—The weight of a vehicle with standard equipment, maximum capacity of fuel, oil, and coolant. This does not include optional equipment or passengers.

Gross Axle Weight—The weight that is loaded on the front or rear axle.

Gross Axle Weight Rating—The amount specified by the manufacturer as the maximum weight that can safely be loaded onto the axle.

Gross Combined Vehicle Weight (GCVW)—The actual weight of the loaded truck and the loaded trailer combined.

Gross Combination Vehicle Weight Rating (GCVWR)—The value specified by the manufacturer of the tow vehicle that is the maximum the total trailering combination can safely weigh. This includes the combined weight of the tow vehicle, the trailer, passengers, horses, plus all equipment and supplies carried in the tow vehicle and in the trailer.

Gross Vehicle Weight (GVW) also *Gross Weight (GW)*—The actual weight of a single vehicle and its complete load.

Gross Vehicle Weight Rating (GVWR)—The value specified as the maximum loaded weight of a single vehicle. For the tow vehicle, this includes the weight of the tow vehicle, fuel, all passengers, equipment, and the tongue weight of the trailer, either tag-a-long or gooseneck. For the trailer, this includes the weight of the trailer plus mats, spare tire, horses, hay, feed, supplies, etc.

Payload—Gross payload is the weight of all passengers, options, and cargo that is being carried in and on the vehicle. Net payload is the weight that can be placed in and on the vehicle after the weight of the passengers, optional equipment, and cargo has been subtracted.

Payload Rating—The maximum allowable payload for the vehicle.

Tongue Weight—The amount of the trailer's weight that presses down on the trailer hitch (tag-a-long) or the rear axle (gooseneck). Too much tongue weight can cause suspension and drive train damage and can press the vehicle down in back, causing the front wheels to lift to the point where traction, steering response, and braking are severely decreased. Too little tongue weight can actually lift the rear of the vehicle, reducing rear-wheel traction and causing instability that may result in tail-wagging or jackknifing. On trailers over 2,000 pounds, tongue weight should be 10 percent to 15 percent of trailer weight. For gooseneck trailers, tongue weight should be 25 percent of trailer weight.

Selecting a Tow Vehicle

In chapter 1, we recommended that the tow vehicle you select should be chosen after you have first decided on the trailer that will meet the needs of the horses you will be hauling and that will also fulfill your requirements.

To choose the proper tow vehicle, you must first add the actual weight of the trailer (including optional equipment), the weight of the horses you will be hauling in the trailer, the weight of any equipment, feed, water, or anything else you will be carrying in the trailer. This will be the GVW of the trailer. You should also have an idea of how many passengers and how much equipment will be carried in the tow vehicle. This last figure will come into play later.

Every major automobile and truck manufacturer has a published towing vehicle guide. These guides give the manufacturer's specific tow vehicle ratings for every vehicle in each particular product line.

The tow vehicle ratings are determined by very specific calculations. The combination of the engine size, the axle ratio, and the transmission are the factors that are used by the manufacturer to determine the towing capacity. Also, the frontal surface of the trailer is a consideration in this determination. (It takes almost one horsepower per square foot of frontal area to move a truck and trailer at highway speeds.)

The engine needs to have enough power to pull the combination not only in normal driving conditions, but also on hilly terrain, and to be able to blend and move with traffic conditions. It should also be able to perform in adverse weather conditions and, if applicable, in high altitudes.

The next important factor is the axle ratio. This is the gearing in the differential that multiplies torque to the rear wheels. Torque is responsible for getting the load moving and providing pulling power at higher speeds. The higher the gear ratio (4.56:1, for example), the more torque. The lower the gear ratio (3.08:1, for example), the better the fuel efficiency, but the less torque. It is important to have a vehicle equipped with a proper rear-axle ratio for the amount of weight you will be hauling. However, if the ratio is too high, you will be using more fuel than necessary, but if the axle ratio is too low, the vehicle may not be able to pull the load and will suffer excess wear and tear on the power train. Getting just the right rear-axle ratio is important to the long life of your vehicle and for the best fuel economy. If you must choose one over the other, it is better to choose the higher ratio over the lower.

The transmission provides the lower gears to start the load moving and then changes to direct drive or overdrive to reduce engine speed while the vehicle is driving at the desired speed. An automatic transmission is usually recommended because the torque converter multiplies the engine torque smoothly, making the first-gear ratio twice as effective as that of a manual transmission. This means more start torque to get the load moving, plus ease of operation. In most trailering guides, you will find that the towing capabilities of vehicles with equal gear ratio and engine size will be *less* when the vehicle is equipped with a manual transmission.

Four-wheel drive and diesel engines do not figure in the equation for towing power. If you need four-wheel drive in your normal driving regime without the

A gooseneck trailer is classified as a semitrailer because some part of its weight rests directly on the self-propelled towing vehicle.

trailer, this may be an option for you, but it will not increase towing capacity if the engine and gear ratio are not adequate. Diesel engines are fuel efficient, but you must still have all the aforementioned ingredients for the rating to be equal to the task.

There are more factors to consider in this equation. Once you have determined that the recommended towing capacity of the vehicle will work for you, you must also consider the GCWR that is specified for that particular vehicle. If the vehicle is rated to tow a trailer of 7,100 pounds and the GCVWR of the vehicle is 12,000 pounds, you have 4,900 pounds left for the tow vehicle and its contents. If the tow vehicle actually weighs 4,900 pounds and you add 750 pounds for five passengers and 350 pounds for luggage, the trailer towing capacity is reduced to 6,000 pounds. The GCVWR should never be exceeded. The performance will also be compromised by hilly terrain, high altitudes, and trailer frontal area. Wheelbase must also be considered, but we'll talk about that in the hitch section.

A HORSE IS NOT A BOAT

There are also some important considerations that are only important to those who are hauling horses. All manufacturers' ratings are based on hauling travel trailers and boat trailers in normal driving conditions. When you talk to auto salespeople, you will be very lucky to get one who has any knowledge of horses at all, and even though you know the difference, they may not know that a horse is not a boat.

One of the most important parts of safely hauling any trailer is the proper securing of the load. Commercial cargo drivers can be fined for losing control of a vehicle because of a shifting load. Included in every commercial driver's handbook are strict instructions for properly packing a load. These procedures require that a load be balanced properly over the axles, that it be centered on the trailer, and that the heaviest part of the load be at the bottom. (Weight that is loaded with a high center of gravity causes a greater chance of rollover.) Cargo trailers must have the load secured to keep it from shifting.

These requirements are important for all trailers because to do otherwise compromises safety. Travel trailers and boat trailers can easily be packed according to these guidelines. However, in order to load a horse trailer this way, we would have to ask the horses to lie on their backs with their feet up in the air. Horses are top heavy, shifting, live cargo who have definite minds of their own. They put more strain on the stability of the load than an inanimate object. Horses move around, whether from a loss of balance or a tantrum, which can make for a dangerous driving situation that is not a factor with other kinds of trailers.

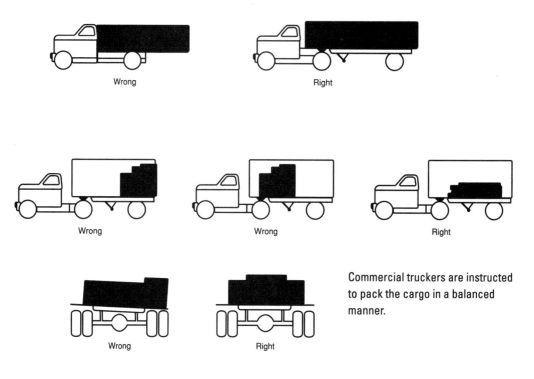

Wrong   Right

Wrong   Wrong   Right

Wrong   Right

Commercial truckers are instructed to pack the cargo in a balanced manner.

This is why you have to be careful when you talk to auto salespeople. They may not understand that you are pushing the limits by hauling horses instead of boats. They may not understand that you are hauling a cherished live companion that cannot be replaced by just an insurance check. It is common for auto salespeople to sell vehicles that are underqualified for the job. Ask to see the trailer towing guide that has been published by the manufacturer of your prospective vehicle. If there is no guide available at the dealership, call the manufacturer. Information is also available on the Internet. These guides have been available for a while, so if you are buying a used vehicle, you should be able to find the same type of information. If you know the GVW and frontal area of the trailer you will be towing, you can check the chart to make sure that the vehicle you want to buy has been rated to tow that particular trailer. You can also consult with your horse trailer dealer or manufacturer, but still, do not buy the vehicle until you actually see the desired rating in print. If the vehicle rating is borderline, go to the next higher option.

For all these reasons, you must be cautious of "downsizing." People who are hauling two-horse trailers are usually the only ones who are looking to haul with the family vehicle. The recent popularity of sport utility vehicles has also fueled the fire. The tendency is to look for a lightweight trailer to pull with a smaller vehicle, but more than the weight of the trailer, you must consider the weight of the horses that will be hauled in the trailer. For instance, if you have two Arabian horses that weigh 950 pounds each, you can probably pull it off. The horses weigh 1,900 pounds together. Because the horses are smaller, you can buy a trailer that is smaller and lighter. Let's say no more than 2,000 pounds, maybe less. Add 300 pounds for tack, equipment, and a bale of hay, and your GVW is only 4,200 pounds. Since many sport utility vehicles and small trucks can be equipped to haul 5,000 pounds, you will be fine as long as you have the proper weight distribution hitch, properly working brakes, and your GCVWR is not exceeded. You even have a little capacity left for abnormal driving conditions. You could probably even haul horses up to 1,100 pounds, but since you are hauling with a smaller vehicle, your margin for error will be narrow, so it is extra important that all components are working properly.

It's when the horses get bigger that the real problem arises. If you use two warmbloods or other large horses in the same example, a rating of 5,000 pounds, the numbers change considerably. If the horses weigh 1,500 pounds each (a very possible situation, some even weigh more!), you start out with 3,000 pounds of horses. Because the horses are bigger and stronger, the trailer must also be bigger

Sport utility vehicles have become very popular, but extra precautions are necessary to tow a horse trailer safely.

and stronger if you are to use our established criteria for trailer selection. The lightest trailer you should be able to use would probably weigh at least 2,200 pounds, so already you have 5,200 pounds. Since you are overloaded, you are putting yourself and your horses at considerable risk.

For those who are hauling those bigger loads, downsizing is not recommended. You will need a full-size tow vehicle. There are many types of pickup trucks and full-size vans, but not all are equally equipped. Quite a few pickup trucks are equipped for carrying a payload, but not for hauling. There are many of these trucks that do not have the engine, transmission, or axle ratio for hauling a horse trailer. Also, not all trucks are equipped with a trailer towing package that meets your requirements.

STANDARD "OPTIONAL" EQUIPMENT

Because towing creates a higher temperature in the engine coolant, engine oil, and transmission oil, tow vehicles should be equipped with optional equipment that deals with this problem. Engine cooling systems include heavy-duty radiator systems, transmission coolers, and engine oil cooling systems. New trucks can also be ordered with a trailer towing package that includes a weight distribution hitch and a wiring harness already installed in addition to the cooling package. All you have to do is to install the required plug and ball mount for your trailer, and you are ready to go.

Only you can decide what type of vehicle you want or can afford to buy. Even though most people have their own preference, all the major truck brands will do the job. Buy what you want, but do not exceed the manufacturer's recommended towing rating. Buying a tow vehicle that is underrated to haul your trailer will not only be dangerous, but also be more costly in the long run. The money you are trying to save in fuel will be spent on replacing your engine and transmission. If you want to haul your trailer with the family vehicle because you do not want to drive a pickup truck for everyday, consider buying a less expensive car and an older used truck that is in good running condition. Use the truck only for hauling and drive your fuel-economical car around town.

Four-wheel drive is an option that is not necessary for towing unless you need a four-wheel drive vehicle for driving in rough driving conditions, either with or without a trailer in tow. Four-wheel drive makes the vehicle higher off the ground and will take some special care to match a tag-a-long hitch to level with the trailer. Hauling a gooseneck may also present a problem since the higher truck bed may also make it more difficult to haul level.

Hitches

There are two basic types of hitches: weight-carrying and weight-distributing. A weight-carrying hitch supports the weight of the tongue as it presses down on the hitch. The hitch is rated by the tongue weight it can support and also by the trailer weight. A weight-distributing hitch (equalizing) distributes the tongue weight to all the wheels of the tow vehicle and trailer. This allows greater tongue weight to be carried and tends to keep the tow vehicle and trailer more level and stable. A weight-distributing hitch greatly surpasses the capacity of the weight-carrying hitch.

When a weight-carrying hitch is attached to the rear of a vehicle, it acts as a lever with the rear axle as the fulcrum. When the tongue weight of the trailer presses down on the rear of the tow vehicle, it can unload the front axles and transfer the weight back onto the rear axle, causing the front end to "float." This effect is more noticeable when the vehicle has a shorter wheelbase such as a sport utility vehicle than when the vehicle has a longer wheelbase such as a full-size pickup. When the front axles are lifted, the stability of the tow vehicle is greatly compromised. A gooseneck hitch is also a weight carrying hitch, but because the weight is carried over the axle instead of at the outermost extremity of the tow vehicle, this lever action is not as much of a factor. However, the tongue weight of the gooseneck must be added to the payload capacity of the truck and considered in the GVWR of the truck.

A weight-distributing hitch incorporates the use of spring bars attached to the hitch head on one end and to the trailer tongue at the other end. These bars distribute the weight throughout the combination to avoid the unloading of the front axles. This adds a great deal of stability to the towing combination and greatly increases the capacity of the hitch.

When the trailer tongue presses down on the rear of the vehicle, it acts as a lever with the rear axle as the fulcrum. When the wheelbase is short, it is easier for the weight of the tongue to lift the front of the vehicle, unload the front axle, and transfer more weight to the rear axle. A weight-distribution hitch minimizes the effect by spreading the tongue weight between the two vehicles.

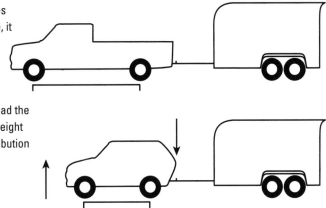

TAG-A-LONG HITCHES

The recommended hitch for towing horse trailers is the Class III or Class IV receiver-type hitch. These hitches are bolted or welded onto the frame of the vehicle and have a square receiver tube where a slide-in ball mount can be inserted. (Bolting is the preferred method and is required by law in some states.)

The Class III hitch is a weight-carrying hitch that is usually rated up to 5,000 pounds trailer weight and 750 pounds tongue weight, although some new ones on the market can handle up to 7,500 pounds trailer weight. Most of these hitches have weight-distribution capability with the addition of a hitch head and spring bars that greatly increases the capacity.

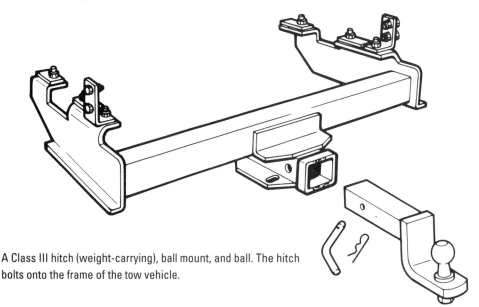

A Class III hitch (weight-carrying), ball mount, and ball. The hitch bolts onto the frame of the tow vehicle.

When the trailer weight is more than 5,000 pounds, or the tow vehicle is downsized and has a shorter wheel base even though the trailer weighs less, a Class IV weight-distribution hitch is highly recommended. Actually, a weight-distribution hitch is desirable on any vehicle combination. The capacity of a weight-distribution hitch can be as much as 10,000 pounds trailer weight and 1,000 pounds tongue weight.

All hitches are available in different weight ratings, so you can't always tell just by looking if the hitch is adequate for the job. If you look closely, the rating will be stamped on the hitch. There will be a rating for tongue weight, weight-carrying capacity, and a rating for weight-distributing capacity. The slide-in ball mount and the ball will also be marked with a rating of capacity. The actual capacity of the entire towing combination will only be the capacity of the weakest part of the hitch, slide-in ball mount, ball, and coupler just as a chain is only as strong as its weakest link. (A hitch rated at 5,000 pounds that has a ball rated at 2,000 pounds will only have a 2,000-pound capacity.)

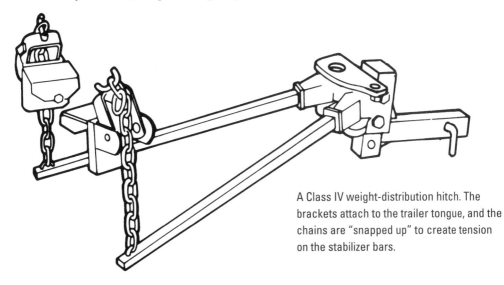

A Class IV weight-distribution hitch. The brackets attach to the trailer tongue, and the chains are "snapped up" to create tension on the stabilizer bars.

An example of a weight-distribution hitch. (Note: The safety chains should be crossed underneath.)

When you choose your hitch, you must again consider the GVW of the trailer. The capacity of the hitch and all its parts must equal or exceed that rating. Always remember that you can pull a lighter load with a heavier hitch, but you can't pull a heavier load with a lighter hitch.

Hitches must be custom fit to the tow vehicle; you can't put just any hitch on just any vehicle. If you have the hitch installed on the tow vehicle at the auto factory, make sure the one that comes on your vehicle matches your trailer requirements. Sometimes a particular hitch will not be available on a particular tow vehicle. There are a few sport utility vehicles that come equipped with a hitch that is rated at 3,500 pounds weight distributing, and there is no other hitch available to increase the rating. Quite often automobile salespeople are confused about the difference between the two types of ratings on the hitch and can give you the wrong answer to the right question. Now that you know what to look for, check it for yourself. If you are adding the hitch onto an existing vehicle, purchase it from a reputable hitch dealer who can be sure you are getting the recommended parts and who can install it for you.

A perfectly level trailer. This is the right way to haul a tag-a-long trailer.

Since it is most important that the trailer is hauled in a level position, the slide-in ball mount can be purchased to drop down or lift up the ball to the proper level of the trailer tongue.

Some vehicles are equipped with a step bumper that has a drilled hole where a ball can be inserted. Do not use one of these to haul your horse trailer. Even if the rating meets your requirements of weight capacity, there are other considerations. This type of a hitch is a weight-carrying hitch, and the weight of your trailer may

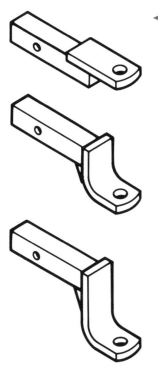

◀ Slide-in ball mounts are available in different drops. They can also be turned over if the trailer tongue is higher than the hitch.

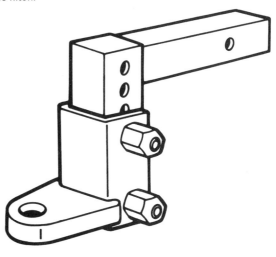

⬒ An adjustable ball mount.

This trailer has a very short tongue and has been hauled too close to the tow vehicle. This damage could have been avoided by using an extended ball mount that would allow more clearance around turns. ➤

unload the front axle too much to be safe. The bumper cannot be adjusted to the level of the trailer tongue and will result in a trailer that is not level, another unsafe situation. Also, the ball is too close to the tow vehicle, limiting the turning radius of the trailer and causing the trailer tongue to hit the bumper if the trailer turns too sharply. Most of these step bumpers are not really designed for towing no matter what the dealers say, and we have seen too many that have twisted and come off the vehicle. It is illegal in some states to tow on a step bumper hitch, and it is illegal for all commercial drivers to haul on a bumper hitch when the trailer weighs more than 5,000 pounds.

By using a slide-in ball mount, the trailer is hauled farther away from the tow vehicle (left). If the trailer is hauled on the bumper (right), it is too close to the tow vehicle, and it is impossible to have a full range of motion.

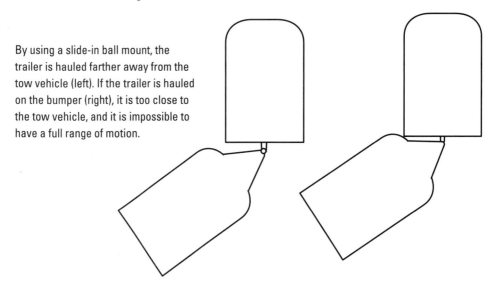

GOOSENECK HITCHES

Gooseneck hitches are less complicated. The standard ball size is $2^5/_{16}$ inches, and the hitch should be installed by bolting onto the frame under the bed of the pickup. Usually the ball is stationary in the bed of the truck and cannot be removed, so it can get in the way of hauling other things in the truck. There are fold-down balls available that fold down out of the way when not needed. Safety chains or cables are required in 29 states. If you have safety chains on your gooseneck, the rings on which to attach them should be adequately rated and should to be attached to the frame of the vehicle or to the hitch itself.

Mini-fifth-wheel hitches can be permanently installed in the bed of the truck, or they can be installed as a removable unit. There is also a convertible-type hitch that can be changed from a ball hitch to a mini-fifth wheel.

This type of fold-away gooseneck ball makes it possible to use the bed of the truck when the trailer is not being towed.

A removable mini-fifth-wheel hitch.

Gooseneck and mini-fifth-wheel hitches are weight-carrying hitches. The tongue weight of the trailer must be considered in the payload capacity and also the GVWR of the truck.

Some trailers have adjustable gooseneck couplers so that the gooseneck can be adjusted to the particular truck so that it hauls level. Some trucks, especially four-wheel drive trucks are very high, and when the coupler is shortened on the trailer to accommodate the truck, there may not be enough clearance between the truck tailgate and the bottom of the trailer gooseneck area. When the truck goes down a grade, the tailgate comes up and hits the trailer from underneath. Trailer manufacturers have recently become aware of this problem and have changed the design of the trailer to eliminate it. However, there are still some trailers that are so designed. If you have a high truck and an adjustable gooseneck trailer, keep this in mind.

15

Driving Tips and Horse Safety

As you have probably gathered by now, there is more to this horse-trailering business than meets the eye. By following some common practices and by being aware of the needs of the horse, you can make intelligent decisions that will keep you safely on the road and will decrease the chances of equine illness or injury.

Horse Safety Tips

DRESSING FOR SUCCESS

So you have a trailer that is modern in safe design. Your hitch is perfectly rated for your trailer, and your tow vehicle is the best money can buy. Your horse jumps on the trailer in anticipation of his next outing. What do you need to worry about?

Well anything can happen. That's why people wear seat belts when riding in a car and helmets when riding a horse. There is safety equipment for horses, too. Leg wraps and other safety equipment can be purchased for the price of one vet bill, so it is less expensive to protect the horse than to take the chance of an injury, no matter how slight, or even the possible loss of the horse.

Most horse trailer injuries happen when the horse is loading or unloading, when the possibility of nicks and scrapes is the highest. Nicking a leg on a step up, slipping off a ramp, jumping into a manger, and rearing backward and bumping a head on the ceiling are problems that can happen even to the quietest, most experienced

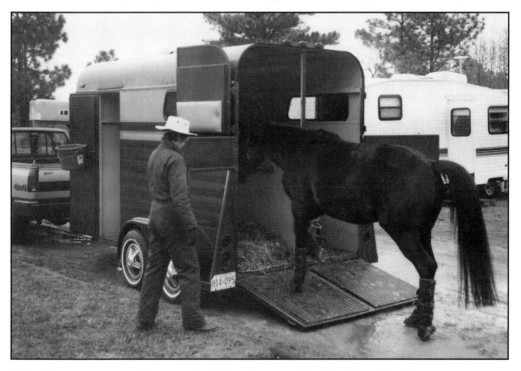

No loading problems here! The mare calmly follows her owner into the trailer while a friend assists by holding the Dutch door open. She will also fasten the butt chain before the mare is tied.

horse. Unforeseen circumstances, such as a bee or wasp inside the trailer, an unexpected noise, or a trailer design flaw are examples of situations that can always cause unsuspected behavior in any horse. Most of these injuries can be avoided by properly wrapping legs and adding a head bumper every time the horse is loaded into a trailer, no matter how short the trip. Protecting the horse should be included in the normal routine for readying the horse for his trip.

Shipping boots can be purchased at any tack store. The better kind is easy to apply and covers the coronary band and hoof as well as the leg. Some more expensive boots cover the knees and hocks as well. Shipping boots will pay for themselves in the long run, since you may avoid expensive medical treatment or permanent injury to the horse.

Standing bandages, instead of commercial shipping boots, may offer more support to the legs in the trailer and are recommended for a long trip. It is important that the coronary band and the hoof also be covered either by the bandage or by bell boots applied below the standing bandage. Before wrapping with standing bandages, make sure that you know how to do it properly because a poorly applied bandage can do more harm than good. If you are unsure about bandaging, ask your veterinarian to teach you how to do it. There are also good books and other sources

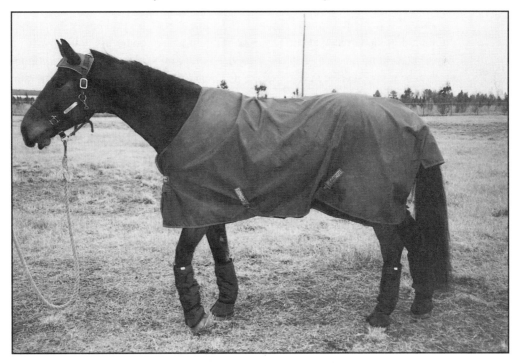

This horse is properly dressed for a winter ride in his stock-combo trailer.

of information about bandaging. The United States Pony Club Manuals of Horsemanship (published by Howell Book House) contain some of the best information about protecting a horse for transport. (Do not be misled by the fact that commercial shipping companies discourage bandaging for horses that are being transported in their vans. This is because they do not want to deal with bandages that may come off during transport, or they do not want to be responsible for bandages that have been improperly applied by the owner.)

Tail wraps can protect the tailbone from damage if the horse tends to lean on the butt bar. This is another type of wrap that can do more harm than good if it is not applied properly. This is another subject that you can discuss with your veterinarian.

TRAILER TRAINING

A horse that is well behaved on the ground will usually be well behaved on the trailer once he understands that the trailer will not harm him. Quiet reassurance will probably be all he needs to load onto the trailer. The more nonthreatening the trailer, the easier it will be to convince him that there is nothing to fear. For horses that are more difficult, it is even more important that the trailer be horse-friendly. By remembering the nature of the horse as we have previously discussed, it should be apparent that the horse needs help to overcome his natural fear of small places and unsteady footing. Patience is very important, but it is also important to be intuitive enough to know the difference between a frightened or inexperienced horse and one that is just being difficult. Good training is good training whether on the ground, in the saddle, or on the trailer. When horse and handler learn to respect and trust each other, the safety margin is markedly increased for everyone.

The following suggestions may help you gain that relationship:

- Make sure the trailer is as user-friendly as possible for both horse and handler.

- Do not use unnecessary force to train a horse to load. Abuse only adds stress to an already stressful situation.

- Do not get angry and punish the horse for behavior that is not his fault. Punishment should be used only at the very moment of bad behavior, not fearful behavior, and reward should be given immediately for good behavior. Reward can be praise, a treat, or the release of the aids. Many recent books have been published by well-known trainers—information is readily available. Research which methods may be suitable for you and your horse.

- For those who may not be experienced enough to feel confident about training, ask for help from a competent professional. Check references and watch training sessions with other horses before subjecting your own horse to someone else's methods. The trainer should allow you to watch your horse being trained and should teach you to continue the training at home. Trailer training is a special discipline and requires a certain expertise. Follow your own instincts and if you have any doubts, look for someone else. A bad experience for your horse may have irreparable consequences.

- Do not try to teach your horse to load when you are going to the horse show or somewhere else where you need to be on time! Training sessions should be devoted only to the subject at hand when you have plenty of time and no one is in a hurry. After the horse is confident about the trailer, you will be free to travel untroubled by loading woes!

- Since accidents and injuries are possible even on a short trip, always carry a first-aid kit on board. Water should be considered part of that first-aid kit—as much as 20 gallons is not too much to have on board. You may need that water if you have a breakdown with horses in the trailer, not only for drinking and for washing cuts, but also for a cooling bath if the weather is hot.

REDUCING RESPIRATORY STRESS

Even though it can stress the respiratory tract, most horses like to have hay in the trailer. (The very act of chewing is a stress reducer for the horse.) A lot of horses don't actually eat while the trailer is in motion but like to take a few bites when the trailer stops even for a few minutes. Some horses are too nervous to eat at all, and of course, there are many seasoned travelers who eat everything in sight. No matter what style of trailer the horse is traveling in, there are some simple ways to improve the environment and still feed hay.

For those horses that won't eat while the trailer is moving: When you make rest stops for yourself on long trips, give the horse a chance to eat some hay and drink some water. Leave them in the trailer unless you have a safe place to unload. Do not unload horses on the highway or in rest areas or anywhere else where an escaped horse can be a danger to himself or others. (*Warning:* Grass in rest areas, parks, or other public places may be treated with toxic chemicals.)

Use the cleanest hay available. Pull the hay apart and shake it with a pitchfork to remove excess dust before putting it into the trailer. Or even better, soak the hay for at least 15 minutes—up to 12 hours—before putting it into the trailer. Besides completely eliminating the dust problem, there is the benefit of adding moisture to the diet while the horse is traveling. This can be a great help on a long trip when the horse will not drink. Be very careful not to let the hay become moldy, and throw out what the horse does not eat in one feeding.

Use a walk-through type trailer with solid hay bags that hang lower than the horse's head. The hay bags may have ventilation holes in the back, but there should be no openings for the horse to catch a leg in the front.

Keep windows open for ventilation. Certain styles of roof vents can be adjusted to remove stale air out of the trailer, which greatly improves the environment and keeps heat from building inside. If there are no screens on the trailer windows, put a fly mask on the horse to avoid eye injuries from flying objects. If it is cold, blanket the horse accordingly instead of closing in the trailer.

If you still must use a nylon or rope hay net, it must be tied high enough that the horse cannot get a leg caught in it. This makes it too high to be healthy, but the threat of permanent injury makes it too dangerous to do otherwise. The hay net should also be tied securely enough that it does not come loose and work its way down where it becomes dangerous. Tie the net up in front of the horse, not next to his head. A hay net that swings around next to the horse's head can be responsible for eye injuries. To minimize dust, put the hay in the net and dip the whole thing into a tub of water for a while before putting it in the trailer with the horse. Keep a sharp knife handy so that you can quickly cut the hay net if the horse should become entangled in it.

Good ventilation is crucial not only to clear the air of hay dust, but to remove noxious gasses created by urine and manure, which are harmful to the horse's respiratory tract. Frequent removal of urine and manure helps maintain a clean environment in the trailer. It is a common practice to add shavings on the floor of the trailer to absorb liquids and to encourage the horse to urinate on a long trip. This is a good habit, although removal of soiled shavings throughout the trip is important so buildup of ammonia does not occur. Shavings can also be a source of flying dust, so it can help to dampen the shavings before loading the horse. Shavings should be unnecessary on a short trip if floor mats are non-slip.

TYING

There are several good reasons that horses should always be tied in the trailer. If there are dividers in the trailer, a horse can put his head over or under them and get himself stuck. It is even possible for a horse to break its back or neck by getting into this kind of trouble. Two or more horses in the trailer can start playing or fighting with each other if they can reach noses, and not only can they hurt each other, the balance of the trailer can be compromised, making for a dangerous driving situation. This is also true of an open stock trailer. Horses may like to move around, but in this case it is not good for them or for you.

This could have been a major disaster! A horse can easily get stuck under a divider or breast bar if he isn't tied.

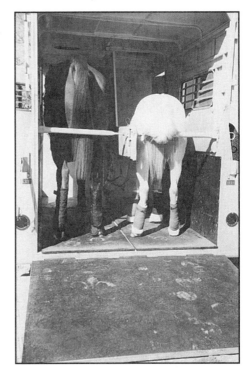

Horses break halters and lead ropes, get the rope over their heads, untie the knot, and do many more imaginative things to make trouble. Most of these problems occur because they have not been tied properly. We have seen more mistakes about tying a horse in a trailer than one would think possible.

There are three hard and fast rules about tying a horse in a trailer. The first one is to always use a quick-release snap or quick-release knot to tie the horse. The second is to always put the butt bar up before you tie the horse, and the third is to untie the horse before the butt bar is taken down.

If the horse walks into the trailer by himself, you can stand behind him and lift the butt bar or close the slant divider as soon as he gets far enough inside that you can do so. Hopefully, if the horse starts to back out, the butt bar or slant divider will have a safety catch that prevents the horse from pushing it out of the latch before you can secure it properly. If you must walk into the trailer to lead the horse, try to have a friend lift and secure the butt bar for you. The horse may back out before you can get out of the trailer and get behind him to lift the bar. If the trailer is a slantload, you can lead the horse into the stall and close the divider behind him as you back out.

After you secure the bar or divider, walk around the trailer to the horse's head and tie him before you load the next horse. The horse should be tied long enough so he can walk back and touch the butt bar. This gives him a boundary and prevents him from believing that if he pulls hard enough, he can get out of the trailer. Many horses panic when they reach the end of the rope, and there is nothing behind them. This is the cause of many broken halters and lead ropes. As a result, the horse can be flung

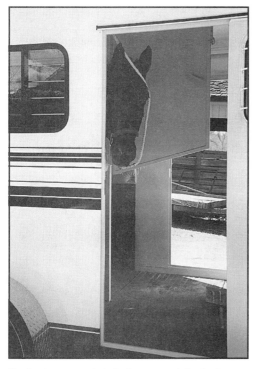

The lead rope needs to be long enough for the horse to reach down to his hay bag, but because the rope was tied under his chin, Rebel was able to get his head tangled in it. (The hay bag was removed for the picture.)

By tying the rope on the side of Tristan's halter, it can be shorter and he can still reach down and have adequate range of motion. He cannot turn his head too far in either direction to get in trouble. This is our favorite method to tie a horse in a walk-through trailer. The lead rope is tied in a quick-release knot, but a quick-release trailer tie would be better.

backward by the quick release of the broken equipment and may be severely injured by falling out the back of the trailer. Some horses like to lean on the butt bar for balance. If you have one of those, wrap his tail and let him do it.

Quick-release trailer ties have many advantages over plain lead ropes for tying the horse in the trailer. If the horse gets into trouble, you can quickly get him out of the situation when you believe it is safe to do so. Trailer ties can be preadjusted to the proper length and left hanging in the trailer. When you load the horse, all you have to do is clip the tie to his halter and remove the lead rope you used to lead him in. Lead ropes can be tied in a quick-release knot, but they sometimes come undone or get longer and longer as the trip goes on. Both trailer ties and lead ropes must be heavy-duty and have very strong snaps. Lead ropes should be at least 5 feet long.

The tie should be long enough so the horse can reach his food, use his head and neck for balance, and lower his head to cough out inhaled debris. It should be short enough that he cannot get his head over or under the head and center dividers or under the breast bar. He should also be unable to get the trailer tie or lead rope over his head or otherwise entangled.

In a straightload trailer, I like to tie the horse to the ring on the sidewall by the escape door, then I tie it to the ring on the side of the halter, not to the ring under the chin. In this way I can make the tie short enough that the horse cannot reach over the head divider but can reach down into the hay bag to eat. The horse also cannot turn his head around too far to look out the back of the trailer. I have also never had a horse get stuck under the trailer tie when tied in this way.

There are many trailers, especially manger trailers and slantloads, that do not have tie rings on the side but only in front of the horse. In this case, the horse should be tied by the normal ring under the chin on the halter.

If the trailer tie is attached by the quick-release snap onto the trailer tie ring, the tie will still be attached to the horse's halter for an emergency lead line if you have to use the quick-release function. Also, you will be able to quickly reach the snap and keep out of harm's way if the horse panics.

The choice of halter to use is open for discussion. Although nylon halters without breakaway devices are not recommended for other uses, they *may* be acceptable for trailering. Trailer ties and lead ropes must always have a breakaway function, but if a halter breaks in a trailering emergency, the horse may be running loose without a halter. Leather halters may break too easily and leave you in a lurch just because of a slight behavior problem. Probably the best option is to use a leather halter to tie the horse and to put a spare halter under it. Whichever system you use, always keep an extra halter aboard the trailer.

Cross tying a horse may be too restrictive unless a horse has a particular problem that makes it necessary to tie him this way. In a three-horse or six-horse side-by-side unit, it may be necessary to cross tie the middle horse(s) so he cannot reach the horses on either side of him.

When it is time to unload the horse, untie him before the butt bar is taken down. He will know it is time to come out of the trailer and may forget to wait for the signal from the handler. If he starts out before he is untied, it is another chance for him to panic and break the halter or trailer tie. Horses that are trained to back out of the trailer quietly and slowly have the best chance of safe unloading. If the horse is reluctant to unload and the divider can be moved over, allow him to turn around and walk out headfirst if there is enough room. This is an instance where the design of the trailer can help increase safety.

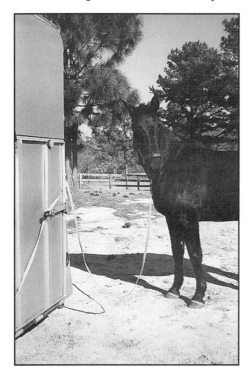

Never tie a horse to a trailer like this. This horse could easily get tangled in the long rope and suffer permanent injury.

If you tie the horse to the outside of the trailer when you are at a show or other event, make the tie only as long as it needs to be to let the horse stand comfortably and eat his hay out of the hay net. Never let the rope get long enough for the horse to get tangled in it or to get it caught under the fender or any other part of the trailer. A lead rope can come untied or the horse can gradually work at it until it gets too long. If you use a lead rope to tie the horse, it should also be tied with a quick-release knot. Quick-release trailer ties are the best choice because they do not get longer, and you have the same quick-release benefit that you do when the horse is in the trailer. Hay nets should also be tied high enough to keep the horse out of trouble. Hay that is put into hay nets can scratch the finish of the trailer. There are soft enclosed hay bags available that are better to use than the old-style hay net. Never put the hay on the ground for the horse to eat while he is tied to the trailer. Do not leave a horse tied to the trailer unsupervised, and never tie a horse to an unhitched trailer.

You might want to leave the horse in the trailer during a one-day event instead of tying him to the outside. If you can let the ramp down or leave the doors open, he is likely to be happier standing in the shade of the trailer eating his hay, and he will certainly be safer. Most horses will stay calm, especially if there is more than one horse in the trailer or if he can see others close by.

These horses are tied correctly with quick-release knots. Some horses may not be so content to stand so quietly without hay, or so close together without kicking each other.

There are two more no-no's that should be mentioned. Never put a horse in a trailer backward when the trailer is not designed for it, and never let the horse put its head out the back opening or outside the window of a slantload or any other trailer while the trailer is in transit. We have seen these situations on the road but still find it hard to believe that someone would actually do this.

The Railroad Crossing

In all our years of experience, one story defines everything that we have found to be true. Something so inconceivable happens that only God, fate, or luck, or wherever you put your faith, can pull you through.

Bobbie left her driveway hauling her two-horse manger step-up trailer to a trail ride. Her passengers were her Quarter Horse, Doc, and BJ, a rather large draft-cross gelding that belonged to a friend. Both horses were tied with leather halters. She was driving a ³/₄-ton pickup truck with a good weight-distribution hitch and safety chains. Bobbie had driven down this road many times before. The railroad track she was about to cross was very near her home. No lights were flashing, but, good driver that she was, she looked both ways anyway. All was clear.

As she pulled onto the tracks, she noticed that the railroad crews had put fresh new gravel over the crossing. As Bobbie carefully crossed the double track, she felt the truck bog down. Her truck wheels made it over the first track, but she sunk deeper into the new gravel, and the trailer hitch caught on the railroad track. She could not go forward or backward. The truck was across the second track and the trailer was on the first track! Bobbie got out of the truck to look over the situation.

Concern turned to fear as the lights started flashing and bells started ringing. Her blood ran cold when she heard the long whistle warning of the train's approach. The train came barreling around the bend! Bobbie ran to the back of the trailer and opened the trailer doors. The horses had panicked when they heard the train whistle, and both had already broken their halters. Bobbie only had enough time to get Doc's butt chain down, but BJ was strong enough to break his and get out of the trailer. Doc still had his front hooves on the trailer when the train hit. The impact pulled the trailer out from under him, and he was flung backward. The train hit the side of the truck dead on, whipping the trailer back and into the side of the train. The whole rig was dragged on the tracks for several hundred feet before the train stopped. Unbelievably, they had all escaped death. Doc and BJ ran away and were caught by onlookers. Doc suffered a broken rib, but that was the extent of his injuries. The truck was completely crushed. No horse would have survived in the trailer, but it held together better than one would expect, probably because it was steel. The trailer hitch was still intact, and the safety chains had held.

We always say that a trailer should be strong enough that a horse cannot break it. In this rare case, it was a good thing that BJ was able to break his butt chain. He would not have been able to get out in time. Furthermore, this is the only instance in our careers where a step-up trailer was definitely better than a rampload. If Doc had still been standing on a ramp, he may not have been lucky enough to escape with only a broken rib when it was ripped from under him. (However, a railroad crash doesn't come along enough times to use this as a reason to buy a step-up.) Bobbie was a lucky lady that day. Doc and BJ fully recovered, and later, both were happy to load into their new trailer that was paid for by the railroad company.

LONG VERSUS SHORT TRIPS

When horses are being transported on long trips, some management techniques can be used to help them cope with the effects of long-term stress. Talk to your veterinarian about inoculations, electrolytes, bran mashes, mineral oil, and antibiotics that might be recommended. Dehydration, heat exhaustion, colic, and shipping fever are commonly occurring conditions that can be avoided by good prevention techniques. Knowledge is always the best defense, and you should know how to read your horse's vital signs so you can detect a problem before it becomes severe. Your veterinarian is your best source of information. (See *Hawkins Guide: Equine Emergencies on the Road* by James Hamilton, D.V.M. and Neva Kittrell Scheve for more detailed information on this subject.)

Before a trailer trip, make sure your horse is healthy. Take his temperature and check that all his inoculations are up to date. If you will be driving from a colder climate to a warmer one, don't clip the horse the day before you go. Clip him at least a week before and blanket him. Let him get used to his new haircut before he is further stressed by a long trip. Electrolytes may be recommended, especially when traveling in the summer.

Know how to take vital signs and check the horse frequently for dehydration or other signs of stress-related illness. Some horses travel better than others, and you may have to stop after 5 to 10 hours to take a poor traveler off the trailer and let him walk around and drink some water. Always do this in a place that is quiet and off the road, not on an expressway rest area. Don't let him eat grass in a strange place; it may be treated with toxic chemicals. Always consider the possibility that the horse could get loose. It is wise to plan stops along the way. Several publications are available that list stables and veterinarians who offer rest stops. It is really safer to leave the horse in the trailer until you have reached the destination, but longer than 10 to 12 hours can be damaging to his health.

When horses are traveling long distances to compete, they will be further stressed by the competition itself, and then by the long ride home. The most important thing to remember is to keep the horse drinking during the entire trip, including the competition. Dehydration is the first step to colic and heat exhaustion. This kind of stress also subjects the horse to shipping fever, which quite often does not make itself apparent until the horse arrives home.

ADDITIONAL SUGGESTIONS

The following list of additional suggestions should help make trailering easier for you and your horse:

Wear gloves and boots when you are loading and unloading horses.

If the trailer is dark inside when you are loading, open the doors and turn on the lights to make it lighter.

If you are having trouble loading a horse, at least ten well-meaning bystanders will usually show up to help you. Thank them for offering to help but ask them all to leave except those who you know will be able to help. "Too many cooks in the kitchen" can really make a bad situation worse.

Make sure there are no hazards near the trailer when you are loading and unloading farm machinery, fence posts, etc.

Don't let door covers stick out the sides where a horse or handler could get bumped in the head.

If two or more horses are being unloaded from the trailer, keep at least one horse in sight of the last horse until he has also been safely unloaded. The one that is left on the trailer may panic and rush off too quickly. This is more of a problem with inexperienced horses.

If you are hauling your horse in someone else's trailer, do your own safety check. Don't depend on someone else for your safety and the safety of your horse.

If you are hauling someone else's horse in your trailer, insist the horse wear protective bandages, and agree in advance who will be responsible in the event of injury to the horse or damage to the trailer. Check with the insurance company to see who is covered for what.

Don't travel alone if you can help it.

Never lead a horse into the trailer if you do not have an easy escape route.

Never get into a trailer with a panicked horse, and don't open the door if there is a chance the horse could bolt out the door onto the highway.

Never put a horse into a trailer that is unhitched, or unhitch a trailer while the horses are still in it.

Do not use tranquilizers unless you know how. Improper use of tranquilizers can cause death. Discuss the use of tranquilizers with your veterinarian.

Don't Go on the Road Without It!

Store these items in the trailer so you always have them on board:

spare tire	buckets and sponge
jack	spare halter and lead rope
tire iron	spare bulbs
3 emergency triangles	spare fuses if applicable
flares	fire extinguisher
chocks	WD-40 or other lubricant
flashlight	broom
electrical tape and duct tape	shovel
equine first-aid kit with splint	pitchfork
knife for cutting ropes in an emergency	manure disposal bags
water	insect spray (bees and wasps)

During winter months:

shovel	human blankets
sand	candle
red flag (for antenna if stranded)	matches or lighter
	tire chains
horse blankets	

For the tow vehicle:

Hawkins Guide: Horse Trailering on the Road	spare belts and hoses
	tow chain
Hawkins Guide: Equine Emergencies on the Road	cellular phone or CB radio (CB may be more helpful in remote areas where cellular phones may not work)
registration for the vehicle and trailer	
proof of insurance	replacement fuses
jumper cables	road atlas
spare tire	work gloves
jack	portable air compressor
tire iron	cash and credit card
tool kit, including wiring materials	

For crossing state lines:

Certificate of Inspection health certificate)	proof of negative Coggins Veterinary test (Equine Infectious Anemia)

If you are in an accident and you have been injured, the EMS personnel and police will most likely not be capable of taking care of your horses. Prepare for this situation by keeping emergency directions in a visible place. Write the name of someone you know who can be called to help or to advise what to do with the horses if you are incapacitated—a knowledgeable friend, your veterinarian, or someone else who is familiar with your horses and all current telephone numbers.

Driving Safety Tips

BEFORE YOU LEAVE

Ride in a trailer sometime (not on the road in a tag-a-long, it's illegal!) to feel how the horse feels each time you take a turn or make a sudden stop. Careful driving can have a real effect on your horse's attitude about the trailer. Always think about your passenger and he will learn to enjoy his trips.

Practice driving the combination before you ever put a horse into the trailer. Know how to park and back up before you take to the road. We once knew a person who traveled from California to Ohio without knowing how to back the trailer. She always made sure she had plenty of room to turn around whenever she stopped anywhere for food, gas, or lodging. What a pain! Backing a trailer is easy to do when you know how, and you never know when you may get into a situation where you absolutely have to do it.

To back a trailer, tag-a-long or gooseneck, put your hand on the bottom of the steering wheel and turn it in the direction you want the trailer to move. If you want the trailer to move sharply, turn the wheel before you move the vehicle. If you want to turn more gradually, turn the wheel as the vehicle is moving.

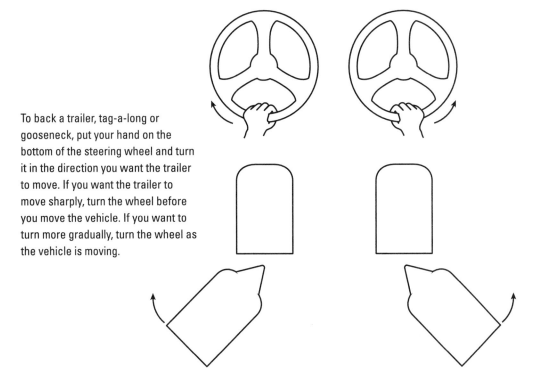

A tag-a-long trailer with a long tongue is easier to back than a trailer with a short tongue. A tag-a-long with a dressing room is also easier than one without a dressing room. The shorter trailer jackknives more easily than the longer trailer.

To back a trailer, tag-a-long, or gooseneck, put your hand on the bottom of the steering wheel. If you want the back of the trailer to go to the left, turn your hand to the left. If you want the back of the trailer to go to the right, turn your hand to the right. Practice until you are familiar with the way the combination handles.

If you are only hauling one horse, put him on the driver's side (roadside) of the trailer. If you are hauling more than one horse, put the heaviest ones on the driver's side. Roads are usually crowned higher in the middle, and putting the heaviest load on this side will help balance the trailer.

If you have a friend with you, familiarize him or her with your rig. If you become incapacitated, your friend may have to take over.

Last-Minute Checklist

- Check the tow vehicle. Check and replenish engine fluid levels and wiper fluid. Towing puts extra stress on the radiator, brakes, and transmission. Make sure fluid levels are correct.

- Make sure the ball on the tow vehicle is the correct size for the trailer.

- Make sure the rearview mirrors are properly adjusted and you know how to use them.

- Check tire pressure in the tires of the tow vehicle and the trailer. Improper tire pressure is responsible for most towing problems. Check tire condition. (See chapter 16, "Operation and Service.")

- Make sure that the trailer is level so the horse is not always fighting his balance by traveling uphill or downhill. This movement can also cause the trailer to sway and cause other safety problems.

- Check lug nuts on the wheels. Wheel nuts and bolts should be torqued before first road use and after each wheel removal. Check and re-torque after the first 10 miles, 25 miles, and again at 50 miles. Check periodically thereafter. (See chapter 16, "Operation and Service.")

- Check inside the trailer for bee and wasp nests.

- Check over your hitch, coupler, breakaway brake battery, and safety chains. Make sure the brakes and all lights are working properly before you load the horses.

- When horses are loaded, make sure all doors are latched properly and horses are tied.

- Drive down the driveway, and before you drive onto the main road, get out and check over everything again. Something you overlooked may make itself apparent by then. (Most accidents happen to people who have been hauling just long enough to get lackadaisical.)

- If you happen to stop somewhere where the rig has been left unattended, check everything all over again. Someone may have been tampering with the trailer or with the horses.

HOW'S YOUR DRIVING

Handling a tow vehicle and horse trailer requires some special precautions. Loaded horse trailers are heavy. The extra weight you are towing will make stopping distances longer, and you will not be able to accelerate as quickly as driving under normal conditions, especially if you have a downsized vehicle. Therefore, drive at least 5 mph under the speed limit, keep a good distance behind the vehicle in front of you, and don't try to dart into traffic. (Some states have a separate speed limit for those hauling trailers.)

Check in your rearview mirror to ensure that you have cleared a passed vehicle or that the lane is clear before you change from one lane to another. Put your turn signals on before you change lanes so that your intentions are clear to the driver behind you. Change lanes gradually.

Loss of control from trailer sway can be prevented by keeping tension on the hitch. The tow vehicle should always be pulling the trailer forward. If the trailer starts to sway or fishtail, apply, in brief spurts, the hand brake on the controller to the trailer only to slow the trailer, but keep a tight hold of the steering wheel and keep the tow vehicle going forward. Do not apply the brakes on the tow vehicle until the trailer is under control.

A jackknife caused by a trailer skid must be handled differently. The earliest way to detect that the trailer has started to skid is by seeing it in the rearview mirrors.

Anytime you apply the brakes hard, check the mirrors to make sure the trailer is where it should be. Once the trailer swings out of your lane, it is very difficult to prevent a jackknife. Stop using the brake. Release the brakes to get traction back. In this case, do not use the hand brake to straighten out the trailer since the trailer brakes have locked up and started the skid in the first place. Once the wheels grip the road again, the trailer will start to follow the tow vehicle and straighten out.

Use a lower gear when traveling up or down steep hills. If you feel the trailer pushing the vehicle when you are going downhill, apply the hand brake to slow the trailer. On long uphill grades, downshift the transmission and slow to 45 mph or less to reduce the possibility of overheating.

Do not park the vehicle and trailer on a grade. If you find yourself in a situation where you must do this, follow these suggestions: Apply regular brakes. Have another person chock the wheels of the trailer. Release the brakes and allow the chocks to absorb the load. Apply regular brakes again, apply the parking brake, and put the transmission into Park. Release regular brakes. To start again, apply regular brakes until the engine is started in Park and the parking brake is released. Release regular brakes and drive until chocks are free. Apply regular brakes and have the other person remove the chocks.

Consider the equine passengers. Give the horses time to prepare for stops, don't accelerate quickly, and make sure the trailer has cleared the turn, has straightened out, and the horses have regained balance before you return to normal speed. Travel over bumpy roads carefully.

Frequently check the trailer through your rearview mirror. Always be aware of what is going on behind you. Driving along with the window closed, the air-conditioning on, and the radio blaring, you could be oblivious to a perilous situation behind you.

Note: If you suspect that you have damaged the trailer in any way or you feel or hear anything that is not normal, pull over and thoroughly inspect the entire combination. Do not drive on until you are sure there is no danger of continuing.

16

Operation and Service

Certain maintenance procedures must be followed to keep your trailer in safe working order. Most horse trailer owners are not very interested in the mechanical aspects of the trailer. If you are like most horse people, you just want to hitch up and go. However, even if you are not interested in working on the trailer yourself, for your own safety, you should at least familiarize yourself with the normal operation of the brakes, coupler, axles, wheels, and tires so you can not only apply the proper maintenance techniques but also tell if something is not working right. More complicated maintenance and repair can be done by a qualified professional.

Safety Notice

Appropriate service methods and proper repair procedures are essential for the safe, reliable operation of all running gear as well as for the personal safety of the individual doing the work. This manual provides general directions for performing service and repair work with tested, effective techniques. Following these guidelines will help assure reliability.

There are numerous variations in procedures, techniques, tools, parts for servicing axles, as well as in the skill of the individual doing the work. It is beyond the scope of this manual to deal with all such variations and provide advice or cautions about each. Accordingly, follow the instructions in this manual and use caution so that you must first neither compromise your personal safety nor the integrity of your vehicle by your choice of methods, tools, or parts.

Refer to the owner's manual for your vehicle and read the manufacturer's suggestions for additional procedures, techniques, and warnings before performing any maintenance or repairs.

For proper performance, all new axles should have the following checked at the specified intervals:

- Wheel nut torque: 10, 25, and 50 miles.

- Brake adjustment: 200 and 3,000 miles.

- Tire pressure: the manufacturers requirements.

- Brake synchronization: set brake controller per controller manufacturer's directions.

Brakes

ELECTRIC BRAKES

Electric brakes on a trailer are similar to the drum brakes on your automobile. The basic difference is that your automotive brakes are actuated by hydraulic pressure whereas your electric trailer brakes are actuated by an electromagnet. With all the brake components connected into the system, the brake will operate as follows:

When the electrical current is fed into the system by the controller, it flows through the electromagnets in the brakes. The high-capacity electromagnets are energized

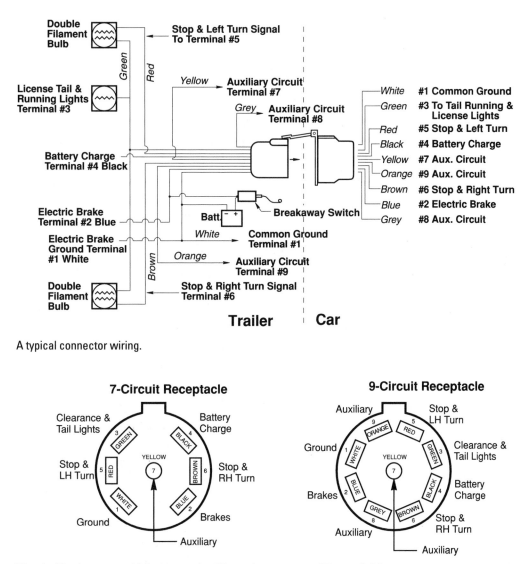

A typical connector wiring.

View looking in to tow vehicle receptacle. *(Illustration courtesy of Dexter Axle)*

and are attracted to the rotating armature surface of the drums that moves the actuating levers in the direction that the drums are turning.

The resulting force causes the actuating cam block at the shoe end of the lever to push the primary shoe out against the inside surface of the brake drum. The force generated by the primary shoe acting through the adjuster link then moves the secondary shoe out into contact with the brake drum.

Increasing the current flow to the electromagnet causes the magnet to grip the armature surface of the brake drum more firmly. This results in increasing the pressure against the shoes and brake drums until the desired stop is accomplished.

The trailer brakes are designed to work in synchronization with the tow vehicle brakes. Never use your tow vehicle or trailer brakes alone to stop the combined load.

Your trailer and tow vehicle will seldom have the correct amperage flow to the brake magnets to give you comfortable, safe braking unless you make proper brake system adjustments. Changing trailer load and driving conditions as well as un-even alternator and battery output can mean unstable current flow to your brake magnets. It is, therefore, imperative that you maintain and adjust your brakes as described in the brakes section, use a properly modulated brake controller, and perform the synchronization procedure that follows.

In addition to the following detailed synchronization adjustment, electric brake controllers provide a modulation function that varies the current to the electric brakes with the pressure on the brake pedal or amount of deceleration of the tow vehicle. It is important that your brake controller provide approximately 2 volts to the braking system when the brake pedal is first depressed and gradually increases the voltage to 12 volts as brake pedal pressure is increased. If the controller "jumps" immediately to a high voltage output, even during a gradual stop, then the electric

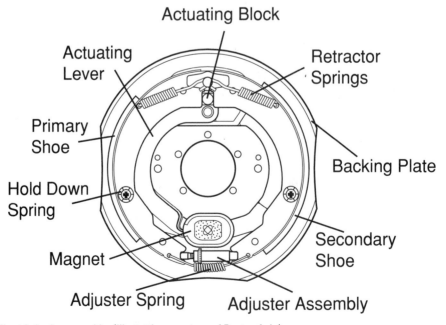

Electric brake assembly. *(Illustration courtesy of Dexter Axle)*

brakes will always be fully energized and will result in harsh brakes and potential wheel lockup.

Proper synchronization of tow vehicle to trailer braking can only be accomplished by road testing. Brake lockup, grabbiness, or harshness is often due to the lack of synchronization between the tow vehicle and the trailer being towed, too high a threshold voltage (over 2 volts), or under adjusted brakes.

Before any synchronization adjustments are made, your trailer brakes should be burnished-in by making 10 to 12 full stops from approximately 20 mph. This allows the brake shoes and magnets to slightly wear into the drum surfaces.

SYNCHRONIZATION

To ensure safe brake performance and synchronization, read the brake controller manufacturer's instructions completely before attempting any synchronization procedures. *Caution:* Before making road tests, make sure the area is clear of vehicular and pedestrian traffic.

Make several hard stops from 20 mph on a dry paved road free of sand and gravel. If the trailer brakes lock and slide, decrease the gain setting on the controller. If they do not slide, slightly increase the gain setting. Adjust the controller just to the point of impending brake lockup and wheel skid.

Note that minimum vehicle stopping distances are achieved when wheels approach lockup. Actual brake lockup should be avoided because it results in poor vehicle stability and control. Not all trailer brakes are capable of wheel lockup; it depends on load, brake type, wheels, and tires.

If the controller is applying the trailer brakes before the tow vehicle brakes, the controller level adjustment should be adjusted so the trailer brakes come on in synchronization with the tow vehicle brakes. For proper braking performance, it is recommended that the controller be adjusted to allow the trailer brakes to come on just slightly ahead of the tow vehicle brakes. When proper synchronization is achieved, there will be no sensation of the trailer's jerking or pushing the tow vehicle during braking. *Caution:* Do not adjust this control outside the parameters outlined in the manufacturer's instructions.

Some controllers have a gain control, to vary the amount of current to the brakes, and a level control that sets the controller's inertia sensor to sense deceleration. The level adjustment also can be used to vary when the trailer braking is felt. The gain or output control adjustment usually controls the maximum amount of amperage available to the brakes. This can be adjusted for varying trailer loads.

BRAKE ADJUSTMENT

Brakes should be adjusted (1) after the first 200 miles of operation when the brake shoes and drums have "seated," (2) at 3,000-mile intervals, (3) or as use and performance requires. The brakes should be adjusted in the following manner:

1. Jack up trailer and secure on adequate capacity jack stands. Follow trailer manufacturer's recommendations for lifting and supporting the unit. Do not lift or place supports on any part of the suspension system. Check that the wheel and drum rotate freely.

2. Remove the adjusting hole cover from the adjusting slot on the bottom of the brake backing plate.

3. With a screwdriver or standard adjusting tool, rotate the starwheel of the adjuster assembly to expand the brake shoes. Adjust the brake shoes out until the pressure of the linings against the drum makes the wheel very difficult to turn. *Note:* With drop spindle axles, a modified adjusting tool with about an 80-degree angle should be used. Sears Craftsman #4736 or K-D #295 are recommended.

4. Then rotate the starwheel in the opposite direction until the wheel turns freely with a slight lining drag.

5. Replace the adjusting hole cover and lower the wheel to the ground.

6. Repeat the above procedure on all brakes.

Caution: Never crawl under your trailer unless it is resting on properly placed jack stands.

BRAKE CLEANING AND INSPECTION

Your trailer brakes must be inspected and serviced at yearly intervals or more often as use and performance requires. Magnets and shoes must be changed when they become worn or scored, thereby preventing adequate vehicle braking.

Clean the backing plate, magnet arm, magnet, and brake shoes. Make certain that all the parts removed are replaced in the same brake and drum assembly. Inspect the magnet arm for any loose or worn parts. Check shoe return springs, hold down springs, and adjust springs for stretch or deformation and replace if required.

Caution: Since some brake shoe friction materials contain asbestos, certain precautions need to be taken when servicing brakes:

- Avoid creating or breathing dust.

- Avoid machining, filing, or grinding the brake linings.

- Do not use compressed air or dry brushing for cleaning. Dust can be removed with a damp brush.

BRAKE LUBRICATION

Before reassembling, apply a light film of Lubriplate or similar grease, or antiseize compound on the brake anchor pin, the actuating arm bushing and pin, and the areas on the backing plate that are touch the brake shoes and magnet lever arm. Apply a light film of oil on the actuating block mounted on the actuating arm. *Caution:* Do not get grease or oil on the brake linings, drums, or magnets.

MAGNETS

Electric brakes are equipped with electromagnets that are designed to provide the proper input force and friction characteristics. Magnets should be inspected and replaced if worn unevenly or abnormally. A straightedge should be used to check wear.

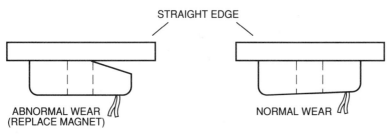

Magnet inspection.

Even if wear is normal as indicated by your straightedge, the magnets should be replaced if any part of the magnet coil has become visible through the friction material facing of the magnet. It is also recommended that the drum armature surface be refaced when replacing magnets. (See Brake Drum Inspection, page 275.) Magnets should also be replaced in pairs—both sides of an axle. Use only parts recommended by the manufacturer. Replacement kits will include more specific instruction for replacement.

SHOES AND LININGS

A simple visual inspection of the brake linings will tell if they are usable. Replace if the lining is worn (to within $^1/_{16}$ inch or less), contaminated with grease or oil, or abnormally scored or gouged. It is important to replace both shoes on each brake and both brakes of the same axle. This is necessary to retain the balance of your brakes. Replacement shoe and lining kits will contain specific instructions for proper replacement.

TROUBLESHOOTING

Most electric brake malfunctions that cannot be corrected by either brake adjustments or by synchronization adjustments can generally be traced to electrical system failure. Mechanical causes are ordinarily obvious, for example, bent or broken parts, worn-out linings or magnets, seized lever arms or shoes, scored drums, loose parts, etc. Voltmeter and ammeter are essential tools for proper troubleshooting of electric brakes.

How to Measure Voltage

System voltage is measured at the magnets by connecting the voltmeter to the two magnet lead wires at any brake. This may be accomplished by using a pin probe inserted through the insulation of the wires dropping down from the chassis or by

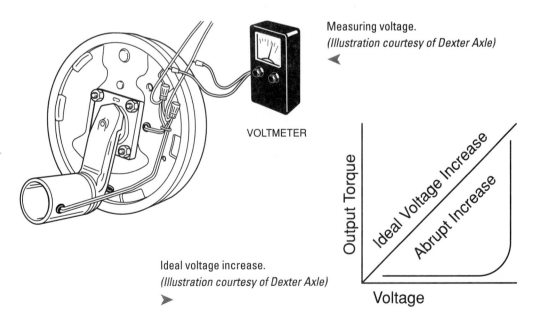

Measuring voltage.
(Illustration courtesy of Dexter Axle)

VOLTMETER

Ideal voltage increase.
(Illustration courtesy of Dexter Axle)

cutting the wires. The engine of the towing vehicle should be running when checking the voltage so that a low battery will not affect the readings.

Voltage in the system should begin at 0 volts and, as the controller bar is slowly actuated, should gradually increase to about 12 volts. This is referred to as modulation. No modulation means that when the controller begins to apply voltage to the brakes, it applies an immediate high voltage, which causes the brakes to apply instantaneous maximum power.

The threshold voltage of a controller is the voltage applied to the brakes when the controller first turns on. The lower the threshold voltage, the smoother the brakes will operate. Too high of a threshold voltage (in excess of 2 volts as is often found in heavy-duty controllers) can cause grabby, harsh brakes.

How to Measure Amperage

System amperage is the amperage being drawn by all brakes on the trailer. The engine of the towing vehicle should be running when checking amperage.

One place to measure system amperage is at the blue wire of the controller that is the output to the brakes. The blue wire must be disconnected and the ammeter put in series into the line. System amperage draw should be as noted in the following table. Make sure your ammeter has sufficient capacity and note polarity to prevent damaging your ammeter.

If a resistor is used in the brake system, it must be set at zero or bypassed completely to obtain the maximum amperage reading.

Individual amperage draw can be measured by inserting the ammeter in the line at the magnet you want to check. Disconnect one of the magnet lead wire connectors and attach the ammeter between the two wires. Make sure that the wires are properly reconnected and sealed after testing is completed.

Measuring amperage.
(Illustration courtesy of Dexter Axle)

AMMETER

By far, the most common electrical problem is low or no voltage and amperage at the brakes. The following are common causes of this condition:

- Poor electrical connections

- Open circuits

- Insufficient wire size

- Broken wires

- Blown fuses (Fusing of brakes is not recommended.)

- Improperly functioning controllers or resistors

Another common electrical problem is shorted or partially shorted circuits (indicated by abnormally high system amperage). These are occasionally the most difficult to find. The following are possible causes:

- Shorted magnet coils

- Defective controllers

- Bare wires contacting a grounded object

Finding the system short is a matter of isolation. If the high amperage reading drops to zero by unplugging the trailer, then the short is in the trailer. If the amperage reading remains high with all the brake magnets disconnected, the short is in the trailer wiring.

All electrical troubleshooting procedures should start at the controller. Most complaints regarding brake harshness or malfunction are traceable to improperly adjusted or nonfunctioning controllers. See your controller manufacturer's data for proper adjustment and testing procedures. If the voltage and amperage are not satisfactory, proceed to the connector and then to the individual magnets to isolate the problem source. Twelve volts output at the controller should equate to 10.5 volts minimum at each magnet. Nominal system amperage at 12 volts with cold magnets, system resistor at 0 and controller at maximum gain should be as detailed in the following chart:

MAGNET AMPERES CHART				
Brake Size	*Amps/Magnet*	*Two Brakes*	*Four Brakes*	*Six Brakes*
$7 \times 1^1/_4$	2.5	5.0	10.0	15.0
$10 \times 1^1/_4$	3.0	6.0	12.0	18.0
$10 \times 2^1/_4$	3.0	6.0	12.0	18.0
12×2	3.0	6.0	12.0	18.0
$12^1/_2 \times 1^1/_4$	3.0	6.0	12.0	18.0
$12^1/_4 \times 3^3/_8$	3.0	6.0	12.0	18.0

TROUBLESHOOTING—ELECTRIC BRAKES

Symptom	Causes	Remedies
Brakes pull to one side	Incorrect adjustment	Adjust
	Grease or oil on linings or magnets	Clean or replace
	Broken wires	Find and repair
	Bad connections	Find and repair
Harsh brakes	Underadjustment	Adjust
	Improper synchronization	Correct
	Improper controller	Change
	Faulty controller	Test and correct
Noisy brakes	Underadjustment	Adjust
	Lack of lubrication	Lubricate
	Broken brake components	Replace component
	Incorrect brake components	Correct
Surging brakes	Grease or oil on linings or magnets	Clean or replace
	Out-of-round or cracked brake drum	Machine or replace
	Faulty controller	Test and correct
Dragging brakes	Overadjustment	Readjust
	Out-of-round brake drums	Machine or replace
	Incorrect brake components	Replace
	Loose, bent or broken components	Replace
	Faulty breakaway switch	Repair or replace
	Loose wheel bearing adjustment	Adjust
	Bent spindle	Replace axle
No brakes	Open circuits	Find and correct
	Severe underadjustment	Adjust brakes
	Faulty controller	Test and correct
	Short circuits	Find and correct
Weak brakes	Grease or oil on magnets or linings	Clean or replace
	Corroded connections	Clean and correct cause of corrosion
	Worn linings or magnets	Replace

(continues)

TROUBLESHOOTING—ELECTRIC BRAKES (continued)		
Symptom	*Causes*	*Remedies*
Weak brakes (continued)	Scored or grooved brake drums	Machine or replace
	Improper synchronization	Correct
	Underadjustment	Adjust brakes
	Glazed linings	Reburnish or replace
	Overloaded trailer	Correct
Locking brakes	Underadjustment	Adjust
	Improper Synchronization	Correct
	Faulty controller	Test and correct
	Loose, bent or broken brake components	Replace components
	Out-of-round brake drums	Machine or replace
	Insufficient wheel load	Adjust system resistor and synchronize
Intermittent brakes	Faulty controller	Test and correct
	Broken wires	Repair or replace
	Loose connections	Find and repair

HYDRAULIC BRAKES

The hydraulic brakes on your trailer are much like those on your car. The hydraulic fluid from a master cylinder is used to actuate the wheel cylinder that, in turn, applies force against the brake shoes and drum. The main differences between automotive hydraulic brakes and hydraulic trailer brakes are the actuation systems that transfer the braking signal from the tow vehicle to the brakes. Descriptions of the most popular hydraulic actuation systems follow.

Vacuum and Hydraulic

The basic actuation system consists of a vacuum booster, synchronizing valve, check valve, and a plumbing kit that includes all lines and fittings. A vacuum supply from the engine manifold is routed to the front of the booster and the top chamber of the synchronizing valve through flexible hoses. The rear of the booster and the lower chamber of the synchronizing valve are connected by a separate line. The vacuum from the engine must pass through a normally closed check valve. The check valve keeps gas vapor out of the system and insures that the highest vacuum available will be kept in the system. With the engine running and with no brake pedal pressure, a vacuum exists throughout the system. The synchronizing valve is connected to the master cylinder hydraulic supply. When the brake pedal is applied, the hydraulic pressure in the synchronizing valve forces a poppet to open that allows atmospheric air to enter the bottom chamber of the valve. Since this part of the valve is connected to the rear of the vacuum booster, the vacuum on this side of the booster chamber is lost. The vacuum on the front side of the booster chamber is maintained, and this atmospheric/vacuum pressure differential causes a piston to move in the booster's slave cylinder. This piston applies the hydraulic pressure to the brakes through the connecting hydraulic line. When the pedal is released, the poppet in the synchronizing valve is closed, and by internal passages, the air in the rear of the booster chamber is removed. This restores a vacuum that is equal to the vacuum in the front part of the booster chamber. The pressure balance allows the slave cylinder piston to be pulled back to its original position, and the hydraulic pressure to the brakes is released.

Air and Hydraulic

Air and hydraulic braking systems are commonly used when the tow vehicle has a diesel engine that does not develop manifold vacuum. The air and hydraulic tow vehicle has an air compressor mounted on the engine to supply compressed air for the braking system and other needs required by the tow vehicle trailer combination. This air is routed to a booster chamber attached to the trailer master cylinder. The air pressure multiplies hydraulic output pressure that then sends fluid to the wheel cylinders. The air over hydraulic systems are often controlled by a series of control valves and servos to insure proper braking under all conditions.

Surge Braking System

The surge braking system uses a specially designed trailer hitch coupler that has a hydraulic cylinder built in. When the tow vehicle applies its brakes, the tow vehicle decelerates, causing the trailer to apply a pushing force against the hitch. This force actuates the surge hitch hydraulic cylinder, transferring high pressure brake fluid to the wheel cylinder. The trailer brakes are now applied.

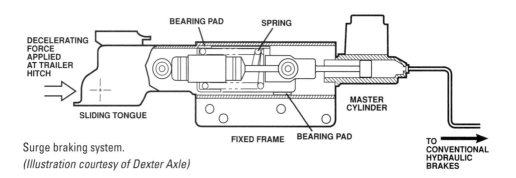

Surge braking system.
(Illustration courtesy of Dexter Axle)

HYDRAULIC BRAKE OPERATION

Duo-Servo

The duo-servo brake uses a dual-piston wheel cylinder to apply the brakes. This type of brake is typically used in a vacuum and hydraulic or air and hydraulic system. A description of operation of this brake is as follows:

When the brakes are applied, the double-acting wheel cylinder moves the primary and secondary shoes toward the drum. The frictional force between the brake drum and lining attempts to turn the primary shoe into the secondary shoe, the secondary

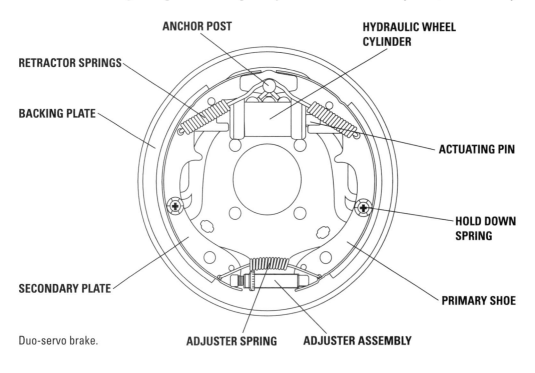

Duo-servo brake.

shoe is forced onto the anchor pin and from this point, the secondary and primary shoes attempt to "wrap around." In essence, the brake has used frictional force to help the applying force on both shoes.

If the brakes are applied while the vehicle is backing, the shoes rotate in the direction of the drum rotation. This causes the secondary shoe to leave the anchor and causes the primary shoe to move against the anchor. Action of the brake is therefore the same in reverse as in forward.

Uni-Servo

The uni-servo brake uses a single-acting cylinder. On actuation, the primary shoe is pressed against the brake drum, which causes the shoe to move in the direction of rotation. This movement in turn actuates the secondary shoe through the adjuster link assembly. Another variation is called a "free backing" brake, which is commonly used on trailers with a surge hitch system. When backing with a surge brake hitch, the brakes are applied through the surge mechanism, and if there is more brake force on the trailer than the tow vehicle can override, no backing is possible. The free backing brake was developed to allow backing in this application. This brake has a primary shoe on a pivot that allows normal application in the forward direction but allows the primary shoe to rotate away from the drum surface when backing.

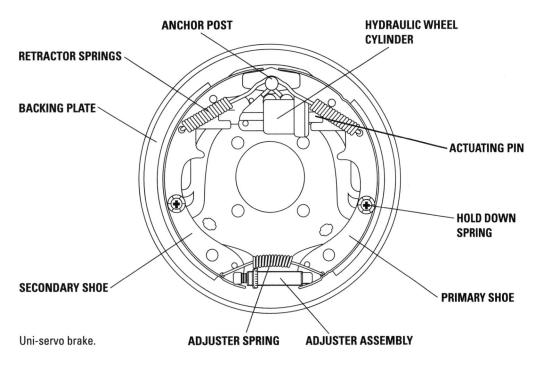

Uni-servo brake.

MAINTENANCE

A properly installed vacuum and hydraulic or air and hydraulic system should not require any special attention except for routine maintenance such as shoe and lining replacement. If problems occur, the entire tow vehicle/trailer braking system should be traced by a qualified mechanic using a methodical approach to determine the exact source of the problem. Typical problems in a hydraulic braking system are as follows:

- Air or vacuum leaks

- Hydraulic system leaks

- Air in brake lines

- Water or other impurity in brake fluid

- Rusted or corroded master or wheel cylinders.

Most of the brake components are very similar to those used in electric brakes, and maintenance is comparable for the hub and drum, shoes and linings, and bearings. Specific maintenance activities are as follows:

- *Brake Adjustment*—As mentioned in the electric brake section, adjustment of your brakes is critical to proper brake performance. Adjustment intervals are after the first 200 miles, and every 3,000 miles thereafter.

- *Wheel Cylinders*—Inspect for leaks and smooth operation. Clean with brake cleaner and flush with fresh brake fluid. Hone or replace as necessary.

- *Brake Lines*—Check for cracks, kinks, or blockage. Flush with fresh brake fluid. Bleed system to remove all air. Replace as necessary.

- *Shoes and Linings*—Inspect visually. Replace if the lining is worn (to within $1/16$ inch or less), contaminated with grease or brake fluid, or abnormally scored or gouged.

- *Hardware*—Check all hardware. Check shoe return spring, hold down springs, and adjuster springs for stretch or wear. Replace as required. Service kits are available.

- *Drums*—Check drums for scoring, cracking, or uneven wear. Turn drum smooth only if under maximum diameter. Replace as necessary.

TROUBLESHOOTING—HYDRAULIC BRAKES

Symptom	Causes	Remedies
No brakes	Broken or kinked brake	Repair or replace
	Severe Underadjustment	Adjust brakes
	Malfunctioning actuation system	Troubleshoot system
Weak brakes	Adjustment not correct	Manual: adjust brakes; Automatic: make several reverse stops
	Excessively worn brake linings	Replace shoe and lining
	Incorrect lining	Install correct shoe and lining
	Grease- or fluid-soaked lining	Repair grease seal or wheel cylinder; install new shoe and lining
	Frozen master cylinder or wheel cylinder pistons	Recondition; replace all cylinders, brake fluid
	Glazed lining	Reburnish or replace
	Excessive drum wear	Replace
	Trapped air in lines	Bleed system
	Overloaded trailer	Correct
	Malfunctioning actuating system	Troubleshoot system
Harsh brakes	Brake adjustment not correct	Manual: adjust brakes; Automatic: make several reverse stops
	Grease or fluid in linings	Replace shoes and linings
Surging brakes	Grease or oil on linings	Clean or replace
	Out-of-round drums or cracked drums	Repair or replace
Noisy brakes	Underadjustment	Adjust
	Lack of lubrication	Lubricate
	Broken brake components	Replace components
	Incorrect brake components	Correct

(continues)

TROUBLESHOOTING—HYDRAULIC BRAKES (continued)		
Symptom	*Causes*	*Remedies*
Locking brakes	Loose, bent or broken components	Replace components
	Underadjustment	Adjust
	Out-of-round drums	Machine or replace
Pulls to one side	Incorrect tire pressure	Inflate evenly to required pressure
	Unmatched tires on same axle	Match tires on axle
	Restricted brake lines or hoses	Repair or replace
	Malfunctioning cylinder assembly	Check for stuck or sluggish pistons
	Defective or damaged shoe and lining	Install new shoe and lining; new axle
	One side out of adjustment	Adjust
Dragging	Improper fluid	Replace rubber parts; fill with DOT4 fluid
	Blocked master cylinder	Open with compressed air or replace cylinder
	Parking brake cable frozen	Free cable and lubricate
	Improper lining, thickness or location	Install new shoes and linings

Hubs, Drums, and Bearings

HUB REMOVAL

Whenever the hub equipment on your axle must be removed for inspection or maintenance the following procedure should be used:

1. Elevate and support the trailer unit according to the manufacturer's instructions.

2. Remove the wheel.

3. Remove the grease cap by carefully prying progressively around the flange of the cap. If the hub is an oil lube type, then the cap can be removed by unscrewing it counterclockwise while holding the hub stationary.

4. Remove the cotter pin from the spindle nut or, in the case of EZ Lube versions, bend the locking tang to the free position.

5. Unscrew the spindle nut (counterclockwise) and remove the washer.

6. Remove the hub from the spindle, being careful not to allow the outer bearing cone to fall out. The inner bearing cone will be retained by the seal.

BRAKE DRUM INSPECTION

There are two areas of the brake drum that are subjected to wear and require periodic inspection. These two areas are the drum surface where the brake shoes make contact during stopping and the armature surface where the magnet contacts (only in electric brakes).

The drum surface should be inspected for excessive wear or heavy scoring. If worn more than .020 inch oversized or if the drum has worn out of round by more than .015 inch, then the drum surface should be turned. If scoring or other wear is greater than .090 inch on the diameter, the drum must be replaced. When turning the drum surface, the maximum rebore diameter is as follows:

7-inch brake drum—7.090 inch

10-inch brake drum—10.090 inch

12-inch brake drum—12.090 inch

12¹/₄-inch brake drum—12.340 inch

The machined inner surface of the brake drum that contacts the brake magnet is called the armature surface. If the armature surface is scored or worn unevenly, it should be refaced to a 120 micro inch finish by removing not more than .030 inch of material. To insure proper contact between the armature face and the magnet face, the magnets should be replaced when the armature surface is refaced; the armature surface should be refaced when the magnets are replaced.

Note: It is important to protect the wheel bearing bores from metallic chips and contamination that result from drum turning or armature refacing operations. Make certain that the wheel bearing cavities are clean and free of contamination before reinstalling bearing and seals. The presence of these contaminants will cause premature wheel bearing failure.

BEARING INSPECTION

Wash all grease and oil from the bearing cone, using a suitable solvent. Dry the bearing with a clean, lint-free cloth and inspect each roller completely. If any pitting, spalling, or corrosion is present, then the bearing must be replaced. The bearing cup inside the hub must be inspected. *Important: Bearings must always be replaced in sets of a cone and a cup.*

When replacing the bearing cup proceed as follows:

1. Place the hub on a flat work surface with the cup to be replaced on the bottom side.

2. Using a brass drift punch, carefully tap around the small diameter end of the cup to drive out.

3. After cleaning the hub bore area, replace the cup by tapping in with the brass drift punch. Be sure the cup is seated all the way up against the retaining shoulder in the hub.

Caution: Be sure to wear safety glasses when removing or installing force fitted parts. Failure to comply may result in serious eye injury.

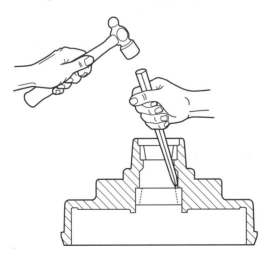

Bearing removal technique.
(Illustration courtesy of Dexter Axle)

BEARING LUBRICATION

Along with bearing adjustment, proper lubrication is essential to the current function and reliability of your trailer axle. Bearings should be lubricated every 12 months or 12,000 miles. The method to repack bearing cones is as follows:

1. Place a quantity of grease into the palm of your hand.

2. Press a section of the widest end of the bearing into the outer edge of the grease pile closest to the thumb, forcing grease into the interior of the bearing.

3. Repeat this while rotating the bearing from roller to roller.

4. Continue this process until you have the entire bearing completely filled with grease.

5. Before reinstalling, apply a light coat of grease on the bearing cup.

Lubricating the bearings.
(Illustration courtesy of Dexter Axle)

E-Z LUBE

If your axle is equipped with the E-Z Lube feature, the bearings can be periodically lubricated without removing the hubs from the axle. This feature consists of axle spindles that have been specially drilled and fitted with a grease zerk in their ends. When the grease is pumped into the zerk, it is channeled to the inner bearing and then flows back to the outer bearing and eventually back out the grease cap hole.

The procedure is as follows:

1. Remove the rubber plug from the end of the grease cap.

2. Place a standard grease gun onto the grease zerk located in the end of the spindle. Make sure the grease gun nozzle is fully engaged on the fitting.

3. Pump the grease into the zerk. The old, displaced grease will begin to flow back out the cap around the grease gun nozzle.

4. When the new, clean grease is observed, remove the grease gun, wipe off any excess, and replace the rubber plug in the cap.

Note: The E-Z Lube feature is designed to allow immersion. Axles not equipped with E-Z Lube are not designed for immersion and bearing should be repacked after each immersion.

If hubs are removed from an axle with the E-Z Lube feature, it is imperative that the seals be replaced *before* bearing lubrication. Otherwise, the chance of grease getting on brake linings is greatly increased.

If your axles are equipped with oil lubricated hubs, then your lubrication procedure is to periodically fill the hub with a high-quality hypoid gear oil to the level indicated on the clear plastic oil cap. The oil can be filled from either the oil fill hole in the hub or through the rubber plug hole in the cap itself.

The convenient lubrication provisions of the E-Z Lube and the oil lubrication must not replace periodic inspection of the bearings.

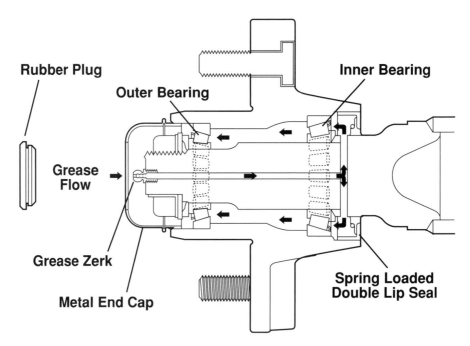

E-Z Lube. *(Illustration courtesy of Dexter Axle)*

SEAL INSPECTION AND REPLACEMENT

Whenever the hub is removed, inspect the seal to assure that it is not nicked or torn and is still capable of properly sealing the bearing cavity. If there is any question of condition, replace the seal. Use only the seals specified in the Seal Replacement Chart.

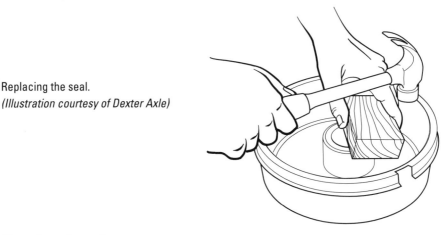

Replacing the seal.
(Illustration courtesy of Dexter Axle)

To replace the seal:

1. Pry the seal out of the hub with a screwdriver. Never drive the seal out with the inner bearing as you may damage the bearing.

2. Apply a Permatex sealant to the outside of the new seal.

3. Tap the new seal into place using a clean wood block.

SEAL REPLACEMENT REFERENCE

Brake Size	Hub	Seal Part Number		
		Std.	*E-Z Lube*	*Oil*
$7 \times 1^{1}/_{4}$	4 or 5 Bolt	10-9	10-60	NA
$10 \times 1^{1}/_{2}$	4 or 5 Bolt	10-42	NA	NA
$10 \times 2^{1}/_{4}$	4 or 5 Bolt	10-4	10-19	NA
12×2	4 or 6 Bolt	10-1	10-10	NA
12×2	5 Bolt Demount	10-1	10-10	10-10
12×2	8 Bolt	10-1	10-10	10-10
$12 \times 2^{*}$	6 Bolt	10-54	NA	NA

*Special application with 2.25 diameter seal journal.

BEARING ADJUSTMENT AND HUB REPLACEMENT

If the hub has been removed or bearing adjustment is required, the following adjustment procedure must be followed:

1. After placing the hub, bearings, washers, and spindle nut back on the axle spindle in reverse order as detailed in the previous section on hub removal, rotate the hub assembly slowly while tightening the spindle nut to approximately 50 pounds per foot (12 inch wrench or pliers with full hand force).

2. Then loosen the spindle nut to remove the torque. Do not rotate the hub.

3. Finger tighten the spindle nut until just snug.

4. Back the spindle nut out slightly until the first castellation lines up with the cotter key hole and insert the cotter pin (or locking tang in the case of E-Z Lube).

5. Bend over the cotter pin legs to secure the nut (or locking tang in the case of E-Z Lube).

6. Nut should be free to move with only restraint being the cotter pin (or locking tang).

Suspension

The three functions of a suspension system are to attach the axle to the trailer, to dampen the effects of road shock, and to provide stability to the trailer.

DOUBLE-EYE LEAF SPRINGS

Double-eye springs have eyes formed in each end of the spring and are attached to the trailer as follows:

1. The front spring eye is attached directly to the front hanger with a bolt and nut.

2. The rear spring eye is attached to a pair of shackle links that are attached to either a rear hanger (in the case of single axle installation) or to an equalizer (in the case of a multiple axle installation).

The articulation of this suspension occurs when the spring becomes loaded and consequently lengthens. The double pivot action of the shackle links accommodates this articulation and allows the system to move freely.

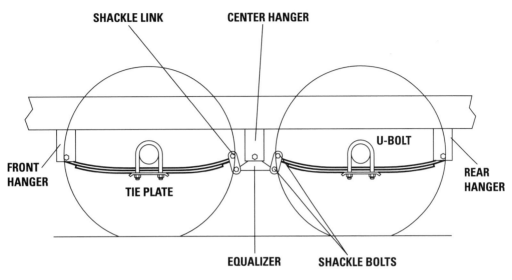

Double-eye leaf springs.

In multiple axle installations the action is the same but with the additional movement of the equalizer assembly that serves to transfer instantaneous loads from one axle to another in an effort to "equalize" the load between the axles.

GREASE LUBRICATED SUSPENSION BUSHINGS

In the optional heavy-duty attaching parts kits, the suspension bolts have grease zerks that provide a lubrication path to the bronze bushing located in the spring eyes and equalizer. These parts should be periodically lubricated and inspected for signs of excessive wear, cracking, or hole elongation.

SLIPPER-LEAF SPRINGS

Slipper springs have an eye formed in one end only with the other end formed into a reverse curve. The attachment of these springs is as follows:

1. The front eye is attached directly into the front hanger with a bolt and nut.

2. The rear end of the spring is captured in the rear hanger or equalizer with a "keeper bolt" that prevents the spring from coming out when the trailer is jacked up for service.

The articulation of this suspension occurs when the rear end of each slipper spring slides against the wear surfaces provided in the rear hangers or equalizers.

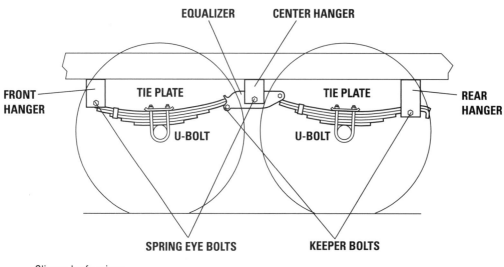

Slipper-leaf springs.

TORSION SUSPENSION

This suspension system is a torsion arm-type suspension that is completely self-contained within the axle tube. It attaches directly to the trailer frame with brackets that are an integral part of the axle assembly. This axle provides improved suspension characteristics relative to leaf-spring axles through the unique arrangement of a steel torsion bar surrounded by four natural rubber cords encased in the main structural member of the axle beam.

Rubber torsion suspension.
(Illustration courtesy of Dexter Axle)

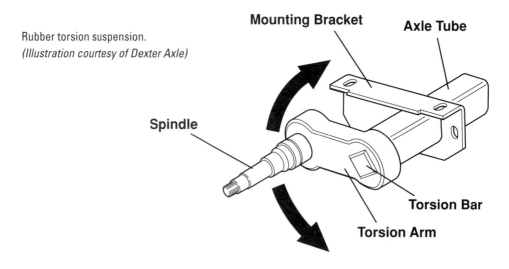

The wheel and hub spindle is attached to a lever, called the torsion arm, which is fastened to the rubber encased bar. As load is applied, the bar rotates, causing a rolling-compressive resistance in the rubber cords. This action provides the same functions as conventional sprung axles with several operating advantages, including independent suspension.

INSPECTION AND REPLACEMENT

All the components of your suspension system should be visually inspected at least every 6,000 miles for signs of excess wear, elongation of bolt holes, and loosening of fasteners. Whenever loose or replaced, the fasteners in your suspension system should be torqued as detailed in the charts that follow.

SUSPENSION FASTENER TORQUE VALUES		
Item	*Torque (lb./ft.)*	
	Min.	*Max.*
$^3/_8$-inch U-Bolt	30	35
$^7/_{16}$-inch U-Bolt	45	60
$^1/_2$-inch U-Bolt	45	60
Shackle Bolt	Snug fit only. Parts must rotate or cotter pins are provided to retain nut-bolt assembly.	
Spring Eye Bolt	Snug fit only. Parts must rotate or cotter pins are provided to retain nut-bolt assembly.	
Equalizer Bolt	Snug fit only. Parts must rotate or cotter pins are provided to retain nut-bolt assembly.	
Shoulder Type Shackle Bolt	30	50

Worn spring-eye bushings, sagging springs, or broken springs should be replaced, using the following method:

1. Support the trailer with the wheels just off the ground. Follow the trailer manufacturer's recommendations for lifting and supporting the unit. Do not lift or place supports on any part of the suspension system.

2. After the unit is properly supported place a suitable block under the axle tube near the end to be repaired. This block is to support the weight of the axle only so that suspension components can be removed.

3. Disassemble the U-bolts, nuts, and tie plates.

4. Remove the spring-eye bolts and remove the spring and place on a suitable work surface.

5. If the spring-eye bushings are to be replaced, drive out the old bushing, using a suitable drift punch. *Caution:* Be sure to wear safety glasses when removing or installing force fitted parts. Failure to comply may result in serious injury.

6. Drive the new bushing into the spring eye, using a piloted drift punch or a close-fitting bolt inserted through the bushing.

7. Reinstall repaired or replaced components in reverse order.

Note: For multiple axle units, the weight of each axle must be supported as outlined in step 2 before disassembly of any component of the suspension system.

If the equalizer or equalizer bushings must be replaced, follow the aforementioned instructions for lifting and supporting the trailer unit and then proceed as follows:

1. With both axles blocked up, remove the spring-eye bolt, shackle bolt, and equalizer bolt from the equalizer to be repaired or replaced.

2. Take the equalizer to a suitable work surface and remove the worn bushings, using a suitable drift punch.

3. Drive the new bushings into place, using a piloted drift punch or a close-fitting bolt through the bushing. *Caution:* Be sure to wear safety glasses when removing or installing force-fitted parts. Failure to comply may result in serious injury.

4. Reassemble in reverse order.

All of the pivot points or your suspension system have been fitted with antifriction-bearing materials that do not require routine lubrication. However, when otherwise servicing the unit, these pivot points may be lubricated if you so desire.

Except for periodic inspection of the fasteners used to attach the torsion axle to the vehicle frame, no other suspension maintenance is required on rubber torsion axles. They are, of course, subject to the maintenance and inspection procedures regarding brakes, hubs, bearings, seals, wheels, and tires as outlined in this chapter.

Warning: Do not weld on the torsion beam. It has rubber cords inside and the heat generated by welding could damage the cord.

Wheels

WHEEL SELECTION

Wheels are a very important and critical component of your running gear system. When specifying or replacing your trailer wheels, it is important that the wheels, tires, and axle are properly matched. The following characteristics are extremely important and should be thoroughly checked when replacement wheels are considered.

1. Bolt Circle. Many bolt circle dimensions are available and some vary by so little that it might be possible to attach an improper wheel that does not match the axle hub. Be sure to match your wheel to the axle hub.

2. Capacity. Make sure that the wheels have enough load-carrying capacity and pressure rating to match the maximum load of the tire and trailer.

3. Offset. This refers to the relationship of the centerline of the tire to the hub face of the axle. Care should be taken to match any replacement wheel with the same offset wheel as originally equipped. Failure to match offset can result in reducing the load carrying capacity of your axle.

4. Rim Contour. *Caution:* Use only the approved rim contours as shown in the *Tire and Rim Association Yearbook* or the tire manufacturer's catalog. The use of other rim contours is dangerous. Failure to use the proper rim contour can result in explosive separation of the tire and wheel and could cause a serious accident.

Warning: Do not attempt to repair or modify a wheel. Even minor modifications can have a great effect. Do not install a tube to correct a leak through the rim. If the rim is cracked, the air pressure in the tube may cause the pieces of the rim to explode with great force and can cause serious injury or death!

TORQUE REQUIREMENTS

It is extremely important to apply and maintain proper wheel-mounting torque on your trailer axle. Torque is a measure of the amount of tightening applied to a fastener (nut and bolt) and is expressed as length times force. For example, a force of 90 pounds applied at the end of a wrench 1 foot long will yield 90 pounds per foot of torque. Torque wrenches are the best method to assure the proper amount of torque is being applied to a fastener.

Note: Wheel nut or bolts must be applied and maintained at the proper torque levels to prevent loose wheels, broken studs, and possible dangerous separation of wheels from your axle.

Be sure to use only the fasteners matched to the cone angle of your wheel (usually 60 to 90 degrees). The proper procedure for attaching your wheels is as follows:

1. Start all bolts or nuts by hand to prevent cross threading.

2. Tighten bolts or nuts in the following sequence.

3. The tightening of the fasteners should be done in stages. Following the recommended sequence, tighten fasteners per wheel torque chart below.

4. Wheel nuts and bolts should be torqued before first road use and after each wheel removal. Check and re-torque after the first 10 miles, 25 miles, and again at 50 miles. Check periodically thereafter.

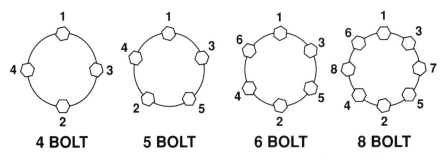

Proper sequence for tightening wheel bolts. *(Illustration courtesy of Dexter Axle)*

WHEEL TORQUE REQUIREMENTS			
Wheel Size	*Torque Sequence*		
	1st Stage	*2nd Stage*	*3rd Stage*
12 inch	20–25	35–40	50–75
13 inch	20–25	35–40	50–75
14 inch	20–25	50–60	90–120
15 inch	20–25	50–60	90–120
16 inch	20–25	50–60	90–120

Tires

Before mounting tires onto wheels make certain that the rim size and contour is approved for the tire as shown in the *Tire and Rim Association Yearbook* or the tire manufacturer's catalog. Also make sure the tire will carry the rated load. If the load is not equal on all tires due to trailer weight distribution, use the tire rated for the heaviest wheel position.

Note: The capacity rating molded into the sidewall of the tire is not always the proper rating for the tire if used in a trailer application. Use the following guideline:

1. LT and ST tires. Use the capacity rating molded into the tire.

2. Passenger car tires. Use the capacity rating molded into the tire sidewall divided by 1.10.

Use tire-mounting procedures as outlined by the Rubber Manufacturers Association or the tire manufacturers.

Tire inflation pressure is the most important factor in tire life. Inflation pressure should be as recommended by the manufacturer for the load. Pressure should be checked cold before operation. Do not bleed air from tires when they are hot. Check inflation pressure weekly during use to insure the maximum tire life and tread wear. The following tire wear diagnostic chart will help you pinpoint the causes and solutions of tire wear problems.

Tire Wear Diagnostic Chart

Wear Pattern		Cause	Action
	Center Wear	Over Inflation	Adjust pressure to particular load per tire catalog.
	Edge Wear	Under Inflation	Adjust pressure to particular load per tire catalog.
	Side Wear	Loss of camber or overloading	Make sure load doesn't exceed axle rating. Align at alignment shop.
	Toe Wear	Incorrect toe-in	Align at alignment shop.
	Cupping	Out-of-balance	Check bearing adjustment and balance tires.
	Flat Spots	Wheel lockup & tire skidding	Avoid sudden stops when possible and adjust brakes.

Tire wear diagnostic chart. *(Chart courtesy of Dexter Axle)*

Note: Tire wear should be checked frequently because once a wear pattern becomes firmly established in a tire it is difficult to stop, even if the underlying cause is corrected.

Storage Preparation

If your trailer is to be stored for an extended period or over the winter, it is important that the trailer be prepared properly.

1. Remove the emergency breakaway battery and store inside, out of the weather. Charge the battery at least every 90 days.

2. Jack up the trailer and place jack stands under the trailer frame so that the weight will be off the tires. Follow trailer manufacturer's guidelines to lift and support the unit. Never jack up or place jack stands on the axle tube or on the equalizers.

3. Lubricate mechanical moving parts, such as the hitch and suspension parts, that are exposed to the weather.

Note: On oil-lubricated hubs, the upper part of the roller bearings are not immersed in oil and are subjected to potential corrosion. For maximum bearing life it is recommended that you revolve the wheels periodically (every 2 to 3 weeks) during periods of prolonged storage.

After Prolonged Storage—Inspection Procedures

Before removing trailer from jack stands:

1. Remove all wheels and hubs or brake drums. Note which spindle and brake the drum was removed from so it can be reinstalled in the same location.

2. Inspect suspension for wear.

3. Check tightness of hanger bolt, shackle bolt, and U-bolt nuts per recommended torque values.

4. Check brake linings, brake drums, and armature faces for excessive wear or scoring.

5. Check brake magnets with an ohmmeter. The magnets should check 3.2 ohms. If shorted or worn excessively, replace.

6. Lubricate all brake moving parts, using a high temperature brake lubricant. (Lubriplate or equivalent). *Caution: Do not get grease or oil on brake linings or on magnet face.*

7. Remove any rust from braking surface and armature surface of drums with fine emery paper or crocus cloth. Protect bearings from contamination while so doing.

8. Inspect oil or grease seals for wear or nicks. Replace if necessary.

9. Lubricate hub bearings. Refer to procedure in this chapter.

10. Reinstall hubs and adjust bearings per instruction in this chapter.

11. Mount and tighten wheels per instructions in this chapter.

Trip Preparation Checklist for Trailer Axle Assembly

There are a number of simple rules to follow in caring for your trailer axle assembly that can add to its life—and in the case of some of these rules, you may be protecting your own life as well. Using the following checklist before starting a trip with your trailer is highly recommended. Some of these items should be checked 2 to 3 weeks before a planned trip to allow sufficient time to perform maintenance.

1. Check your maintenance schedule and be sure you are up to date.

2. Check hitch. Is it showing wear? Is it properly lubricated?

3. Fasten safety chains and breakaway switch actuating chain securely. Make certain the breakaway battery is fully charged.

4. Inspect towing hookup for secure attachment.

5. Load your tag-a-long trailer so that approximately 10 percent of the trailer's total weight is on the hitch. For light trailers this should be increased to 15 percent.

6. Do not overload. Stay within your gross vehicle rated capacity.

7. Inflate tires according to manufacturer's specifications; inspect tires for cuts, excessive wear, etc.

8. Check wheel mounting nuts and bolts with a torque wrench. Torque, in proper sequence, to the levels specified in this chapter.

9. Make certain brakes are synchronized and functioning properly.

10. Check tightness of hanger bolt, shackle bolt, and U-bolt nuts per torque values specified in this chapter.

11. Check operation of all lights.

Check that your trailer is towing in a level position and adjust hitch height if required.

MAINTENANCE SCHEDULE*					
Item	*Function Required*	*Weekly*	*3 Mo.*	*6 Mo.*	*12 Mo.*
Brakes	Test they are operational	At every use			
Brake adjustment	Adjust to proper operating clearance		X		
Brake magnets	Inspect for wear and current draw			X	
Brake linings	Inspect for wear and contamination				X
Brake controller	Check for correct amperage and modulation			X	
Brake cylinders	Check for leaks, sticking				X
Brake lines	Inspect for cracks, leaks, kinks				X
Trailer brake wiring	Inspect for bare spots, fray, etc.				X
Breakaway system	Check battery charge and switch operation	At every use			
Hub/drum	Inspect for abnormal wear or scoring				X
Bearings and cups	Inspect for corrosion or wear; clean and repack				X
Seals	Inspect for leakage; replace if removed				X
Springs	Inspect for wear, loss of arch				X
Suspension	Inspect for bending, loose fasteners, wear			X	

MAINTENANCE SCHEDULE* (continued)					
Item	*Function Required*	*Weekly*	*3 Mo.*	*6 Mo.*	*12 Mo.*
Hangers	Inspect welds				X
Wheel nuts/ bolts	Tighten to specified torque values		X		
Wheels	Inspect for cracks, dents, distortion			X	
Tire inflation pressure	Inflate to manufacturer's specifications	X			
Tire condition	Inspect for cuts, wear, bulging, etc.		X		

* All service information in the chapter supplied by Dexter Axle.

Jacks

The jack on your trailer can be easily taken for granted, but remember these few things to keep it from being damaged and working properly.

1. Make sure the jack is in the "up" position before pulling the trailer away.

2. Crank the jack to its shortest length to minimize bending stress on the jack.

3. When cranking the jack up or down, chock the trailer to minimize rolling.

4. If the jack has a removable foot plate or caster, remove it before hauling the trailer.

The internal gearing and bearings of the jack must be kept lubricated. Follow the instructions in the manual for your particular type of jack. In the absence of a manual use a small amount of automotive grease to accomplish this purpose. An enclosed jack tube may have a lubrication opening through which the grease may be pumped, using a needle-nosed applicator. Lightly grease the inner tube of the jack, using the same type of grease. A lightweight oil must also be applied to the handle unit.

Couplers, Latches, and Locks

Couplers should be kept in perfect condition and checked often. Any doubt whatsoever about the coupler should be referred to a professional. To insure properly working mechanisms, frequently lightly lubricate all moving parts of the coupler. Also lightly lubricate the interior of the socket. The hitch ball may also be lightly lubricated to reduce friction.

Latches and locks can be kept in good working condition with the application of a lubricating fluid such as WD-40. If the lubricant drips onto the surface of the trailer, wipe it off immediately because it may damage the finish.

Prolonging the Life of the Trailer

In chapter 10, "Construction Materials," we discussed maintenance of each type of construction material. No matter what the trailer is made of, some type of maintenance and care is required to prolong the life of the trailer.

The most important thing you can do for your trailer is to keep it clean and dry. After each use, completely sweep out every bit of manure, urine, shavings, and hay. Sweep it from the corners, under the mats, and out of the springs and hinges. If any moisture has collected on the floor, whether wood or aluminum, hose the floor and put the mats up to the side until the floor is completely dry. Aluminum floors should be washed with a mild soap and water and thoroughly rinsed. Sweep hay out of mangers and do not let hay or any other material collect in the seams around the manger and the outer wall. Don't let mud, tar, salt, or any other such road crud dry on the exterior surface. Jack the trailer up and hose off the undercarriage as well as possible.

If you don't hose out the trailer with each use, at least sweep it well and hose it every few times you use it. Don't let wet hay and horse mucous dry onto the walls. Wipe off the walls after each trip. Several times during the season, wash the trailer with a mild detergent.

If you can store the trailer out of the sun, it will add many years to the life and beauty of the finish. FRP is especially sensitive to UV rays, and some paints will fade rather quickly. Putting a nonporous tarp over the trailer may trap moisture under the tarp and could do more harm than good.

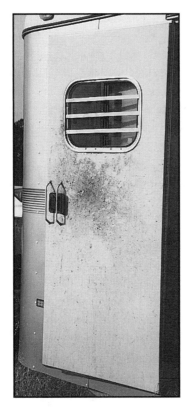

Clean off this kind of dirt after every use and you will add years to the life of your trailer.

Any chips in the paint should be touched up immediately to prevent moisture from seeping under the paint, and deep scratches in FRP should be professionally repaired before moisture can leak into the interior. Waxing a painted or FRP trailer twice a year will protect the finish. A paste wax applied to painted interior walls of the trailer will make it surprisingly easy to clean and will protect the surface from the abuse of the horses. Follow the manufacturer's recommendations for the type of wax to use. FRP and fiberglass need a particular kind of wax.

Follow the manufacturer's suggestions for maintaining the finish of your trailer. If you have purchased a used trailer and have no manual, call the manufacturer for instructions.

Following these suggestions not only will give you many years of satisfactory trailering, but also will make your trailer a valuable commodity when you decide to sell it.

Appendix

Manufacturers

Al-Ray Manufacturing
P.O. Box 355
Raymond, MN 56282
(612) 967-4470

American Trailer Mfg.
8645 Westpark
Boise, ID 83704
(208) 375-0019

Arndt Trlr. Mfg. (Collin-Arndt)
1019 Pondtown Rd.
Dillsburg, PA 17019
(717) 432-5476

Barrett Mfg.
1137 Oak Park
Corpus Christi, TX 78407
(512) 882-9941

Bear Cat Conversions
808 Logan St.
Goshen, IN 45626
(Living qrtrs.) (219) 533-0448

Bee Trailers
Rte. 2
Climax, GA 31734
(912) 246-2052

Bellamy Mfg. & Repair
P.O. Box 55
Hiltons, VA 24258
(703) 386-9471

Big Valley
P.O. Box 246
Wynne, AR 72396
(501) 238-8429

Bison
71913 CR 23
New Paris, IN 46553
(219) 831-6800

Bonanza Corp.
P.O. Box 596
Conway, AR 72033
(501) 327-0189

Boerne Trailer Mfg., Inc.
28991 I.H-10 W
Boerne, TX 78006
(800) 666-8724

Brenderup Trailer
P.O. Box 3126
Midland, TX 79702
(915) 684-8372

C M Trailer Mfg.
P.O. Box 680
Madill, OK 73446
(800) 845-5339

Chaparral Trailer of Ark.
P.O. Box 169
Quitman, AR 72131
(501) 589-2741

Cherokee Ind., Inc.
11301 S. I-44 Service Rd.
Oklahoma City, OK 73173
(405) 691-8222
(800) 654-4967

Cherokee Mfg. Co.
Industrial Park Rd.
Sweetwater, TN 37874
(800) 523-8114

Circle J Trailers
200 N. Kit Ave.
Caldwell, ID 82605
(800) 247-2535

Circle M Supreme Mfg. Co.
I-423
Knoxville, TN 37932
(615) 693-1783

Corn Pro
Oden, IN
(812) 636-4319

Cotner
P.O. Box 347
Revere, PA 18953
(215) 847-2237

Cowboy Trailers
P.O. Box 331
Burleson, TX 76028
(817) 556-2417

Crescent Limited, Inc.
184 Industrial Loop
Orange Park, FL 32067
(904) 269-9991

Diamond D Trlr. Mfg.
1000 N. Hwy. 48
P.O. Box 33
Shenandoah, IA 51601
(712) 246-5375

EBY
4435 SR 29
P.O. Box 137
W. Jefferson, OH 43162
(904) 351-4019
(800) 752-0507

Elite Tlr. Mfg.
8220 SW 8th St.
P.O. Box 270603
Oklahoma City, OK 73137
(405) 787-1115

EquiSpirit
P.O. Box 1987
Southern Pines, NC 28388
(910) 692-1771

Exiss Alum. Trailers
P.O. Box D
1512 S. Rock Island
El Reno, OK 73036
(405) 262-6471

Featherlite Mfg. Inc.
Hwy. 63 & 9
P.O. Box 320
Cresco, IA 52136
(319) 547-6000

Four Star Trailers
10000 NW 10th St.
Oklahoma City, OK 73147
(405) 324-7827

Gantway Trailer Mfg.
3860 N. Federal Hwy.
Del Ray Beach, FL 33483
(407) 737-4999

Gooseneck Trailers
P.O. Box 832
Bryan, TX 77806
(409) 778-0615

Gore's Trailers Mfg., Inc.
Rt. 3 Box 369
Whiteville, NC 28472
(800) 334-3488

Grand Prix Trailer Mfg.
4800 Ballenger Creek
Frederick, MD 21701
(301) 662-0616

Hart Trailers
P.O. Drawer C
Chickasha, OK 73018
(405) 224-3634

Hawk Trailers, LLC
1220 Depot St.
P.O. Box 270
Manawa, WI 54949
(920) 596-3080
(920) 596-3155 fax

Heliarc Alum Horse Trailers
3110 Riverside Dr.
Clarkston, WA 99403
(509) 758-1257

Jackson Mfg. Co.
Rte. 1 Box 185
Chickasha, OK 73018
(405) 224-6013

Kiefer Built, Inc.
P.O. Box 88
Kanawha, IA 50447
(515) 762-3201

Kingston Trailers, Inc.
136 Wapping Rd.
Kingston, MA 02364
(617) 585-4337

Lazy N Custom Mfg.
Hwy. 121
Warrensburg, IL 65273
(217) 672-3281

Logan Coach
P.O. Box 746
Logan, UT 84323
(800) 742-7047

Monarch Trailer Co.
2832 N. Bowman St.
Mansfield, OH 44903
(419) 747-2848

Nationwide Mfg., Inc.
5005 Crittenden Dr.
Louisville, KY 40213
(502) 366-0335

North Shore Conversions
67928 A US 33 S.
Goshen, IN 46526
(Living qrtrs.) (219) 642-4310

Ponderosa Trailers
1985 Favre Ln.
Conway, AR 72032
(501) 329-1267

S & H Trailer Mfg. Co.
800 Industrial Dr.
Madill, OK 73446
(405) 795-3080

Shoop Trailers
715 Range End Rd.
Dillsburg, PA 17019
(717) 432-5212

Show Me Trailers
P.O. Box 397
Smithton, MO 65350
(816) 343-5362

Sidekick Trailers
5700 Industrial Blvd.
Milton, FL 32583
(800) 627-4335

Sooner Trailers
P.O. Box 1323
Duncan, OK 73534
(405) 255-6979

Steel Prod. & Design
1530 S. 280 W.
Salt Lake City, UT 84115
(801) 487-8945

Sterling Trailers
826 Pensy Rd.
Willow St., PA 17584
(800) 392-2630

Sundowner Trailers
HC 61 Box 27
Coleman, OK 73432
(405) 937-4256

Titan Trailer Mfg., Inc.
125 W. Railroad
Waterville, KS 66548
(913) 785-2101

Trail Magic Mfg.
P.O. Box 278
Coleman, OK 73432
(405) 937-4238

Trail-et
107 Tower Rd.
P.O. Box 499
Waupaca, WI 54981
(800) 344-1326

Trailers USA
8280 NW 121st Ave.
Ocala, FL 34482

Truxall Corp.
RR 2 Box 46
Jackson Center, PA 16133
(412) 376-3792

Tuff Cat Trailers
Goodwin Mfg.
P.O. Box 207
Tekonsha, MI 49092

Turnbow Trailers, Inc.
P.O. Box 300-8
Oilton, OK 74052
(800) 362-5659

Valley
2525 State Hwy. 41
Cynthiana, OH 45624
(614) 634-2875

Ventura Trailers
Medford, NY
(516) 475-7968

Vogt Mfg.
1441 W. 2550 S.
Ogden, UT 84401
(801) 627-1017

WW Trailers
P.O. Box 807
Madill, OK 73446
(405) 795-5571

Wil-Ro, Inc.
1155 Hwy. 109 N.
Gallatin, TN 37066
(615) 452-7078

Wilson Trailer Mfg.
P.O. Box 388
Anson, TX 79501
(915) 823-2541

Wright Trailers, Inc.
45 Old Fall River Rd.
Seekonk, MA 02771
(508) 336-8530

Index

A

Aerodynamic nose, 50–51
Aluminum, 160–166
    alloys, 160–161
    corrosion, 164
    electrolysis, 164
    extrusions, 161–162
    floors, 162
    maintenance, 166
    structure, 161–164
    subframe, 163
Anxiety (horse),
    manifested in trailering problems,
        1–2
    responses, stress, 2–4
    separation anxiety, 3
Autonomic nervous response, 2–3
Axles, (*See also* Suspension)
    136–140, 194–195, 257
    axle ratio, 223–225
    bearings, *see* Bearings
    maintenance checks, 258
        trip preparation checklist, 290
    weight, 222

B

Backing a trailer, 253–254
Backwards, hauling horses, 32

Bearings, 141, 194
    servicing, 276–280
Behavioral responses, 2
Brakes, 131–133, 195–196
    electric, servicing, 258–268
    emergency breakaway, 133–134,
        196
    hydraulic, servicing, 268–274
Breast bars and doors, 81, 85–87,
    192
Butt bars and chains, 81–85, 192

C

Capacity, 149–157
    GCVW (gross combined vehicle
        weight), 222
    GCVWR (gross combination
        vehicle weight rating), 151,191,
        222, 225, 229
    GVW (gross vehicle weight), 150–
        151, 222–223, 226, 232
    GVWR (gross vehicle weight
        rating), 149–151, 191, 222
        measuring the trailer, 151–157
Centerload trailers, 32–34
Certificate of Origin, 191
Checklist (last minute), 254–255
Chest bars, *see* Breast bars
Commercial cargo drivers, 225–226

Commercial vehicles
    classifying, 143–144
    FMCSR regulations, 143–146
Connector wiring diagram, 259
Construction materials, 159–180
    aluminum, 160–166
    hybrids, 172–179
        fiberglass, 174–175
        FRP (Fiberglass Reinforced
        Product), 175–176
        wood, 176–179
    steel, 166–170
Couplers, 123–128, 197–198
Criteria for selecting a trailer, 7–9,
    191–198
    safety in design, 8, 191–192
    size, 7–8, 191–192
    ventilation, 8, 197
Curb weight, 222

D

Dealers, 210–212, 215–218
    survey results, 212–215
Diesel engines, 224–225
Dividers, 27–37
    center dividers, 74–79
    head dividers, 79–81
Door latches, 118–121
Dressing rooms, 44–49
Driving tips, 253–256
    backing a trailer, 253–254
    checklist, 254–255
Drums (brake), 141, 259–260, 262–275
Dutch doors, 62–63

E

Electric brakes, servicing 258–268
Electrical system, 196–197
Emergency breakaway brake,
    133–134, 196
Emergency items, 251–252
Environment, interior,
    color, 105–107
    contaminants, 6, 23, 26, 242
    controlling environment, 99–109
    size, 7
    ventilation, 6, 8, 242
Exterior features and options, 111–122
    colors, 107
    door latches 118–121
    exterior tie rings, 116–117
    fenders, 111–113
    gravel guards, 113–114
    lighting, 108–109
    roof rack and ladder, 121–122
    running boards and steps, 114–115
    water tanks, 122
Exterior measurements, 157
E–Z lube, 277–280

F

Fans, 9, 109
Federal Motor Carrier Safety
    Regulations (FMCSR), 143–146
        requirements for exterior lights, 144
Fenders, 111–113
Fiberglass, 174–175

Fiberglass Reinforced Product (FRP), 175–176

Financing, 218–219

Flight or fight response, 3–4

Floorboards, 176–178, 194

Four-horse trailers, 29–34

Four-wheel drive, 224–225, 228

FRP, *see* Fiberglass Reinforced Product

Full-height doors, 63–64

G

GCVW (gross combined vehicle weight), 222

GCVWR (gross combination vehicle weight rating), 151, 191, 222, 225, 229

Gooseneck trailers, 41–51
    dressing rooms, 44–49
    hitches, 234–236
    jacks, 129–130

Gravel guards, 113–114

Gross axle weight, 222

GVW (gross vehicle weight), 150–151, 222, 226, 232

GVWR (gross vehicle weight rating), 149–151, 191, 222

H

Hay bags, 26, 32, 89–90, 242

Hay nets, 26, 117, 242

Head dividers, 79–81

Height, 151–152
    legal clearance, 157

Herd behavior, 3
    flight or fight, 3–4
    separation anxiety, 3

Hitches, 229–236
    gooseneck, 234–236
    tag-a-long, 229–234
        Class III, 230
        Class IV, 230–231
    types
        weight-carrying vs. weight-distributing, 229–231

Hubs, 141, 194
    service, 274–280

Hybrids (construction), 172–179

I

Inline trailers, 34–35

Interior environment controlling, 99–109
    colors, 105–107
    insulation, 100–102
    lighting, 108–109
    windows and vents, 102–105

Interior features and options, 73–98
    breast bars and doors, 85–87
    butt bars and chains, 81–85
    dividers, 74–81
        center dividers, 74–79
        head dividers, 79–81
    hay bags and mangers, 89–94
    mats, 95–97
    padding, 94

Interior features and options, *cont.*
  sidewall and back door
    linings, 98
  tie rings, 88–89

J-K

Jacks, 128–130, 194

L

Ladders, 121–122
Latches, door, 118–121
Leasing, 218–219
Legal limit (height clearance), 157
Length, 155–157
Lighting interior/exterior, 108–109
Living quarters, 44–49, 181
  appliances, 182–184
  interior decor, 185
  maintenance, 186
  regulations and safety
    codes, 187
  structural accommodations, 186
Loading and unloading (features
  and options, 53–71
  front and side ramps, 66–71
  hold-backs (tie-backs), 64–66
  rear entry, 54–64
    ramps, 54–59
    rear doors and windows, 59–64
      dutch doors, 62–63
      full-height doors, 63–64
      tail door covers 61–62
    step-up, 54
Long trips, 5, 249–252

M

Manger, 22–24, 31, 90–94
Maintenance, *see* Service
Manufacturers, 295–298
Mechanical parts, 123–147
  brakes, 131–133
  couplers, 123–128
  emergency breakaway brake, 133–134
  exterior lights and plugs, 143–146
  hubs, drums, and bearings, 141,
    194, 276–280
  jacks, 128–130
  plugs and wiring, 146–147
  safety chains, 130–131
  suspension and axles, 136–140
    leaf spring suspension, 137
    rubber torsion suspension,
     135–141
  wheels, tires, and spares,
    142–143, 254, 285, 287–289
    torque requirements, 286

N

NATM (National Association for Trailer
  Manufacturers), 210
NEC (National Electric Code), 187
Neuroendocrine response, 2–3
New trailers, buying, 207–219
  getting best deal, 215–218
Noses, aerodynamic vs. flat, 51

O

One-horse trailers, 34

P-Q

Padding, 94

Payload, 222

Plugs, 146–147, 210

Plywood, 178–179

Prolonging life of trailer, 293–294

Purchasing a horse trailer, 11–20,
   new, 207–219
   used, 189–205

R

Ramps, 31, 54–59, 62, 191
   front and side, 66–71

Ratio, axle, 223–225

Rear doors and windows, 59–64

Respiratory stress, 5
   reducing, 241–242
   shipping fever, 6

Responses, stress, 2–4

Roof rack and ladder, 121–122

Rubber torsion suspension 135–141,
   282–283

Running boards and steps, 114–115

Rust, 166–169, 192–194

RVIA (Recreational Vehicle Industry
   Association), 187

S

Safety chains, 130–131, 198

Safety tips, 238–252
   emergency items, 251–252
   long vs. short trips, 249–252
      reducing respiratory stress, 241–242
   safety equipment, 238
      bandaging, 239–240
      head bumper, 239
      shipping boots, 239
      tail wraps, 240
   trailer training, 240–241
   tying, 242–249

Service (and maintenance), 257–294
   axles, 258
   bearings, 276–278
      adjustment, 280
      E-Z lube, 277–280
      inspection, 276
      lubrication, 276–277
      seal inspection and
         replacement, 279
   brakes, electric 258–268
      adjustment, 262
      cleaning and inspection, 262–263
      drum inspection, 275
      lubrication, 263
      magnets, 263
      shoes and linings, 264
      synchronization, 261
      troubleshooting, 264–268
         chart, 267–268
         measuring amperage, 265–266
         measuring voltage, 264–268
   brakes, hydraulic, 268–274
      air and hydraulic, 269
      maintenance, 272
      operation, 270–271
         Duo-servo, 270
         Uni-servo, 271
      surge braking system, 269–270
      troubleshooting, 273–274
      vacuum and hydraulic, 268–269

Service (and maintenance), *cont.*
  couplers, 293
  hubs, 274
    removal, 274–275
    replacement, 280
  jacks, 292
  latches and locks, 293
  maintenance schedule, 291
  prolonging life of trailer, 293–294
  suspension, 280–285
    double-eye leaf springs, 280–281
    inspection and replacement,
     283–285
    slipper leaf springs, 281–282
    torsion suspension (rubber),
     282–283
  tires, 287–288
    wear diagnostic chart, 288
  trailer storage, 288–290
  trip preparation checklist for axle
   assembly, 290
  wheels, 285
    torque requirements, 286–287
Shipping boots, 239
Shipping fever, 6
Sidewall and back door linings, 98
Slantload trailers, 26–32
  measuring, 26–27
Slide-out (living space), 185
Steel, 166–170
  corrosion, 166–169
  galvanealed steel, 168–169
  Kote steel, 168
  maintenance, 170
  raw steel, 167
  rust, 166–169, 192–194
Step-up trailers, 31, 54, 63, 192
Stock and stock-combo trailers,
  36–39

Storage, trailer, 288–290
Stress, 2
  elimination, 7–8
  external influences, 4
  negative effects, 5
  respiratory stress, 5, 214–242
Structure (frame), 194
Subframe, 163
Suspension, 9, 136–140, 194–195
  axle weight rating, 222
  drop leaf (leaf spring), 39,
   137–138, 194
    service, 280–285
  maintenance schedule, 291
  rubber torsion, 9, 39, 138–139, 195
    service, 280–285

T

Tack areas, 47
Tag-a-long trailers, 39–41
  dressing rooms, 44–48
  hitches, 229–234
Tail door covers, 61–62
Three-horse trailers, 35–36
Tie rings
  exterior, 116–117
  interior, 88–89
Tires, 142–143, 194, 254,
  287–289
Title, 191
Tongue weight, 222, 229
Torque
  axle ratio, 223–224
  wheel, 258, 286–287
Tow vehicles, 221–228
  axle ratio, 223–224
  cooling systems, 228

definitions, 222

diesel, 224–225

downsizing, 226–227

engine, 223

four-wheel drive, 224–225, 228

torque, 223

transmission, 223–224

selecting, 223–228

Trailers, choosing

horse needs, 13–17

buyer needs, 17–19

Trailers, types and variations

aerodynamic nose vs. flat nose,
50–51

dressing rooms, living quarters,
and tack areas, 44–50

styles, 22–32

centerload, 32–34

four-horse and larger, 26–34

manger, 22–24, 31, 90–94

one-horse, 34

slantload, 26–32

stock and stock-combo, 36

three-horse side-by-side, 35–36

two-horse inline, 34–35

walk-through, 24–26

types of trailers (hitches), 39–44

gooseneck, 41–51

tag-a-long, 39–41

Trailering (from horse's point of view),
1–6

Trailering problems

effects of stress, 4, 241–242

emergency items, 251–252

safety tips, 238–252

Training, 240–241

Transmission, 223

TV cameras, 9,109

Tying, 242–249

U

USDOT (United States Department
of Transportation), 12, 143–146

Used trailers, 189–205

bill of sale, 202

buying 189–202

determining value, 198, 202

transfer of title or CO, 202,
204

when to trade up, 205

V

Ventilation, 8, 242

Vents, 102–105

W–Z

Walk-through trailers (Thoroughbred),
24–26

Water tank, 122

Weight definitions, 222

Wheel base, 225

Wheel torque, 258, 286–287

Wheel wells, 27

Wheels, service, 285

Width, 152–155

Windows, 102–105

Wiring, 146–147, 196, 210

Wood construction, 176–179

floorboards, 176–178

oak, 176

plywood, 178–179

pressure-treated, 176